The Chinese Theatre in Modern Times

The Chinese Theatre in Modern Times

From 1840 to the Present Day

COLIN MACKERRAS

UNIVERSITY OF MASSACHUSETTS PRESS

AMHERST

© 1975 THAMES AND HUDSON LTD, LONDON

Published in the United States of America by the
University of Massachusetts Press

International Standard Book Number 0–87023–196–0

Library of Congress Catalog Card Number 75–13827

PRINTED IN GREAT BRITAIN
BY WESTERN PRINTING SERVICES LTD,
BRISTOL

CONTENTS

CONTENTS

Preface

This book has been written primarily for the general reader, who may not necessarily wish to consult my sources. For the benefit of those who wish to do so, I have added brief bibliographical notes at the end of the book; I have also given references for excerpts quoted *verbatim*, and in cases where an author or book is specifically mentioned in the text as an authority. Otherwise, notes have been kept to the minimum.

Many people have helped me in preparing this book for publication. I should like to thank particularly Professor Liu Ts'un-yan, of the Department of Chinese, Australian National University, and Professor John Frodsham, of the School of Human Communication, Murdoch University, Perth, who made many helpful suggestions and pointed out a number of errors in my original text, my wife Alyce, who read through the manuscript and suggested many improvements both to the content and to the style, and Mr Peter Daniell, of the Department of Geography, Australian National University, who drew the original on which the map is based. I should also like to thank Professor A. M. Nagler, of Yale University, for permission to quote from his work *A Source Book in Theatrical History* (New York, 1959).

Colin Mackerras

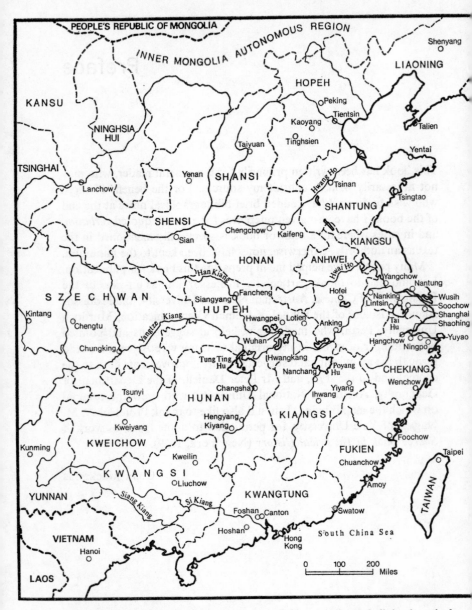

Fig. 1 Map of China, showing the provincial boundaries and all the theatrical centres mentioned in this book.

10

Introduction*

It is a truism that the Chinese rank high among the world's peoples in the quality and quantity of the artists, in many media, that they have produced over the past three millennia. Chinese painting, pottery and literature have aroused the admiration of both the specialist and the non-specialist, and many Western writers have made the history of these art forms in China the subjects of scholarly and penetrating works. The quality of the Chinese drama has also been recognized, but European and American scholars have paid less attention to China's theatrical art than to its other outstanding cultural achievements. Although a few excellent works have been written, most have tended to concentrate to a great extent on acting techniques, costumes and the stories of famous dramatic pieces. In view of the material already available, I have decided to deal only briefly with these subjects in the present book.

It may be helpful to comment here on a few salient features of the Chinese drama, and thus draw attention to some differences and similarities between the drama of China and that of the West, with which most readers will be familiar. In the first place, until the present century there was no such thing in China as a 'spoken play' – that is, a dramatic performance in which music, singing and chanting find no place. Dramas consisted of sung verses, or 'arias', interspersed with percussion-accompanied sections of stylized chanting in prose or, sometimes, spoken dialogue. The orchestral accompaniment was totally different from that represented by a Western orchestra. Instruments were normally played in unison, harmony in the European sense being unknown. The music was very much simpler than that of a Western opera, and only in rare cases is it possible to ascribe a particular drama or melody to a 'composer'. The musicians rarely had a score before them as they played; they knew the music by heart. In

* See Ills. 1–11, pp. 129–33.

11

any case, before the twentieth century, the music of the popular drama was never written down but passed on from master to student over generations. Tablatures of theatre music existed only for the drama of the aristocracy, and even these indicated only the pitch or series of pitches which corresponded to a word. They did not show the rhythm or give instructions to the orchestra, which simply followed the singer.

The visual aspects of the Chinese drama were also highly stylized, and I shall be describing the conventions later in this introduction. In view, however, of the great differences between Western opera and the theatre of China, I have chosen to use the vaguer word 'drama' when referring to the latter, except in standard terms, such as Peking Opera.

Over the past few centuries there have developed in China some three hundred different kinds of drama. They vary primarily in their music, and can be referred to collectively as 'regional theatre'. Each type tends to be found in one particular district of China. Whereas a Western opera-lover identifies the music by its composer, a Chinese will know it by its provenance. Only the most famous forms are found in many areas and none can be called a truly national theatre. Even the Peking Opera, which is the most widespread of the regional forms, is heard only seldom in southern provinces, such as Kwangtung. In a brief study it is not possible to review all these forms, so I have selected a few provinces and regions which are especially important and interesting in this context and have considered some of the main types of drama which have flourished in each. For two reasons, I have devoted more space to Peking Opera than to any other regional form. Firstly, since much more primary material is available on it than on any other type of Chinese drama, we know much more about it. Secondly, since it has become the most popular of the regional forms, it is therefore the most important.

Many of these local dramatic types have produced actors of very great stature. Those best known to the West performed principally in Peking and Shanghai. Yet, apart from Mei Lan-fang (1894–1961), even these have attracted very little attention from Western writers. It is my hope to interest the reader in China's most outstanding stage personalities of the last century, to describe the kind of life that they led, their guilds, their non-professional activities and their place in society.

Not only is the position of the actor in Chinese society of great interest, but a study of the role of the theatre in the community can throw much light on the reasons for its rise and decline in China. Moreover, it is possible to find in the social function of the Chinese theatre many illuminating points of similarity and contrast with its counterparts in other parts of the world. I intend, then, to describe the types of theatre found in China, their methods of organization and the people who patronized them. By drawing occasional comparisons with other countries, I hope to set the history of the theatre of China since the Opium War in some kind of international setting and hence show that it is in the mainstream of the development of world theatre.

To bring the main theme of this book into better focus it will be useful to begin with a brief history of the Chinese theatre down to the eighteeenth century, followed by accounts of the principal musical instruments employed and of the main stage conventions.

HISTORICAL OUTLINE OF THE CHINESE THEATRE

The history of the Chinese drama is very long indeed. Ancient texts attest to the existence of a flourishing acting profession and theatre well before the time of Christ, both among the population at large and at the courts of kings. Most scholars have believed that stage representation took its origins from shamanistic religious ceremonies, especially those in honour of harvest gods. While this is undoubtedly possible, the theory has yet to be proved by detailed research.

From c. 200 BC many records of the theatre refer to the central court and show that the emperors sponsored drama both for enjoyment and to accompany sacrifices to ancestors and the gods. By far the most important early imperial patron of the theatre was Ming-huang (AD 712–56), of the T'ang dynasty (618–907). Not only did he greatly enjoy drama, he also set up special training-schools for actors and actresses and took part in instructing them himself. Of the schools, the one best remembered by posterity is that in the Pear Garden, which lay north of the main walled city of the T'ang capital Ch'ang-an (now called Sian). The students at the school were known as 'the children of the Pear Garden', a title sometimes used even today to refer to Chinese actors.

The Sung (960–1279) and Mongol Yüan (1280–1368) dynasties saw the growth and flowering of a northern style of drama called *tsa-chü*. Indeed, the Chinese have traditionally considered their dramatic literature to have reached its apogee under the Yüan, and Kuan Han-ch'ing (*c*.1245–*c*.1322), the most brilliant of the many *tsa-chü* writers of the period, is often regarded as China's greatest playwright.

At the same time, important developments were taking place in the south. There, the *nan-hsi*, or Southern Drama, arose in Chekiang province in the twelfth century. It was based partly on folk songs and also appears to have been influenced by Indian drama. No early *nan-hsi* drama survives in full, only excerpts having been preserved. However, there do exist complete texts of several *nan-hsi* dramas dating from the late years of the Yüan dynasty. Although the form of these was similar to that of the original Southern Drama, they were called *ch'uan-ch'i*. The new name probably represented an attempt by the authors of the late Yüan dramas of south China to suggest that they were creating a different form, and not merely carrying on an old tradition.

The Northern and Southern types of drama of the Sung and Yüan periods are the first in China's theatrical history to demonstrate clearly the differentiation of dramatic styles by region, a feature which has been retained right down to the present day. At the same time, the process of interchange among different forms of drama was already apparent even in Yüan times, and some dramatists used tunes from both Northern and Southern dramas in a single work. Moreover, the Northern Drama began to spread southwards, and by the end of the Yüan period could be seen in most if not all of China's provinces.

There were many differences between the *tsa-chü* and *ch'uan-ch'i* in music, in feeling, and in the categorization of actors. The dramatist Wang Shih-chen (1527–90) sums up some of the distinct characteristics as follows: 'In the northern [drama] there are many words and the melody is hurried . . . in the southern words are few but the melody is slow. . . . So in the north there are many emotions in the words but few emotions in the sounds, while in the south, there are few emotions in the words but many in the sounds. The strength of the northern is in string [instruments], while the strength of the southern is in the beat. . . . The spirit of the northern tends to be coarse, and that of the southern to be soft.'[1]

The four-stringed lute (*p'i-p'a*) which the author had mainly in mind when mentioning stringed instruments is still in widespread use in Chinese drama, not only in the north, but also in the south. When he writes that the 'strength of the southern is in the beat', he is referring to the drum and wooden clapper. These instruments are also played nowadays in virtually all types of Chinese regional drama, and I shall discuss them in greater detail later in this introduction.

Although the distinctions in musical accompaniment to which Wang draws attention no longer hold good, I think one could still state as a very broad generalization that drama in north China tends to be more vigorous and bold than in the south, where softer and gentler melody is more usual. However, one major feature that the two types shared—and still share—is that both were primarily operatic – that is, neither could be categorized as a 'play' in which singing found no place.

Although there were differences between Northern and Southern drama in the categorization of actors, a person familiar with Western opera will notice that both types have one striking feature in common: in the casting of the players, the main emphasis is on the kind of person portrayed, not on the range or pitch of the actor's voice. In a Western opera, the tenor, for example, is very frequently the hero or main male character, but the crucial factor is not his importance in the story but his high male voice. In the Chinese theatre, not only of the Yüan but also of later times, there are certain 'stock' characters, each of whom is not necessarily associated with one particular vocal compass. In the Southern Drama, there were four main character types, called *sheng*, *tan*, *ching* and *ch'ou*. These were, respectively, the leading male character, the principal woman, the rough, strong character with the painted face, and the clown. These classifications were carried over, with variations, into virtually all the later forms of Chinese drama.

With the accession to power of the Ming dynasty (1368–1644) we find a considerable flowering and diversification of regional drama, and the growth of three broad streams or 'systems'. These were called *Yiyang ch'iang* (Tunes of Yiyang), *Pang-tzu ch'iang* (Clapper Opera) and *K'un-ch'ü* (Drama of K'unshan).

The *Yiyang ch'iang* system was based on folk tunes and arose in the sixteenth century in Yiyang county, Kiangsi province; hence the name by which it is called. Throughout its development over the years one feature remained constant: the use of the chorus. In the original drama of Yiyang, there were no musical instruments to accompany the singers, apart from percussion; we see here the influence of the Southern Drama of earlier times. The melody was given added interest by the sung comments of a group of artists not involved in the plot, like the chorus in ancient Greek tragedy. The percussion players usually sang with the chorus. Even though an accompanying orchestra was occasionally added in later variants of the *Yiyang ch'iang*, the practice of adding choral variety was always maintained and to this day may be found in regional dramatic forms based on the *Yiyang ch'iang*.

Although it does not appear to have lasted very long in its town of origin, the *Yiyang ch'iang* quickly spread to other places along various lines of communication, showing a strong tendency to follow the trade routes. Wandering companies took their art from one town to another and, with the passage of time, the *Yiyang ch'iang* had been performed and had become popular in most of the main provinces of southern China; it had even been accepted in Peking. The music of the *Yiyang ch'iang* was improvised and adapted to suit the tastes of the populations of the various districts which the actors visited. Local folk tunes became absorbed into the *Yiyang ch'iang* drama, and the words were modified according to regional dialect. Over the years, the music performed in any particular district might become so transformed that it would be quite unrecognizable to an inhabitant of Yiyang itself.

While the music of Yiyang was spreading throughout the south, the Clapper Opera was, similarly, becoming widely popular in north China. Probably first heard in eastern Shensi in the sixteenth or seventeenth century, the Clapper Opera was distinct from its southern counterpart in that it did not employ a chorus and its rhythm was beaten out with a clapper made of datewood. By the middle years of the eighteenth century, Clapper music of one kind or another was being heard all over north China and had even spread to several provinces of the south.

The dramas of both the *Yiyang ch'iang* and the Clapper Opera were popular entertainment. Both their words and their music were expressly composed for the ordinary listener. Such was not the case with a third kind of theatre, which, originating in K'unshan near Soochow, Kiangsu province, became widespread from the end of the sixteenth century. This was the *K'un-ch'ü*, which found most of its admirers among the gentry, officials and scholars. Its music was softer and more melodious than that of the popular drama and it was accompanied principally by the *ti-tzu*, or Chinese transverse flute. Educated persons always despised the popular theatre, which they considered vulgar, noisy and lacking in rhythm. Since the tastes of the *literati* went beyond the enjoyment of folk melody, the music of the *K'un-ch'ü* remained fairly constant in all the regions where it was performed, although local dialect was taken into account in the pronunciation of the words.

The *K'un-ch'ü* developed a significant body of written dramatic literature and was in this respect the successor of the Northern Drama of the Yüan and of the southern *ch'uan-ch'i*. In fact, many dramas composed in the earlier forms were taken over by *K'un-ch'ü* writers and adapted to its repertory. Although only a very few scripts of *Yiyang ch'iang* dramas of the Ming period are extant, many texts of the more genteel *K'un-ch'ü* dramas survive. Moreover, though none of the 'popular' dramas can be ascribed to an individual dramatist, most being merely arranged from *K'un-ch'ü* texts, the names of many *K'un-ch'ü* authors have been preserved. The earliest known *K'un-ch'ü* musician was Wei Liang-fu, who lived in the sixteenth century. He combined many elements of the earlier drama in his work and is usually given the credit for the creation of the *K'un-ch'ü* form that we know today.

Wei appears to have used his newly developed music only in dramas on a small scale. However, one of the principal characteristics of the major *K'un-ch'ü* dramas of the Ming and Ch'ing periods was their enormous length. A complete performance of one of these works would take several days. The first dramatist to establish this precedent was Liang Ch'en-yü (*c*. 1520–*c*.1580), from K'unshan, a man of very strong personality and imposing appearance who became an idol in theatrical circles during his own lifetime. He was mainly a poet-playwright, and his principal work was *Huan-sha chi* (sometimes rendered as 'The Beauty Trap'), which he wrote especially for adaptation to the music of Wei Liang-fu's compositions. The play relates how Hsi-shih, a famous beauty of the fifth century BC, was used by the leaders of Yüeh, an ancient Chinese state, to bewitch the ruler of an enemy principality and thus effect its conquest. Later *K'un-ch'ü* texts usually give the author's name and the titles of the tunes which are to be sung. These tunes were not necessarily composed by the author, but might be based on earlier melodies by Wei or by some other person unknown. Liang was the earliest famous author of texts for *K'un-ch'ü* music.

From about 1580 the *K'un-ch'ü* split into various schools, each with its own special characteristics. By the beginning of the seventeenth century it was popular in Peking and in other parts of north China, and it later became a significant element in the Peking Opera. Among the many *K'un-ch'ü* dramatists of Ming times one stands out, perhaps the most famous of all post-Yüan Chinese playwrights.

T'ang Hsien-tsu (1550–1617), a contemporary of Shakespeare, came from Kiangsi province and passed the highest civil service examinations (*chin-shih*) in 1583. Although his success might have led to a distinguished career in the bureaucracy, he was not interested in power and neglected his duties in favour of singing and drama. He withdrew from office and spent most of his adult life in retirement in his home town. T'ang was a romantic at heart and expressed his attitude to writing as follows: 'There are four essential factors in any form of good writing: (1) the theme, (2) vivid and interesting presentation, (3) the style and (4) beauty. With these four vital principles in mind, the fine quality of the lines and sound will naturally come into effect. Then who cares about what kind of tune or tone should be used? If one has to follow a certain pattern of form in writing, one will surely suffer from the difficulty of constructing a decent sentence with coherence and clarity.'[2] It should be noted here that T'ang, in accordance with these principles, refused to write rigid *K'un-ch'ü* music. However, because his contemporaries adapted his works to that form, he is generally known as a representative of *K'un-ch'ü*. In any case, the romantic themes of his dramas were eminently suitable to its soft and melodious music.

His greatest drama, called *Huan-hun chi* (*The Return of the Soul*), was completed in 1598. It concerns the girl Tu Li-niang and the scholar Liu Meng-mei. The two fall in love in a dream, and so strong is Tu's passion that she dies of love-sickness, even though she has not actually met Meng-mei in the flesh. Three years later she is resurrected, Liu passes his examinations and Tu's father then consents to her marriage with the scholar. This drama became widely loved in China, and several scenes from it formed part of the *K'un-ch'ü* repertory until very recent times. It is a typical *K'un-ch'ü* story: soft and romantic, with a vivid appeal to the imagination.

The Ming period saw the apex of *K'un-ch'ü* development. During the Manchu Ch'ing dynasty (1644–1911) this form of aristocratic drama began to decline and was finally all but submerged in the Taiping war of the mid-nineteenth century. Yet the Ch'ing did produce some *K'un-ch'ü* writers of note, the most famous one being Hung Sheng (1645–1704). He wrote eleven plays of which only one survives complete: *Ch'ang-sheng tien* (*The Palace of Eternal Youth*). This deals with the love of Emperor Ming-huang of T'ang (the famous patron of the theatre, whom I have mentioned earlier) for his concubine Yang Kuei-fei. Upon the outbreak of the rebellion of An Lu-shan in 755, the two flee the capital together. Because the troops accompanying them threaten mutiny, Kuei-fei hangs herself to save the emperor, after which she is taken to the moon. The emperor follows her thither, and the lovers are reunited.[3]

This theme had often been used before in Chinese dramas, as well as in novels and poems, and it was to form the basis of many later dramas. Like T'ang Hsien-tsu's works, it was admirably suited to *K'un-ch'ü* music, with its imaginative romanticism, element of sadness, and traditionally happy ending. It won passionate praise from contemporary and later theatre-goers, but was also the cause of its author's exile from Peking. At that time there was a taboo on the performance of drama during a period of mourning for an empress or emperor. In 1689, the year after its completion, *The Palace of Eternal Youth* was performed on a proscribed day in Peking. Although the Emperor K'ang-hsi (1662–1722) was an ardent admirer of the work, Hung was punished for his part in arranging the performance and was never again allowed to take up an official post. Some years later he accidentally fell from a boat while drunk, and was drowned.

Probably the most important development in the Chinese theatre of the early Ch'ing period was the growth of the *P'i-huang* system, or group of similar styles of local drama, which was based upon two melodies: *Erh-huang* and *Hsi-p'i*. Both of these can be varied endlessly, both rhythmically and emotionally, but in general *Erh-huang* 'is used for more serious occasions', while *Hsi-p'i* is 'happy and spirited in feeling'. At the same time there is for each tune a set of variations termed 'counter' (*fan*), which 'are used for sad and tragic occasions or during a kind of lament which is a feature of some roles'.[4] For regional forms of drama in the *P'i-huang* system a stringed bowed instrument, such as the *hu-ch'in*, is used in the accompanying orchestra.

The two components of this system are probably separate in origin. There has been great debate among Chinese scholars over the genesis of *Erh-huang*. However, in my view, it is most likely that its place of origin was Ihwang country, in Kiangsi province, and that its name was derived from the place where it was first heard.[5] *Hsi-p'i* was probably a variant of Clapper Opera and seems to have originated in the northwestern provinces. According to the modern scholar Ou-yang Yü-ch'ien, the character *p'i*, which normally means 'skin', is used to mean 'singing' in Hupeh province. He believes that the name referred to the 'singing' of the west (*hsi*), because the style had spread from western China (that is, from Shensi province) to Hupeh and other regions.[6]

By the eighteenth century the two styles *Erh-huang* and *Hsi-p'i* had amalgamated to form a single system. From that time onward they have always been used together, hence the term *P'i-huang*. Wandering players brought the styles to all the main provinces of south China and eventually to the Chinese capital itself, where they formed the basis of the Peking Opera, the most important of all the regional forms. Just as with the *Yiyang ch'iang* drama, in each area the original melodies were adapted to suit the tastes of the local inhabitants, and the appropriate dialects were used for the texts. Possibly somebody from Ihwang, hearing *Erh-huang* in another region, would not even recognize it as the music of his home town, but there are nevertheless firm structural similarities which enable us to relate the regional variants to the original melody.

By the reign of the famous Manchu emperor Ch'ien-lung (1736–96), Chinese drama was divided into two categories: *ya-pu*, or 'elegant drama', and *hua-pu*, or 'flower drama'. These two terms were used to refer respectively to what had previously been known as *K'un-ch'ü* and popular drama. (In effect, the term *hua-pu* was used to refer to any dramatic piece which was not *K'un-ch'ü*.) In the major theatrical cities, dramas of both types were frequently performed, and in some cities the range of 'flower' drama available was very wide indeed. Among the main centres were Yangchow, in Kiangsu province (the most important city in China for the lucrative salt trade), Nanking and Soochow, also in Kiangsu, Anking, in Anhwei province, Canton, and the national capital, Peking.

A highly significant development during the eighteenth century was the beginning of the breakdown of prejudice against the 'flower' drama among the educated classes. Although the feeling that the popular theatre was vulgar remained strong and did not die out altogether until after the Communists came to power, we find scattered references of approval in the literature on drama from the time of Ch'ien-lung onward. One particularly striking example comes from the brush of Yen Ch'ang-ming (1731–87), a scholar-official from Nanking, who wrote a lengthy paeon of praise for the Clapper Opera of Shensi.[7] In Yangchow the salt merchant Chiang Ch'un, who differed from most Chinese traders of those days in being very high in the social scale, patronized both the 'elegant' and the 'flower' drama.

MUSICAL INSTRUMENTS

Just as in the West, musical instruments in China can be classified in the string, wind and percussion categories. For the regional theatre the most important of these groups is probably the percussion. To this day some forms of drama have been accompanied only by percussion instruments. The various local styles differ in their combinations of percussion instruments. In some regions one finds instruments not often used elsewhere; in some cases they have (especially in combination) a particular texture of sound which gives an individual flavour to the local form.

Percussion instruments are of four kinds: drums, clappers, gongs and cymbals. The small drum (*hsiao-ku*) is of the greatest importance because its player functions as the 'conductor' of the orchestra. It is he who beats out the rhythm which the others must follow. The *hsiao-ku* is of hardwood, with pig's hide stretched tightly over the top, and gives out a sharp, metallic sound. The larger drum (*ta-ku*) is barrel-shaped, with ox hide. It is not often used in Peking Opera, and in *K'un-ch'ü* is reserved mainly for the entrances of emperors or other high-ranking persons.

Like the small drum, the clapper (*pan*) beats out the rhythm and is normally played by the same man, who holds it in his left hand as he strikes the drum with a bamboo stick held in his right. The clapper consists of three pieces of redwood, of which two are fastened together, so that the player can produce rhythmic sounds by flicking his wrist. However, the clapper used in Clapper Opera is called *pang-tzu*, not *pan*, and is a block of datewood which is beaten with a wooden stick.

Gongs and cymbals, like drums, are divided into large and small. In Peking Opera and many other styles, they are normally silent when actors are singing, but they can be very expressive when played as an accompaniment to certain actions. In particular, the small gong and cymbal are highly appropriate for the fighting scenes in military dramas and are usually played simultaneously.

The stringed instruments are divided into two principal categories: that in which bows are used and that in which the instruments are plucked, and bows are not used.

The most important of the bowed instruments is the *hu-ch'in*, vital to the *P'i-huang* system. In the past a famous actor usually employed his own *hu-ch'in* player, who accompanied nobody else. There are two silk strings, and a horsehair bow is fitted between them in such a way that the musician plays one string when he pushes and the other when he pulls. The sound-box of the instrument is a hollow cylinder, or elongated hexagon, made of bamboo, with a snake-skin cover; it rests on the player's thigh, with the strings pointing upwards. The pitch of the *hu-ch'in* is high and the tone somewhat shrill.

The term *hu-ch'in* is also used generically for all bowed stringed instruments. Other members of the family are the *erh-hu* and *pan-hu*. The first of these is longer than the *hu-ch'in* discussed above; it is lower in pitch and rather softer and mellower in tone. It was introduced into the Peking Opera in the days of the great Mei Lan-fang (see Chapter Three). Although the *hu-ch'in* and the *erh-hu* are often played simultaneously, the former is normally allowed to dominate when accompanying the singers of male roles; the latter, when accompanying the singers of female roles. The *pan-hu* is the principal stringed instrument of the Clapper Opera. Its shape is similar to that of the *hu-ch'in*, but its cylindrical base is shallower and entirely wooden. It gives a very strong, high-pitched sound.

Of the plucked, non-bowed stringed instruments the most significant is the pear-shaped *p'i-p'a*. Like the *hu-ch'in*, it is played held upright on the thigh. The musician plucks the strings with his right thumb and first finger, sometimes protected with a plectrum, and determines the pitch with three of his left fingers. This is an extremely ancient instrument; it has found its way into innumerable forms of regional drama and story-telling, and a large repertoire of solo melodies has developed for it. Its tone is mellow and extremely refined. The other principal plucked instruments are the *yüeh-ch'in* and the *san-hsien*, both of which function as secondary accompanying instruments in many dramatic styles. The *yüeh-ch'in* has four strings, a large round soundbox and a very short neck. The name *san-hsien* means 'three strings'. In contrast to the *yüeh-ch'in* its neck is extremely long, and its soundbox, covered in snakeskin, oval in shape and small. It produces a characteristic twanging sound.

In general, stringed instruments are much more important in Chinese drama than wind instruments, especially in the northern styles. Some wind instruments, however, should be mentioned.

The *ti-tzu*, or Chinese flute, is made of bamboo and, like its European counterpart, is played transversally. It is a little over two feet in length and just under one inch in diameter. There are ten holes, of which one is covered with a thin piece of bamboo paper. This gives the *ti-tzu* a strikingly wistful and lyric tone. As noted above, it is the chief instrument of the *K'un-ch'ü* orchestra; it is also played solo, or as an accompaniment to folk songs. It is, however, rarely used in the Peking

Opera. Another member of the flute family is the *hsiao*, which has six finger-holes, and is end-blown, not blown transversally.

Reed instruments are not of great significance in Chinese drama. The only one that need be mentioned here is the *so-na*, which has eight finger-holes and a double reed. Though in this way similar to the Western oboe, the *so-na* is rather shrill and piercing in tone. It is used in some forms of drama to add lustre or colour to the entrance of an emperor or other dignitary, and is also sometimes played when ceremonial or joyous occasions, such as weddings, are represented on the stage.

In former times the musicians who played these various instruments sat not in a pit but on the stage, in full view of the audience and to its right. Generally the player of the small drum and clapper sat in the central position as conductor. In front of him was the *hu-ch'in* and behind were the *san-hsien* and *yüeh-ch'in*.

This mention of the stage brings me to the subject of the conventions followed there, which it was the function of the musical instruments to accompany.

STAGE AND ACTING CONVENTIONS

The stage for a Chinese drama was very simple. There was a backdrop curtain, but no curtain in the front. The audience could thus see any change that took place between scenes, but since there was rarely any scenery, this was not a serious problem. The stage was, in fact, normally rather bare, with no more than a carpet, table and two chairs; sometimes there was only the carpet. The significance of the action was portrayed not by elaborate and heavy stage properties but by a highly complex set of formal, symbolic gestures and portable objects. Although a foreigner might find them confusing, the Chinese audiences knew them from childhood and understood all the nuances of the symbolism. For instance, by carrying an oar an actor indicated that he was in a boat, and a special jumping and swaying movement showed that he was going on board. If he wished to indicate that he was riding a horse he carried a riding whip with heavy silk tassels; a formal upward kick represented mounting.

In contrast to the simplicity of the stage itself, the categorization of the actors, their costumes and make-up, the gestures which each makes with the finger, hand and foot, and their facial expressions are symbolic and extremely complicated. Each of the character types *sheng*,

Fig. 2 The four principal character types in the classical Chinese theatre. From left to right: the *ch'ou* (the clown); the *ching*, who may represent one of a variety of male roles, such as warriors, officials or gods; the *tan*, or female character; the *sheng*, who represents one of several different male character types, which differ, however, from *ching* roles. Drawings by Josephine Huang Hung.

tan, *ching* and *ch'ou* can be subdivided, and in most of the main regional styles are classified also as civilian (*wen*) or military (*wu*).

The principal male *sheng* characters are *lao-sheng*, *hsiao-sheng* and *wu-sheng*. The *lao-sheng* is the old man, such as a court official or general. He always wears a long beard which varies in colour and style according to the character of the person portrayed, and sings with a rich baritone voice. The *hsiao-sheng* is the scholar and lover. In contrast to the *lao-sheng*, he does not wear a beard and his voice is high-pitched (not the full voice of the Western tenor, but usually falsetto). His make-up is similar to that used in female roles. The *wu-sheng* is the military man. His costumes are very colourful and are designed to symbolize armour. He must be highly skilled in acrobatics, which, especially in the *P'i-huang* style, represent battles and vigorous fighting.

In the past, female roles (*tan*) were played by men (except in all-female troupes). Like the *sheng*, they were divided into civilian and military types. The *wu-tan*, or military *tan*, must, like her male counterpart, be a good acrobat. The main civilian *tan* was the *ch'ing-i*, who was the faithful wife or lover or virtuous daughter. The actor sang with a fairly high falsetto voice, his movements were graceful and his eyes normally lowered. *Ch'ing-i* characters did not take part in fighting or acrobatics. The *hua-tan*, or 'flower', *tan* was a 'faster' woman. The player was very coquettish in his movements and gestures, and his costumes more stylish than those of the *ch'ing-i*. There was great emphasis on facial and eye expression, and on methods of smiling and laughing.

In general, actors of female roles adopted a standard make-up, which consisted of a layer of white cream all over the face and one or two layers of pale powder or rouge, leaving the mouth, chin and nose white, and the eyes and cheeks pink. The corners of the eyes were then pencilled in black.

In contrast to the actors of *tan* roles, where make-up is relatively simple, the actors of *ching* roles are required to paint their faces to a high degree, for which reason they are often called *hua-lien* (painted face). Their make-up is almost infinitely varied in colour and form, each pattern symbolizing particular characteristics of good (red), treachery (white) or wildness (blue). A *ching* must have a very strong and versatile voice, for of all the categories of actor he is the one from whom an audience expects the greatest volume. The painted-face players 'portray brave warriors, swashbuckling bandits, crafty and evil ministers, upright judges and loyal statesmen and there are some who represent gods and supernatural beings'.[8] As with the *sheng* and *tan*, some *ching* characters are classified as 'military', in which case they must excel in acrobatics.

Finally, there is the clown (*ch'ou*), who is often a stupid or ribald person, though he can also be evil. The *ch'ou* is allowed more improvization than other actors, and spontaneous or local jokes are very much a part of his technique. The special feature of the clown's make-up is a white patch round the eyes and nose, and it is this which makes him instantly recognizable. His costumes, on the other hand, may be elaborate or simple, depending on the social status of the character whom he is portraying.

It will be clear from the foregoing that Chinese drama is both an aural and a visual art. It would be quite impossible to conceive of a great Chinese actor who could sing magnificently but looked bad on the stage, although it is true that, for some character types, it is not the singing which is of paramount importance. This is in contrast to traditional Western opera, in which aural pleasure is more important than visual. Chinese drama depends much more on its symbolism, costumes and make-up than does Western opera, and is in this sense a more integrated art. Indeed, it may be this factor as much as any other which has aroused world-wide interest in the Chinese theatre in recent decades.

1 The Development of the Peking Opera until 1860

The period which saw the rise of the Peking Opera was politically one of sharp descent from great splendour to the near collapse of the existing order. The Manchu Ch'ing dynasty, after reaching its apogee in the early and middle years of the reign of the Emperor Ch'ien-lung (1736–96), began to decline sharply in the 1780s. Corruption became widespread, being in no way restrained by the fact that Ch'ien-lung's chief minister Ho-shen (1750–99) was just as corrupt as any of his subordinates. In 1793, the first British ambassador, Earl George Macartney, arrived in Peking and tried unsuccessfully to persuade the emperor to open his country to foreign trade. In later decades further such attempts were made, and eventually the Chinese gave way. In 1839 the Emperor Tao-kuang (1820–50) sent Lin Tse-hsü to Canton to ban the import of opium, to which the British responded by sending armed forces into China in 1840 to force the Chinese government to maintain the trade. The Treaty of Nanking, which ended the First Anglo-Chinese War (or Opium War), was signed in 1842; according to its provisions five Chinese cities (Canton, Amoy, Foochow, Ningpo and Shanghai) were opened as trade ports (in fact, they became known as 'treaty ports') in which England could establish trading facilities. In addition, the Chinese agreed to pay a substantial indemnity to the British and ceded to them the port of Hong Kong. Similar conflicts continued to occur, as a result of which the Western powers made further encroachments on Chinese sovereignty. In October 1860 British and French troops actually occupied Peking.

The Chinese empire now seemed to be in a hopeless condition. The inroads of the Western powers were by no means the only problem which faced it. Economically, it was on the point of breakdown and, on top of that, it was rent by civil war. The Taiping uprising had broken out in 1851, and the rebel forces had succeeded in occupying large areas of China, including some of the main cities. This rebellion was primarily of peasant origin, and its ideology was a blend of traditional Chinese egalitarianism and Protestant Christianity. At about the same time the Nien insurrection had spread rapidly from its source in Anhwei to several other provinces. By 1860 many contemporary observers were predicting the imminent collapse of the Ch'ing dynasty.

At the time of Ch'ien-lung's greatest glory there were three major categories of theatre available in Peking: the *K'un-ch'ü*, Clapper Opera and *Yiyang ch'iang*. The first found its clientele largely in the imperial court, where in about 1740 the emperor, a great devotee, set up a special organization to look after its development. It appears, however, that the elegant drama was not particularly popular outside the palaces, even among the gentry, and we are told that 'if they hear *K'un-ch'ü* sung, [the people] always leave noisily'.[1] The Clapper operas of Shensi and Shansi, on the other hand, were well loved in the capital by the middle of the century and were played by various troupes from these two provinces.

But the main style of Peking drama during the early and middle years of Ch'ien-lung's reign was the *Ching-ch'iang* (Music of the Capital), which had evolved from *Yiyang ch'iang*. There were six famous *Ching-ch'iang* troupes, of which the best was the Wang-fu hsin-pan, or the New Company of the Princely Mansions. As its name suggests, it performed mainly for the aristocracy, but there is evidence that its most popular actors could also be seen in the ordinary playhouses of the capital.

The New Company of the Princely Mansions reached its apogee in the 1770s, but in about 1778 an event occurred which cast a cloud over the troupe and caused a serious falling-off in the aristocracy's patronage of the *Ching-ch'iang* companies. The troupe was to perform during a banquet. One of the actors arrived late for the performance and even spoke very impolitely to an official who happened to be present. The official flew into a rage and slapped the actor in the face, for which he was quickly dismissed. Though the incident seems trivial, the troupe was henceforth considered ill-omened and, according to one writer, 'from then on friends would caution each other when they held banquets and there was nobody who dared listen to the great company of the Princely Mansions again'.[2]

THE CLAPPER ACTORS OF THE 1780s

In 1779 the great actor Wei Ch'ang-sheng (1744?–1802), popularly known as Wei San (Wei the Third), made his appearance in Peking. He came from Kintang county in Szechwan province and, together with his numerous followers, introduced to Peking the form of opera popular in the south-west, which was a kind of Clapper Opera. It is difficult to overestimate the importance of Wei Ch'ang-sheng in the history of the Peking theatre. He was the first of the great stars and his career in the capital resulted in a tremendous revival of interest in the theatre there, just when the dynasty itself was beginning its rapid decline. Wei Ch'ang-sheng was a *tan*, a male impersonator of female characters, and it is possible that until the arrival of the brilliant Mei Lan-fang in the second decade of the present century no other exponent of this kind of role exercised a more profound influence on the theatre of Peking.

At the time of Wei Ch'ang-sheng's arrival in Peking there existed a *Ching-ch'iang* troupe called the Shuang-ch'ing company. Since it was not highly regarded by the people Wei, anxious for a challenge, asked to join it, guaranteeing to increase its prestige within two months. He performed in *Kun-lou*, a bawdy drama the subject of which is unfortunately not known in detail, and won immediate fame. People flocked in their thousands to see him, and the former darlings of the stage were pushed aside.

Wei's acting was generally somewhat risqué, which brought down upon his head the anger and suspicion of the government. In the autumn of 1782 the government actually forbade him to continue acting, on the grounds that his performances were exercising a harmful moral effect on the people. Ch'ang-sheng did not leave the stage for long. He soon founded a new company, the Yung-ch'ing, and was able for a while to escape the ire of the authorities by toning down the bawdy features of his performances. However, in 1785 an edict was issued banning not only Wei but all the actors of the Clapper Opera from the stage. This time Wei Ch'ang-sheng was forced to obey. He left Peking and sought employment in other parts of the country; he may well have returned to his native Szechwan. In 1788 he was in the cosmopolitan city of Yangchow and soon after performed in Soochow. He aroused great interest and enthusiasm in both cities, but inevitably also drew attack both from those who feared the adverse effect which the new drama might exercise on the popularity of the aristocratic *K'un-ch'ü* and from those who considered his acting immoral.

29

Late in 1800 Wei made a return visit to Peking. By this time he had eliminated the bawdy element in his acting. He still commanded a great following, and one author wrote that 'his voice and facial expression were as of old, and his poise and bearing of the utmost distinction'.[3] For the first time audiences praised him for his spectacular acrobatics. Unfortunately, the last phase of Wei's career did not last long, and he died a pauper in 1802, after a fit of faintness on the stage. Despite his impoverished circumstances at the time of his death Wei Ch'ang-sheng had been extremely wealthy. He was able to afford a magnificent house and rode about in carriages of a kind normally only used by senior officials. He also had friends in high places. For instance, he was on very good terms with Ch'ien-lung's notorious minister Ho-shen and, according to an unnamed old man who had 'caught a glimpse of them',[4] the relationship between the actor and the minister was homosexual. In Yangchow, Wei Ch'ang-sheng was sponsored by the most eminent merchant and patron of the arts in the city: Chiang Ch'un, whose success in the all-important salt trade had made him fabulously wealthy.

Throughout his career on the stage Wei Ch'ang-sheng had acquired many disciples. In Peking, especially, we know the names of several actors who benefited from his instruction. By far the most famous and important of them was the *tan* performer Ch'en Yin-kuan, who, like his master, was a Szechwanese.

Ch'en arrived in Peking shortly after Wei Ch'ang-sheng, in 1780 or 1781 when still in his teens, and joined the Shuang-ch'ing company. He was noted for the verve and wit of his performances, which were, like those of Wei, considered bawdy. He refused to obey the edict of 1785 banning Clapper actors but was not able to escape the watchful eye of the government for long. In about 1786 he was arrested and the cangue of a criminal was placed round his neck. The authorities planned to exile him to the frontiers, but certain influential friends interceded on his behalf and he was sent back to his native city instead.

Ch'en Yin-kuan was highly sociable. He would drink with his admirers after his performances and in this way formed many friendships. He was attractive not only on the stage, dressed as a woman, but also off-stage. He was treated like a *prima donna* and given a large number of valuable gifts, including jades and silk. He quickly became extremely rich, and soon owned two mansions in Peking.

Ch'en gained a reputation for loose morals and vanity. In some respects he was not unlike a high-class male prostitute. On one occasion

30

he was approached after a performance by a man of impressive appearance who described himself as an official from Kwangtung but declined to give his name. Through flattery and generous gifts this 'official' wheedled from the young actor an invitation to dinner at one of his mansions, and after a sumptuous meal the two retired together to bed. Unfortunately for Ch'en, however, the intentions of the self-styled official were not what they seemed. 'At midnight, when people fell silent, he secretly drugged the wine and passed winecups round to everybody. After a little while they all collapsed in a stupor; the guest gave a call to his host of servants, who jumped down from the roof [having earlier hidden there]. They emptied all the coffers [containing] Ch'en Yin [-kuan's] property, which he had been accumulating over several years and used to persuade [his guests] to drink or to go to bed with him, and departed.'[5]

Stories of this kind illustrate that the Clapper actors, of whom Wei Ch'ang-sheng and his famous disciple were only the most prominent among many fine artists, fulfilled a social role as homosexual favourites in addition to their importance in the theatre. We may probably say, therefore, that one reason for their undoubted success was that they were able to capitalize on the growing corruption among the richer citizens of the time. There were, of course, other reasons. The extraordinary novelty and magnificence of their art must have attracted many people. Moreover, they filled a vacuum in Peking's theatrical life, for they flourished at a time when the popularity of the capital's other dramatic forms, *Ching-ch'iang* and *K'un-ch'ü*, was dwindling. The decline of both these kinds of drama was greatly accentuated by the arrival of the Clapper actors.

When the latter were banned in 1785 and departed from the Peking stage, they in their turn left a void made all the more serious by the fact that they had themselves stimulated such widespread interest in the theatre. It was inevitable that a new form of drama, new actors and new companies should now be introduced into Peking.

THE ANHWEI COMPANIES

The Emperor Ch'ien-lung made a habit of holding lavish celebrations in honour both of his own and of his mother's birthday and loved to include drama in the festivities. In 1752 fell the Empress Hsiao-sheng's sixtieth birthday (by Chinese reckoning), which was commemorated with elaborate celebrations. Theatrical performances were part of the occasion and in one large part of the city 'there were stages set up every twenty or thirty steps, on which both northern and southern dramas were given'.[6] Similar celebrations were held on the empress's eightieth birthday in 1772.

But in terms of the history of drama in Peking, the most important of these occasions, as far as they are recorded,[7] took place in 1790. In that year, various companies came to Peking to celebrate Ch'ien-lung's eightieth birthday. They included the San-ch'ing, which was led by Yü Lao-ssu. By 1793 this troupe included the famous *tan* actor, Kao Lang-t'ing, the first man known to have performed in Peking in the *Erh-huang* style.

The introduction of *Erh-huang* into the capital is of great significance for the Peking theatre, since it formed (and still forms) the basis of Peking Opera. Probably Kao Lang-t'ing also sang in the livelier *Hsi-p'i* style, the other major component of contemporary Peking Opera, so that we may date the origin of China's best known form of opera to the 1790s. Already by the early years of the eighteenth century there had been several regional forms in south China based on *Erh-huang* and *Hsi-p'i*. These two musical forms were especially popular in Anhwei province, the capital of which, Anking, was famous for actors who could sing in them. For this reason the groups which sang *Erh-huang* came to be known as 'Anhwei companies'.

At the time of Kao Lang-t'ing's arrival in Peking, the most striking characteristic of his new music was that it was accompanied by the Chinese fiddle, or *hu-ch'in*. There is a tradition that the Emperor Chia-ch'ing (1796–1820) objected to the use of this instrument and ordered it to be replaced by the more melodious flute. This story cannot be confirmed from primary sources and is based on the hearsay of old actors. Whether it is true or not, there is no doubt that the *hu-ch'in* was the principal instrument of the *Erh-huang* orchestra in the 1860s and has remained so ever since.

Despite the importance of Kao Lang-t'ing in the history of *Erh-huang* and the Peking Opera, very little indeed is known about his life. He was born a few years before or after 1770 and came from Yang-chow. As a child he lived also in Hangchow, the capital of Chekiang, and he later went to Anhwei. During the period just before his arrival in Peking he worked in his native city, and it was from there that he journeyed to the capital.

Kao Lang-t'ing's career on the Peking stage was short, and we shall see that in this respect he was like other *tan* actors of the Anhwei companies at this time. By 1800 he was already past his prime. He probably retired from the stage altogether in about 1808, but may well have worked as a teacher long after that time. Certainly he was active in the actors' guild, which had become an important feature of the Peking theatre, until well into the 1820s, and he may have died in about 1830.

The San-ch'ing, in which Kao Lang-t'ing came to hold so prominent a place, was by no means the only Anhwei company to go to Peking in 1790 for Ch'ien-lung's birthday celebrations. Others included the Ssu-hsi, Ho-ch'un and Ch'un-t'ai, all of them large companies. During the decades after 1790 more Anhwei companies were formed, while others declined and were eventually disbanded. By the 1820s, four companies had come to occupy a dominant position in the Peking theatre. These were the San-ch'ing, Ch'un-t'ai, Ssu-hsi and Ho-ch'un, which became known as the 'Four Great Anhwei Companies'. Apart from the Ho-ch'un, which was disbanded in about 1850, these troupes retained their following until the end of the nineteenth century.

The Anhwei companies were noted for their superb stagecraft, especially in military scenes, which involved complicated acrobatics. Although spectacular acting of this sort had been significant in the drama of Anhwei for some time, it was fairly new to the audiences of Peking and had not been a characteristic of the Clapper companies of the 1780s. There is, for instance, no record that Wei Ch'ang-sheng could perform acrobatics until his last return to Peking in 1800, and by that time he, too, had been influenced by the art of the Anhwei companies. The splendid prowess in acrobatics of the Peking Opera's actors has thrilled millions of people since the 1790s and remains even today one of its chief attractions.

Neither the popularity of their art nor their original purpose in coming to the capital prevented the Anhwei companies from arousing the suspicion of the authorities. According to one tradition, based on the oral evidence of old actors, the Emperor Chia-ch'ing forbade the use of the name *Erh-huang*. He considered it to be blasphemous because one homophone of the name means 'two emperors'. In 1798 the government, alarmed at the continuing decline of the elegant *K'un-ch'ü* and *Ching-ch'iang*, forbade the performance of several other forms of drama, including *Erh-huang*. Unlike the Clapper companies of the 1780s, however, the Anhwei troupes were very little affected by government pressure. Firstly, they were extremely adaptable and could placate the authorities by performing *K'un-ch'ü*. Secondly, though the use of the name *Erh-huang* was discontinued, there was no need to change the style of the music. In fact, the edict of 1798 appears to have become ineffective very quickly, and the Anhwei companies remained as firmly entrenched in Peking as ever.

At the same time there was a partial revival of the Clapper companies after Wei Ch'ang-sheng's second visit to Peking. Though they were never again able to rival the Anhwei troupes in their appeal to the people, they continued to function throughout most of the nineteenth century, and in the traditional Peking Opera of recent times a number of pieces have been performed with music which reveals their origin as Clapper drama. The Clapper Opera was not alone among the older forms to acquire a new lease of life. The *Ching-ch'iang* of the 1770s, which had been virtually destroyed by Wei Ch'ang-sheng's arrival in 1779, was also to some extent resuscitated. Never before had the variety of drama seen in Peking been so wide.

In the late 1820s the theatrical life of the capital began to be complicated by another factor. Certain actors had begun to move from Hupeh to Peking and to introduce a new dramatic form called *Ch'u-tiao*, or the Tunes of Hupeh. A work of 1832 records that 'the capital honoured the *Ch'u-tiao*. Among its performers, men like Wang Hung-kuei and Li Liu were praised by all for their excellence in the new sounds.'[8]

The arrival of the Hupeh actors was not nearly as great an event in the history of the Peking Opera as that of either Wei Ch'ang-sheng or Kao Lang-t'ing. In the first place, neither Wang nor Li was particularly eminent as an actor, and neither is mentioned much in the sources of their period. We know practically nothing about them beyond the fact that both were *lao-sheng* actors. Secondly, the *Ch'u-tiao*, like the drama of the early Anhwei companies, was based on the *Erh-huang* and *Hsi-p'i* forms. Although these two forms were not performed in exactly the same way in Anhwei and Hupeh, the innovations introduced into Peking by the Hupeh actors of the 1820s were but slight in comparison with those of Wei or Kao. Finally, the new actors arrived as individuals. They did not bring new companies to the capital but joined those already there. The Four Great Anhwei Companies were in no way superseded. On the contrary, they were strengthened by the influx of new talent and of new approaches to fundamentally similar dramatic styles.

During the two decades after the arrival of Wang Hung-kuei and Li Liu, these four companies maintained their prominent position in

Peking. Apart from another Anhwei company (the Sung-chu, apparently formed in the early 1820s), none could rival them either in popular appeal or in artistic standards. The Four Great Anhwei Companies provided the people of Peking with an excellent variety of entertainment, each company becoming famous for a particular characteristic. For example, the San-ch'ing was distinctive in that it often performed long dramas in episodes. This was in contrast to the normal custom of the time, whereby short scenes were acted individually, and successive items did not necessarily tell a connected story.

The companies of the Peking Opera were certainly quite equal to the task of satisfying the theatrical needs of the capital, with the result that the *K'un-ch'ü* and other forms of drama tended to disappear. Indeed, so successful was the Peking Opera that it spread throughout most of the country and by the middle of the twentieth century had approached as near as any theatrical form to the status of a national drama.[9]

2 Actors of the Late Ch'ing Period

This chapter covers approximately the last fifty years of the Ch'ing dynasty – that is, roughly from 1860 to 1911. I noted in Chapter One that the occupation of Peking by foreign forces in 1860 had brought the dynasty to the point of near-collapse, but in fact the following years saw a slight revival. Under the leadership of men like Prince Kung (1833–98), the sixth son of Emperor Tao-kuang, and Tseng Kuo-fan (1811–72), the Chinese and Manchus succeeded in establishing what became known as the T'ung-chih Restoration (1861–74). The Taiping and Nien rebellions, as well as other serious local uprisings, were suppressed. Relations between China and the Western powers were put on a more equal basis, and the economy was partly restored. The leaders of the T'ung-chih Restoration were deeply conscious of the moral decay of the Chinese empire and strove to remedy this fundamental defect by a return to the traditional Confucian values. They were also aware of the significance of Western technology and, with the support of the intellectuals, made a serious attempt to introduce it into China by establishing industry and by manufacturing arms along Western lines.

The decades which followed this 'Restoration' saw a tremendous upsurge of nationalist feeling, and of nationalist reaction, in China. Her intellectual elite and its supporters searched for ways to strengthen their country through modernization and the adoption of Western technology. On the other hand, many people saw no need for China to absorb Western culture, even if she was to adopt Western technology, and believed that they could bring about a revival of Chinese greatness without it. In particular, there was very strong anti-missionary feeling, and it was believed in many quarters that the carriers of religion were merely a front for imperialist penetration. It was largely hostility towards Christianity, and consequently towards the West, that caused the Boxer uprising. In 1900 revolutionary troops stormed the foreign legations in Peking, burned down churches in the city and killed many Christians, both Chinese and foreign. The Ch'ing government gave some support to the insurgents and it was only after the Western powers and Japan had intervened and slaughtered the Boxers in large numbers that the uprising was put down.

Another aspect of nationalism was the strong feeling against the Manchus. Chinese resentment towards a foreign dynasty believed to be dominated by imperialist powers was growing, and it was only a matter of time before movements to overthrow it would gain momentum. Anti-Manchu feeling was given impetus by the reactionary character of the Ch'ing government, notably embodied in the person of the Empress Dowager Tz'u-hsi. Since 1875, when she contrived to have her three-year-old nephew and adopted son the Emperor Kuanghsü (1875–1908) placed on the throne, the Empress had been the effective wielder of power at court. In 1898 a group of reformers, led by K'ang Yu-wei (1858–1927), succeeded in persuading the emperor to adopt their programme, but the Empress moved quickly to suppress the proposed innovations. She placed Kuang-hsü under house-arrest and had several of the leading reformers arrested and executed. K'ang Yu-wei himself managed to escape her clutches and fled to Hong Kong.

Although the Empress Dowager had crushed the reform movement of 1898 so effectively, she completely failed to appease her subjects' demand for change and after 1900 even adopted most of the reform programme herself. But the reforms were adopted too slowly and too late, and the Chinese turned increasingly to revolution as a solution for the country's problems. Both the Empress and Kuang-hsü died in 1908, and it was their successor, Hsüan-t'ung (1909–11), who bore the full impact of the revolutionary movement led by Sun Yat-sen. In October 1911 Sun's followers took the strategic city of Wuchang and the tottering Manchu dynasty fell soon afterwards.

At first, the Peking Opera was only marginally affected by the political upheavals of the period. Although the Ho-ch'un troupe had disbanded in about 1850, the other three 'Great Anhwei Companies' (the San-ch'ing, Ch'un-tai and Ssu-hsi) continued to dominate the Peking stage until late in the nineteenth century. The great actors of the time joined their ranks and gave them able leadership. During the period of the T'ung-chih Restoration, the Ch'un-t'ai company was headed by the famous *tan* Hu Hsi-lu, and the Ssu-hsi by Cheng Hsiu-lan and Mei Lan-fang's grandfather Mei Ch'iao-ling, who became the company's most important *tan* actor. The San-ch'ing was led by Ch'eng Chang-keng (discussed below), who took charge of the company in about 1845 and retained control until his death in 1880.

The last two decades of the century saw a marked decline in the standing of the three remaining 'Great Anhwei Companies'. Many of their finest members died or left Peking, and some of the best actors of the day founded their own companies rather than join the old ones. For instance, in 1887 T'an Hsin-p'ei established a company called T'ung-ch'un. Later, after making two brief attempts to revive the San-ch'ing, he combined the best actors from both this company and the T'ung-ch'un to form the T'ung-ch'ing troupe, which is listed among the capital's foremost troupes in a Peking guide-book of 1907.[1]

The most striking feature of the Peking Opera's history in the period 1840–1911 was the rise of the great *lao-sheng* actors. This was caused by the growing interest in China's heroic past, and consequently in heroic drama, which was possibly aroused in China by the country's humiliation at the hands of foreign powers during this period. In earlier times *tan* players had dominated the stage, but with the appearance of the great Mi Hsi-tzu, who died in 1832, and the growing demand for heroic drama, in which *tan* actors of necessity took a subordinate place, the performers of *lao-sheng* roles became increasingly important. Indeed, although many fine *tan*, *ch'ou*, *hsiao-sheng* and *hua-lien* (painted face) actors remained on the stage, most of the greatest artists of the theatre belonged to the *lao-sheng* category. Such names as Chang Erh-k'uei, Yü San-sheng, Wang Kuei-fen, and Wang Chiu-ling are well known to enthusiasts of the Peking Opera. Yet even they should probably be ranked below three other *lao-sheng* actors of the period: Ch'eng Chang-keng, Sun Chü-hsien and T'an Hsin-p'ei. These three men contributed more than any of their contemporaries to the Peking theatre, and it is to them that I intend to devote most of the remainder of this chapter.

CH'ENG CHANG-KENG

Ch'eng Chang-keng is generally considered the greatest Peking actor of the nineteenth century. He was born in Anking, Anhwei province, in 1812. In his early years he learnt to sing *K'un-ch'ü* and it is said that his training in the elegant drama made his diction unusually clear.

Ch'i Ju-shan claims that he studied under Mi Hsi-tzu,[2] in which case he must have arrived in the capital before 1832.

Ch'eng Chang-keng's first reported public performance was not a success and the audience ridiculed his acting. The story goes that he was so ashamed of this failure that he avoided public appearances for three years while he worked hard to perfect his art. One day, a certain noble held an important banquet to which Manchu aristocrats, high-ranking officials and other dignitaries had been invited. The host wanted to try out a number of new actors at this function. Among them was Ch'eng Chang-keng, whose performance proved to be so magnificent that the guests, several hundred strong, stood up and shouted aloud with surprise and delight.

Over the succeeding decades Ch'eng's reputation grew by leaps and bounds. He was extremely versatile, and his repertoire was among the widest of any actors' of the time. In 1860, when the court invited actors from the Outer City of Peking to perform in the palaces for a few months, Ch'eng achieved the ultimate honour of being among those who were invited to act in the imperial presence. Ch'eng died in 1880 at the age of sixty-eight, apparently from exhaustion. He had already arranged for the leadership of the San-ch'ing company to devolve upon the *lao-sheng* Yang Yüeh-lou. Chang-keng left no family, apart from an adopted son, the actor Ch'eng Chang-pu.

Ch'eng was noted not only as a player but also as a teacher. A number of performers who later achieved fame received instruction at his hands, and his disciples included Yang Yüeh-lou and T'an Hsin-p'ei. Like all senior performers, he was able to teach all types of roles; though he was himself a *lao-sheng*, there were *tan*, *hsiao-sheng* and *hua-lien* among his students. The training which Ch'eng gave was extremely thorough. Dialogue, singing and walking on the stage were all taught with the greatest care. Ch'i Ju-shan writes: 'After [the students] had learned [this art], he would again divide them up into *sheng*, *tan*, *ching*, *ch'ou* and so on, so that each [group] formed a company; and he would make the best student act as leader. Each company would walk for one or two hours every day, while the teacher superintended from the side. Whenever someone did the walking badly, he would immediately correct the fault. This process would continue over one or two years.'[3]

A number of Ch'eng's personal characteristics are described in the sources, which record several revealing incidents from his life and also some of his habits. We learn that Ch'eng was a strict man. This is already clear from what I have written of his qualities as a teacher, but it is shown also in the rigid discipline which he imposed on the members of his company. Boys in his care had to call him 'master', and he would punish or reprimand those who made mistakes during a performance. Disapproving of the rather free and easy behaviour allowed in many troupes, he also forbade actors who were off-stage to laugh or play when a drama was in progress. Chou Tzu-heng, an actor in the San-ch'ing company, has recalled how one day he was acting with Ch'eng at a party. Chou was off-stage and, 'mistakenly thinking that Chang-keng had gone on stage, he played around and laughed. . . . Suddenly someone struck his head from behind. [Looking round], he saw that it was the boss.'[4]

It was consistent with his strictness that Ch'eng should not have been afraid of high-ranking persons, as the following story shows. One day Prince Kung, one of the chief architects of the T'ung-chih Restoration, wanted to rest from state affairs and invited Ch'eng to come and perform for him. Ch'eng was at the time feeling slightly ill and refused the invitation, at which Prince Kung insisted, with signs of irritation. Ch'eng complied to the extent of coming into the statesman's presence, but protested that he did not feel well and would not be able to perform. The prince became even more infuriated and had Ch'eng tied up. The actor then shouted, 'There is in reason [no distinction between] the high and the lowly. Why do you, O Prince, go against reason as recognized by everybody? Even if you should put me, your slave, to death, I cannot perform for Your Highness.' After a protracted argument Prince Kung smiled and sent Ch'eng away.[5]

Ch'eng Chang-keng is described as having been very patriotic. He is said to have been extremely upset by the disasters which befell China at the hands of the foreign powers. He was enraged by the Opium War, and is reported to have wept bitterly at China's humiliation when British and French troops occupied Peking in 1860. During the 1850s he stopped acting for a time, but with the accession of the T'ung-chih Emperor in 1861, and the establishment of improved conditions during the Restoration period, he was once more seen on the Peking stage. It is said that he liked performing only patriotic dramas about ancient heroes and patriots, and that he acted such parts with such intense emotion that his audience were reduced to tears.

This great actor emerges from the sources as a superlative performer, an excellent teacher, and a man with a character patriotic, strict, just, strong and honest. In short, he was the model of a truly virtuous actor, and the only blemish on his character which I have found mentioned was his love for opium. It is difficult to avoid the suspicion that the men who wrote about him were biased in his favour. It would be interesting to know how an enemy regarded him, but no such record survives. In any case, it seems beyond doubt that Ch'eng was widely respected and loved.[6]

SUN CHÜ-HSIEN

It was Ch'eng Chang-keng who was chiefly responsible for strengthening the influence in Peking of the *Erh-huang* music of Anhwei province. At the same time Yü San-sheng was fulfilling the same role for the rather similar but by no means identical theatre of Hupeh. One of the actors who did most to weld the two dramatic styles into a harmonious whole was Sun Chü-hsien, who was deeply influenced by both men. He was endowed with extraordinary vocal versatility and was equally at home in both the high and the low registers.

Sun Chü-hsien was born in Tientsin on 23 January 1841 of an old merchant family. From an early age he took an interest not only in scholarship but also in military matters, and it seemed likely that he would follow an army career. This ambition appeared to hold good prospects when he passed an important military examination in 1858 and, three years later, entered the service of Ch'en Kuo-jui (1837–83), who was at that time engaged in suppressing the rebellion of the Nien. Sun was wounded in action twice. In 1867 he was transferred to a different unit, and remained in the army until 1870, when his new commander was dismissed for gambling.

Sun Chü-hsien had always had a liking for the theatre and had taken up acting as an amateur even in his Tientsin days. He now decided to devote his life to promoting the drama and went to Shanghai, where he assisted in the management of several theatres. In 1876 he moved to Peking, where he happened to see a performance by Wang Kuei-fen which impressed him so deeply that he determined to make his own name as a *lao-sheng*.

Sun Chü-hsien was immediately successful and caught the eye of Ch'eng Chang-keng. The two men became acquainted through an opium dealer, who was a mutual friend, and Ch'eng invited Sun to undertake training to succeed him as leader of the San-ch'ing company. Despite his high regard for Ch'eng, Sun declined the offer, and instead joined the Ssu-hsi company, of which he remained a member throughout his years in Peking. Like Ch'eng, he was invited to act at court, but in this respect his experience was different from Ch'eng's. Previously, there had been only one brief period, in 1860, when actors (including Ch'eng) were invited from the city to perform before the emperor. But in 1884 the Empress Dowager altered this policy and engaged many eminent artists to entertain her. Sun Chü-hsien was invited to be a teacher in the imperial palaces and to perform in them. Indeed, he made such an impression on the Empress that she offered him an official rank, which, however, he declined.

Sun's position in the palaces got him indirectly involved in politics. However, he seems to have taken this in his stride despite the dangers inherent in being involved in such activities.

During the coup of 1898 [when the Empress Dowager suppressed the Reform Movement] there was an actor called T'ien Chi-yün who was taking part in its affairs. Disaster was coming. Chü-hsien was rather sympathetic towards him and said to some friends: 'I'm on his side. It would be a great pity if he got killed.' He discussed it with the eunuch Li Lien-ying [the Empress's favourite eunuch]. When Lien-ying heard what he had said, he changed colour because of it and said in a low voice: 'It's just as well it's me you spoke to. Don't tell anybody else. The Empress is trembling with rage, so don't say any more.' Chü-hsien said magnanimously, 'What does it matter if I get killed? If a wise person like the Empress should mistakenly kill an actor, she would bring scorn on the empire. That's why I pity the Empress and am willing to remonstrate with her loyally and to the utmost.' Because of this Chi-yün was eventually released, as a result of what he [Chü-hsien] said [to the Empress].[7]

In 1900 Sun's house in Peking was burned down during the Boxer uprising, and at about the same time both his wife and his concubine died. He therefore left the capital for Shanghai, where he lived for many years, acting and assisting in the management of the city's main theatres. It was at this time, too, that he came under the patronage of Tuan-fang (1861–1911), who was governor-general of the lower Yangtze provinces in 1904 and again from 1906 to 1909. Tuan-fang loved to encourage scholars and other men of talent and would frequently invite Sun Chü-hsien to perform.

Sun lived in Shanghai until 1917, when he returned to Peking. Soon afterwards he went back to his native Tientsin, where he lived in semi-retirement, making occasional appearances on the stage and teaching. He died in Tientsin on 29 July 1931, at the age of ninety.

Sun Chü-hsien's career offers an excellent illustration of the high standing which amateurs have been able to achieve in the Chinese theatre. Sun never underwent the gruelling training provided by the drama schools of the time, nor did he take up acting seriously until the late age (by Chinese standards) of sixteen. Moreover, he was nearly forty when he won his first great successes in Peking late in the 1870s. Yet he was able to reach the summit of his chosen profession. The fact that he was the most long-lived of all the famous actors is irrelevant, since his main activities on the stage ended in 1900, when he was still only fifty-nine and had thirty-one years to live.

Sun was a kind-hearted man who always went out of his way to encourage younger actors and supported charitable causes with all his power. He was also prepared to devote large sums of his own money to helping his friends or people whom he admired. Once an old friend of his fell sick and died while the two were travelling northwards together by boat from Shanghai, and the body was about to be buried at sea. 'Chü-hsien was afraid that his old friend's corpse would be buried in the stomach of a fish or sea turtle. So he hid the corpse and waited till the boat was anchored. He then took it single-handedly ashore. After it had been shrouded and placed in a coffin, he sent it back to [his friend's] native town. All this cost him several thousand cash.'[8]

For much of his life Sun Chü-hsien was interested in Buddhism and abstained from meat. He also placed a high value on learning and sought the company of scholars. Like other progressive actors of his time he felt strongly that actors should acquire an education for the sake of their art. He would say, 'Performing drama and writing essays are essentially the same kind of thing. Those who know no characters cannot write essays. Those who cannot write essays lack the qualifications for performing.'[9]

Sun's interest in scholarship may have been partly due to the influence of his elder brother, who was highly educated and took up a career as an official. Sun had three sons, the eldest of whom went into the civil service. The other two both became soldiers, reflecting the earlier enthusiasm of their father for military affairs.

T'AN HSIN-P'EI

Despite the length of his career and his undoubted magnificence on the stage, Sun was somewhat overshadowed by 'the great king of the acting world', as he was generally called, T'an Hsin-p'ei, who was certainly the most famous and popular of Ch'eng Chang-keng's immediate successors. T'an was born on 23 April 1847 in Hwangpei county, Hupeh province. This district was also the birthplace of Li Yüan-hung (1864–1928), one of the early Republican presidents, and Li's accession to leadership gave rise in Peking to the saying that he, T'an and the courtesan Hsiao-a-feng were the 'three famous natives of Hupeh'.

T'an Hsin-p'ei's father was also an actor. Little is known about this man except that he performed as a *tan* in the Ssu-hsi company in the 1850s and died in 1877. It soon became clear that Hsin-p'ei would follow his father's profession and he entered a training-school at the age of ten. After graduation he went to Tientsin, but soon afterwards he returned to Peking, where he joined the San-ch'ing company as a disciple of Ch'eng Chang-keng. He was not very successful at first, and his difficulties were increased when his voice lost its power after it broke, and he was compelled to abandon *lao-sheng* roles for the vocally less strenuous military male roles (*wu-sheng*).

After this early period of failure, T'an Hsin-p'ei left Peking and formed a wandering company in the districts east of the city. He was joined by a number of other actors who later became famous, including the amateur Liu Ching-jan. The troupe met with some success in its travels and even founded an attached training-school. A story survives from T'an's years as an itinerant actor. One day he was travelling with his company and had decided on a particular village some distance away in which to spend the night. His companions had grown very tired and wanted to stop. It so happened that T'an was acquainted with a young girl in a nearby village; he told his followers that he knew of a hotel there where they could sleep. When the company arrived they found no hotel, and so T'an went to the girl's house and asked for lodging. He knew very well that she would refuse because there were no men in the family. T'an began to insist. 'It is just because there are no men that we [thought we could] stay,' he said. As he expected, the girl took fright and aroused the neighbours. Everybody was so shocked at T'an's impertinence that they chased the whole company from the village. T'an, who had anticipated this, then guided his colleagues in the direction of the village where he had originally hoped to spend the night. Through this ruse he succeeded in persuading his troupe to reach his intended destination.[10]

This story suggests that T'an was a man of some determination. It is therefore not surprising that, despite the setbacks which he had suffered, he still aspired to a career on the stage in Peking. In the early 1870s he returned to the capital, where he joined the San-ch'ing company once more. He worked hard, and when his voice fortunately regained its strength, he again began to sing *lao-sheng* roles. Ch'eng Chang-keng was extremely enthusiastic and went so far as to tell T'an that he would eventually become recognized as the greatest actor of his day. T'an was of course flattered, but modestly pointed out that Sun Chü-hsien was not without prestige. Ch'eng replied, 'No, not he. Chü-hsien's voice is of course very fine, but it has a bitter flavour, so it will not suit people's tastes. But *your* voice is sweet and intoxicating. You just wait and see in thirty years' time whether my prediction turns out correct.'[11]

Ch'eng's forecast was indeed to be proved right. Any possibility of rivalry between T'an and Sun was removed when Sun left Peking in 1900. By that year, T'an had founded the T'ung-ch'ing company, with which his name is so closely associated, and in the twenty years since Ch'eng's death had become so successful that there was no section of Peking's population that did not idolize him. He was constantly invited to Tientsin, but the pressure of engagements in the capital ensured that he never stayed in Tientsin for more than two or three days at a time. Socially, he achieved possibly his greatest success when he became the favourite actor of the Empress Dowager Tz'u-hsi. It is true that in her time it was not especially remarkable that good actors should be invited to perform at court, but T'an was seen there unusually often and was even granted the rank of a sixth-degree official. Most of the Manchu nobles followed the Empress's taste, although it is said that Prince Kung did not particularly admire T'an.

In 1913 the 'king of the acting world' visited Shanghai. He had acted there on three earlier occasions, but the acclaim accorded him in 1913 surpassed anything that he had experienced in the city before. According to one account, 'for more than ten days in advance, people displayed advertisements for the great king in large golden characters, they stuck them all over the streets and on the doors of the theatres. They joined electric lights together to form characters, specifically showing his wonderful features. . . . None of this had ever happened before.'[12] T'an earned huge sums of money, and the people flocked in unprecedented numbers to see him.

After he returned to Peking, T'an Hsin-p'ei continued to be engaged to perform privately before high-ranking officials. However, he was now getting old, and declining health caused him to refuse many invitations. In April 1917 he was ordered to act at a party given to welcome the arrival in Peking from Kwangsi of the great southern warlord Lu Jung-t'ing. He wanted to refuse, but it proved impossible for him to do so. The performance was the last that he ever gave. About a fortnight later, on 10 May, he died in his house in Peking.

T'an had four daughters, the eldest of whom married Hsia Yüeh-jun, the famous revolutionary actor of Shanghai. He also had seven sons, of whom two pursued scholarly careers and five became actors. T'an often expressed his disappointment that none of these five achieved great success. However, after T'an's death his fifth son, Hsiao-p'ei, did win a certain degree of fame; and, more important, Hsiao-p'ei's son Fu-ying became one of the most highly regarded *lao-sheng* of his time.

As an actor, T'an Hsin-p'ei was regarded partly as a transmitter, because he learned a great deal from many of his predecessors and absorbed what he had learnt into his own art. On the other hand, he developed his own particular style and would alter the words of a drama quite freely. This was a practice which was looked upon with disfavour by the theatrical profession, and actors who adopted it were sometimes punished by the guild. However, even though T'an did not always alter texts with especial skill, his stature (and probably his leadership of the guild also) ensured that he would not be reprimanded. Indeed, with the passing of time, audiences came to regard T'an's versions of texts as the only correct ones and would criticize anyone who did not follow them.

As a man, T'an was often regarded as intolerant, especially since he did not suffer the faults of others gladly. He was quite unworldly and took no interest in political matters. The revolution through which he lived left him totally unmoved. Even the affairs of the actors' guild, of which he was the leader, failed to arouse his concern. He was indifferent to its activities and only agreed to be its head because he was the leading actor of the time.

In view of his high connections and remarkable self-confidence (which even amounted to vanity), it is perhaps not surprising that T'an Hsin-p'ei was completely unafraid of exalted personages and sometimes even treated them with disrespect. These traits, as well as his sense of fun, emerge vividly from the following story.

One day Prince Ch'ing (1836–1916), one of the many great-grand-sons of Ch'ien-lung, was holding a birthday party to which he had invited various dignitaries, and at which T'an was to act. T'an's arrival was announced, and the Prince took him to a quiet room to dress up. Instead of preparing to perform, T'an took a good rest and smoked opium. After smoking his fill he appeared, and Prince Ch'ing requested him to perform two scenes. 'At first T'an agreed, but demanded that a member of the Grand Council should kneel in front of him to request it before he could obey the order. Prince Ch'ing was caught completely unawares by these words. But just as people were busily trying without success to think what to do, somebody rushed in and, without waiting for T'an to finish talking, said: "The boss has condescended to come." He entreated T'an and prostrated himself before him. Who was this man? It was the Grand Councillor Na-t'ung.' T'an burst into laughter and promptly performed the two scenes.[13]

Apart from his art and his family, T'an Hsin-p'ei had only two main interests. One was his religion: T'an was a fervent Buddhist and made frequent trips to the beautiful temples in the Western Hills outside Peking to pray. The other interest was opium, to which he was addicted for much of his life. It is said that he took to smoking it to drown his sorrows after falling desperately in love with an unsympathetic prostitute in Shanghai. His love of opium aroused no disapproval among his admirers. On the contrary, the story circulated that he sang much better than usual after awakening from an opium dream, and his greatness as an actor was partly attributed to the drug. Some actors, including Yü Shu-yen, went so far as to take up smoking opium to improve their art.

These biographical sketches leave us in no doubt that the great actors of the Ch'ing's last half-century were quite different in kind from those of the preceding period. They owed their success much more to their art than had their predecessors (whose popularity, in many cases, had been derived from their status as homosexual favourites); their personalities were far stronger and more mature, their careers much longer. It is not surprising, therefore, that they made a firmer imprint on the Peking theatre. They consolidated the work of earlier masters and expanded its scope by supplementing their predecessors' repertoire of small-scale comedies, love stories and such relatively slight pieces by introducing heroic drama, to which they gave central importance. Recent players of the traditional Peking Opera have regarded them as models and have ignored the actors of the early nineteenth century.

The title 'father of the Peking Opera' is applied most often not to Wei Ch'ang-sheng nor to Kao Lang-t'ing, but to Ch'eng Chang-keng.

One wonders whether the 'patriotic' Ch'eng, had he lived forty years later, would have been as little interested in the revolution as T'an was. Certainly the acting community included many artists who did not share T'an's attitude, and it seems appropriate to end this chapter with a short discussion of them.

Possibly the most important were T'ien Chi-yün and Wang Chung-sheng. T'ien was known in Peking for his revolutionary ideas. In particular, he pressed for the abolition of the houses in which boy actors lived and were trained. These had acquired a sordid reputation owing to the high incidence of homosexuality in them. T'ien was sometimes invited to act at court and would take advantage of these occasions to introduce progressive literature into the palaces. In 1898 he became actively involved in the Reform Movement, with the result that the Empress Dowager ordered his arrest. As mentioned earlier, however, she later released him, and he escaped to Shanghai. After the storm had blown over, T'ien returned to Peking, where he founded the Yü-ch'eng company. This group was noted not only for its repertoire of Peking Opera and Clapper pieces (T'ien was himself a magnificent exponent of the Clapper Opera), but also for its modern dramas with social and revolutionary content. In the last years of the Ch'ing period, theatrical pieces of this kind became important vehicles of propaganda. T'ien was keenly aware of their value for the revolution and actively promoted progressive drama in his company. He invited from outside Peking several actors who were known as supporters of Sun Yat-sen, and these players performed as members of the Yü-ch'eng company.

The most noted of them was Wang Chung-sheng, who had been among the leading exponents of the new progressive spoken drama (discussed in Chapter Seven) since its inception in 1907. In that year, to spread its influence, he helped to found the Ch'un-yang she (Spring Society) in Shanghai. As a visiting member of the Yü-ch'eng troupe, Wang mounted several revolutionary plays in Peking. He also went to Tientsin, whither he was accompanied by several of the permanent members of T'ien Chi-yün's company. Wang Chung-sheng's political sympathies made him an object of intense suspicion to the tottering Ch'ing dynasty. After the Revolution broke out in 1911 he was soon arrested, together with several other actors of similar persuasion. At his interrogation he made no attempt to disguise either his earlier revolutionary activities or his intense hope that the Revolution would soon triumph. As a result, he was sentenced to death, and was executed towards the end of 1911.

Wang's death naturally caused him to be regarded as a martyr to Sun Yat-sen's cause. When the Manchus were in fact overthrown a few weeks later, it became obvious to the revolutionaries that if the theatre could be used to uphold the *status quo*, then it could also function as an effective weapon against those in power. We shall see in later chapters that the adherents of successive revolutionary movements were to remember this lesson.

3 The Peking Theatre of the Republic*

Despite Sun Yat-sen's success in overthrowing the Ch'ing dynasty, his revolution was in many respects a failure. The social reforms on which he had set his heart were not carried out, and he himself was forced to hand over the reins of administration to Yüan Shih-k'ai, a former official of the Ch'ing government who enjoyed greater military support than Sun, had little interest in the revolutionary cause, and in 1915–16 even tried to proclaim himself emperor. During the years after 1911 China was not the united, democratic nation for which the revolutionaries had striven, but a country in which warlords competed for power.

The outbreak of the First World War produced in China a feeling of deep disillusionment with the West, and the events which followed the war intensified their disappointment. The Chinese hoped that at the Versailles Peace Conference of 1919 the great powers would arrange for the return to China of certain rights held by Western interests in China, especially those previously enjoyed by Germany in Shantung and seized by Japan during the war. When their demands were refused at Versailles the anger of the Chinese flared into demonstrations, first on 4 May in Peking and later in many other parts of the country, as a result of which the Chinese government refused to sign the Treaty of Versailles (1919). Chinese nationalism was given a new focus by this show of feeling, which became known as the May Fourth Movement.

This campaign was related to, and gave impetus to, the efforts of a group of Chinese intellectuals to bring about changes in the social and cultural life of the people. The proponents of the New Cultural Movement, which was led by men like Hu Shih (1891–1962) and Ch'en

* See Ills. 12–14, p. 134.

Tu-hsiu (1879–1942), sought to introduce colloquial Chinese as the literary medium, with the intention that it should replace the previously almost universally used classical language. They also advocated radical changes in the strongly hierarchical Chinese family structure and pressed for thorough-going social reforms of the sort that the architects of the 1911 Revolution had espoused but failed to effect.

After the October Revolution of 1917 in Russia, which brought the Communists to power, some thinking Chinese began to favour the adoption of a more radical, left-wing solution of their country's problems. Their position was strengthened by the New Culture and May Fourth Movements. In July 1921 the Chinese Communist Party held its first congress in Shanghai, and its members began to prepare themselves to exert greater influence. Meanwhile, Sun Yat-sen was trying to revitalize the Nationalist Party (Kuomintang). He called a national congress of his party in Canton early in 1924, and from then until 1927 Communists were allowed to become members. After Sun Yat-sen's death in 1925, Chiang Kai-shek made a serious and largely successful attempt to reunify the country under Kuomintang rule. In 1928 he moved the capital to Nanking, where it was to remain until the outbreak of the Sino-Japanese war in 1937.

In 1927, to secure his power and to eliminate potentially dangerous opposition, Chiang Kai-shek reversed Sun Yat-sen's policy of co-operation with the Communists. During that year and the years that followed, his police and armies slaughtered several hundreds of thousands of Communist Party members and their supporters. Contrary to Chiang's expectations, however, the Communists did not give in under the constant pressure which he brought to bear against them. They reorganized their forces and in 1934 began their Long March from their bases in south-east China, eventually establishing themselves in northern Shensi, with their capital at Yenan.

While trying to eliminate Communist opposition and consolidating his authority, Chiang Kai-shek set about attempting to solve the problems of national reconstruction. He achieved only limited success, which was, in any case, completely annulled by the outbreak of war with Japan. The Japanese had occupied Manchuria in 1931, but in 1937 they launched a full-scale onslaught on China. Chiang's forces failed in their initial efforts to repel the Japanese, who drove him from Nanking and occupied the major cities of eastern China, eventually forcing Chiang to seek refuge in inland Chungking, Szechwan Province, which became his wartime capital. The war ended in 1945 with the defeat of the Japanese by the Allies, and with their expulsion from China. But the country as a whole, and the Kuomintang itself, had made very heavy sacrifices, and the ravages of the war were a major cause of the total collapse of Chiang's regime which followed. Civil war broke out in 1946 between the Kuomintang and the Communists, whose victory in 1949 enabled their leader, Mao Tse-tung, to proclaim the People's Republic of China.

The Republican period was one of change not only in China as a whole but also in the Peking theatre. The intellectual calibre of actors and dramatists alike was high, and many reforms (which I shall discuss later in this chapter) were introduced. Yet the Peking Opera was not affected as deeply as other more modern forms of drama, especially the spoken play, and many of its most important institutions and innovations had been introduced earlier, during the late Ch'ing period.

The system of establishing dramatic troupes, for instance, remained as it had been since the fall of the Four Great Anhwei Companies. A distinguished actor could found his own group at any time and name it as he pleased, or he could collaborate with another actor in forming a troupe. Companies often survived for only a short time, since one famous actor might co-operate in successive years with different colleagues. Among the more important troupes[1] were the Ch'eng-hua of Mei Lan-fang, the Wu-ho of Ch'eng Yen-ch'iu, the Ch'ung-ch'ing of Shang Hsiao-yün, the Ch'ing-sheng of Hsün Hui-sheng and the Yung-sheng of Yang Hsiao-lou.

The training-schools, to which I shall return in the next chapter, remained as they had been during the late Ch'ing period, when they were founded, and they continued to produce a large number of splendid actors in all categories. Though there still flourished excellent *lao-sheng*, such as Yü Shu-yen (1890–1943), Yen Chü-p'eng (1890–1942) and Ma Lien-liang (1902–67), they no longer dominated the stage to the extent that Ch'eng Chang-keng and his colleagues had done in earlier times. There were numerous *tan*, such as Ch'en Te-lin (1862–1930), Wang Yao-ch'ing (1882–1954) and the 'four great *tan*', Mei Lan-fang (1894–1961), Ch'eng Yen-ch'iu (1904–58), Shang Hsiao-yün (b. 1900) and Hsün Hui-sheng (b. 1900); among *wu-sheng* there have also been a number of prominent actors, such as Yang Hsiao-lou (1877–1938) and Yü Chen-t'ing (1879–1939). The dates of these actors show that many of them worked during both the Ch'ing and the Republican periods, and that six even lived long enough to be prominent under the Communists, having begun their careers during the Ch'ing era. Possibly the best known actors among what was certainly a galaxy of talent were the *lao-sheng* Yü Shu-yen, the *wu-sheng* Yang Hsiao-lou and the *ch'ing-i* Mei Lan-fang and Ch'eng Yen-ch'iu.

YÜ SHU-YEN

Yü Shu-yen was born on 28 November 1890, the third son of the famous *tan* Yü Tzu-yün, himself the adopted son of Yü San-sheng from Hupeh. Shu-yen belonged, then, to a well known acting family, and his training began extremely early. In 1902 he made his *début* in a guild-hall outside the Front Gate in Peking and was widely praised for his performance.

Thinking that he would be unable to make a success of his art in the fiercely competitive conditions of the capital, Yü Shu-yen went to Tientsin, less than a hundred miles away. Young actors of the period often began their careers in that city, where they hoped to establish their reputations by attracting the attention of less critical audiences and theatre managers before returning to conquer greater heights in Peking. Yü Shu-yen remained in Tientsin for about ten years and succeeded in making his name there.

We shall see in the next chapter that mixed companies were forbidden in Peking until about 1930. In Tientsin they had existed from a much earlier date, owing to the lack of insistence on the separation of the sexes in the foreign concessions. During his stay in the city, Shu-yen performed in the same company as an actress called Wang K'o-ch'in. She and the young actor fell desperately in love and wanted to get married. However, the warlord Chang Hsün (1854–1923), who was to collaborate in 1916 with Yüan Shih-k'ai in his efforts to restore the monarchy and in 1917 was to try to put the last Ch'ing emperor, P'u-i (1909–11), back on the throne, had designs on the actress, who became his concubine. According to Hatano Kenichi, Yü's immediate motive for returning to Peking was his disappointment at the outcome of his love affair with Wang K'o-ch'in.[2]

Back in the capital Yü Shu-yen entered a school for amateurs and made friends with several eminent actors, including the well known *ch'ing-i* Ch'en Te-lin. He worked hard but, being unable for financial reasons to devote all his time to acting, took a job as a minor official in the presidential palace. During this time he studied with T'an Hsin-p'ei and went as often as possible to see the famous actor's performances. He himself was never seen in the great public theatres and acted only at private parties (*t'ang-hui*).

In the autumn of 1918, Shu-yen joined Mei Lan-fang's company and began public performances with him on 17 and 19 October. Yü was received with immediate acclaim, and it was from this time that he became famous as a Peking Opera actor. From then until 1928 he was seen constantly at *t'ang-hui* and in the major playhouses. In 1923 he founded his own T'ung-ch'ing company, which regularly gave performances at the K'ai-ming hsi-yüan, one of Peking's modern theatres.

Yü frequently co-operated with the other great actors of the day. In some years he and Yang Hsiao-lou joined forces to form a troupe, in others Mei Lan-fang was his main partner. With the latter, however, Shu-yen quarrelled because of his jealousy of a rival *lao-sheng*, Wang Feng-ch'ing. Yü refused to remain in the same company as Mei Lan-fang unless Wang were expelled. Mei had good reason to be grateful to his friend Wang, who had been responsible for his first invitation to act in Shanghai (in 1913; see page 59), and refused to dispense with him. As a result, Shu-yen left in pique. We may perhaps agree with Ch'i Ju-shan's judgement that the incident showed 'Mei Lan-fang's virtue and Yü Shu-yen's pettiness'.[3]

Yü had never enjoyed robust health. In 1928 he fell seriously ill, and, after only ten years, his career on the major stages of Peking was effectively finished. However, he did not give up acting altogether, since the rich and eminent citizens of Peking continued to engage him for private performances. After 1937, the war with Japan and his declining health made his appearances increasingly rare, and he died on 19 May 1943.

During Yü Shu-yen's comparatively short life, he made several trips from Peking to other parts of China. In 1919 he acted with Mei Lan-fang in Hankow, where his Hupeh family background made him especially popular. He also paid several visits to Shanghai, of which he undertook the last (in the early 1920s) at the behest of the enormously wealthy family of the famous bibliophile T'ao Hsiang (1871–1940). The dowager of the clan was celebrating her birthday, and her relations decided to include some professionally performed dramas in the festivities. It was the normal practice to hire a local company for such an occasion; the fact that Yü was brought all the way from Peking was a tribute to his reputation, and to the T'ao family's wealth. After the birthday celebrations he was engaged to act in the public playhouses and did so for a month with great success.

Yü's trip to Shanghai was somewhat marred, however, by an anonymous letter which he received demanding money and threatening his life should he refuse to pay it. Robbers were common in Shanghai at the time, and Shu-yen, being a public figure, might well be considered a suitable victim. The actor was terrified and immediately hired a bodyguard to accompany and protect him wherever he went. Whoever he was, Yü's correspondent failed in his objective, but his action did have the effect of preventing Shu-yen from showing himself in the city again. During this last trip to Shanghai Yü Shu-yen was also offered a concubine, and accepted her. A progressively minded friend in Peking heard of his decision, and even though concubines were acceptable socially to many people at the time, came to Shanghai especially to dissuade him. He was successful, and Yü changed his mind.

This little episode in Yü's life can be explained by his bitter disappointment at not having sons. A few years earlier, he had married the daughter of Ch'en Te-lin. She had two daughters by Yü, but she was very delicate and weak and it became plain that she would be unable to bear any more children. It was her failure to bear a son that tempted Yü to take a concubine.

Yü Shu-yen's wife died young, and his friends began trying to find him another bride. A match was arranged with the daughter of a former doctor at the Ch'ing court. Yü accepted her on the strength of a character recommendation and a photograph, and did not even meet her until after he had made up his mind to marry her. His hopes for a son were, however, to remain unfulfilled. His second wife bore him one child – another daughter. Despite his disappointment, Yü was naturally extremely fond of his daughters; he was particularly careful to see that they were well educated and (perhaps less endearingly) made sure that they married well.

Yü Shu-yen's willingness to take a concubine in order to have a son, and his insistence that his daughters should marry husbands of his own choice, were by no means abnormal attitudes and nobody condemned him for them. Yet the outline of his life which I have given leaves little doubt that, in his character, he lacked the power and maturity of his principal predecessor, Ch'eng Chang-keng. It is true that Hatano Kenichi described him as 'by nature intelligent and quick-witted';[4] and one of Yü's closest friends and his principal biographer, Sun Yang-nung, emphasizes his relaxed nature, his splendid and amusing conversation and his love of jokes.[5] On the other hand,

Ch'i Ju-shan writes thus: 'Shu-yen had an eye to power and money (the great majority of people in theatrical circles were like this), and he was happy to entertain anybody with status or influence. So the people who mixed with him were all *literati* or politicians. He also loved to chat and even more to find fault with others. . . . The people who mixed with him flattered him greatly and amateurs felt very kindly towards him.'[6] Ch'i Ju-shan later adds that 'he often looked down on the [ordinary] members of his own profession, and, because of his arrogance towards them, these people harboured ill feelings towards him'.[7]

As an actor, Yü may be summed up as a superlative transmitter of traditional style. He absorbed the best points of his predecessors, especially T'an Hsin-p'ei, but he was not particularly creative. His appearance was 'scholarly and elegant',[8] and his singing was considered magnificent. His voice was somewhat more penetrating than those of most actors contemporary with him, and this made it unusually suitable for gramophone reproduction. Yü made a number of records, between 1920 and 1940, showing all aspects of his vocal art, his power of expression and his mastery of dialogue.

YANG HSIAO-LOU

Yü Shu-yen's career was somewhat shorter than that of the other great portrayer of male roles on the traditional stage of the Republican period. Yang Hsiao-lou, the most famous *wu-sheng* of the age, was born on 14 December 1877 and was consequently thirteen years older than Yü. His native area was Ch'ienshan county, a district in Anking, Anhwei province, where the great Ch'eng Chang-keng had also been born, and he was the son of Yang Yüeh-lou, who in 1880 was to succeed Ch'eng as a master of the San-ch'ing company. Yang was thus a member of an acting family, like many other Chinese actors, such as his contemporaries Yü Shu-yen and Mei Lan-fang. Strong though the hereditary tradition has been in the Chinese acting profession, however, it has not been exclusive, as in the Japanese *kabuki*, in which few aspirants could embark on a career unless they were either members of, or had been adopted into, traditional acting families. By comparison with the *kabuki* theatre, the Chinese stage was reasonably open, for almost anybody with talent could attend a training-school and become an actor. We shall see later an example of this in Ch'eng Yen-ch'iu.

Yang enjoyed an advantage over men like Ch'eng in that he grew up from his earliest years in acting circles and could benefit from his father's guidance. Nevertheless, he needed formal instruction, and accordingly entered the Hsiao Jung-ch'un training-school in Peking, where he came strongly under the influence of the leading *wu-sheng*, Yang Lung-shou (1845–1900), the maternal grandfather of Mei Lan-fang. Yang was later to learn from other distinguished actors, such as Yü Chü-sheng (1838–1913), a member for many years of the Ch'un-t'ai company and the father of Yü Chen-t'ing.

After graduating from the training-school, Yang Hsiao-lou joined the Pao-sheng-ho company, one of Peking's most important theatrical troupes during the first decade of this century. However, since few people took any notice of him, he went to nearby Tientsin (like Yü Shu-yen) in the hope of making his name there. Yang was more than usually fortunate in Tientsin. Before his arrival he had been engaged to perform in two theatres, which now started to compete fiercely for his services. Each produced large numbers of advertisements displaying his name, and after a fairly short time he became extremely famous in the city.

Having established his reputation, Yang Hsiao-lou returned to Peking and there rejoined the Pao-sheng-ho company. The ageing Empress Dowager now took a great interest in his acting. He was frequently invited to the palaces and, according to one account, 'Whenever Hsiao-lou came to perform at court, he was treated just like a small boy in the house of his elder brother's wife'.[9] On one occasion the Empress presented him with a jade ring and embarrassed him by insisting on handing it over to him personally. It was a most unusual honour for royalty to deal directly with an actor without the aid of an intermediary.

After the fall of the Ch'ing dynasty, Yang Hsiao-lou established several of his own companies, the most durable being the Yung-sheng, which lasted from 1927 until Yang's death in 1938. In organizing his troupes, Yang co-operated with several of the leading actors of the time, in particular Yü Shu-yen and Mei Lan-fang. The latter performed with him in what became his most famous piece, *The King Parts from his Favourite* (*Pa-wang pieh-chi*). This drama relates the suicide of Hsiang Yü (233–202 BC) and his favourite consort, after Hsiang has been defeated in battle by the founder of China's first great dynasty, the Han (206 BC–AD 220). Yang portrayed Hsiang Yü,

Mei Lan-fang his beloved. It is in this drama, above all, that the names of the two great actors are linked for enthusiasts for the Peking Opera. Fortunately, their performance has been preserved for posterity on records, which have been reissued in long-playing form by the present government.

The gramophone can never do full justice to the Peking Opera. It is true that Yang's magnificent voice is reproduced fairly well on the record, but, for a *wu-sheng*, singing is less important than stage movement and acrobatics. Indeed, Yang was the first of the great *wu-sheng* to win fame for his excellent singing. He was splendid in appearance, martial yet tragic in parts such as Hsiang Yü, at other times elegant and dignified. In particular, he was well known for the agility of his foot movements, and there was a saying that 'he had eyes beneath his feet'.[10]

It may be that Yang's high standards were due in part to his ability to accept criticism. Unlike Yü Shu-yen, Yang was renowned for his humility and generous personality. Yü kept all his private notes on his performances (including texts, and material on the words, music and stage conventions) well hidden and his wife burned them after his death. Yang, on the other hand, placed no copyright at all on his art and amateurs came in droves to learn his secrets. It is, of course, possible to point out faults in the man (some said he was lazy, and certainly he smoked opium), but his reputation was that of a cheerful, kind and unselfish person.

A good illustration of Yang's nature is provided by a little story related by Ch'i Ju-shan:

> When [Mei] Lan-fang was a few years old, he went to a privately run local school. But because a class-mate made fun of him, he did not dare go to his lessons. His uncle [Mei Yü-t'ien] beat him for it, but he still refused. Hsiao-lou said to Yü-t'ien, 'The more you beat him, the more afraid he'll be. Just let me coax him into it.' He took [the child] for a ride on his back to go to school, but when they got to the entrance of the alley where the school was, Lan-fang cried and would not go in. Hsiao-lou took him on his back by a very round-about way, and only because he had not been on that road before would he go in. When they got to the school, Hsiao-lou explained the circumstances to the teacher, who reprimanded the naughty pupil [who had made fun of Mei] and also comforted Lan-fang. Hsiao-lou stayed at the school for a while to keep him company, and after that the child went to his lessons normally. Lan-fang often mentioned the story to me and Hsiao-lou would often joke about it.[11]

Naturally, Yang Hsiao-lou had interests outside his art. He was married, with a family, although, like Yü Shu-yen, he had no sons. He was also a fervent Taoist and knew the principal Taoist classics well. It is said that once, at a private party, he corrected one of the guests who misquoted from them. During his youth his acting career was interrupted for a time while he spent all his days in the Pai-yün kuan, Peking's main Taoist temple. 'He would wear Taoist clothes, mix with all the priests and squat on the ground chanting scriptures.'[12] So great did his devotion become that several of his friends came to take him back to the stage, lest he neglect his art altogether. Yang agreed to leave the temple, but this in no way impaired his enthusiasm for his religion, and he remained a Taoist adept all his life. It is said that he adopted traditional Taoist sexual practices involving *coitus reservatus*.

Yang Hsiao-lou's attitudes were traditional. As we shall see, he did attempt to come to terms with certain innovations being introduced into the Peking Opera, but he was not nearly as active in this respect as younger men like Mei Lan-fang and Ch'eng Yen-ch'iu. But before considering these innovations, I will briefly outline the careers of these two famous *ch'ing-i*.

MEI LAN-FANG

Mei Lan-fang was born in Peking in October 1894 of an old theatrical family. His grandfather, Mei Ch'iao-ling, had been a famous *tan* and the leader of the Ssu-hsi company; his father, Chu-fen, was also a *tan*, but his career was cut short by his death at the age of twenty-five. Mei Lan-fang's uncle, Yü-t'ien, who became the head of the household in which the child was brought up, was a well known *hu-ch'in* player, for many years the accompanist of T'an Hsin-p'ei.

There was never any doubt about which profession Lan-fang would follow. He received his earliest training from Wu Ling-hsien, a former friend of his grandfather, and made his public *début* at the age of ten. Three years later he enrolled at the Fu-lien-ch'eng training-school, the most highly regarded in Peking.

Mei Lan-fang's real fame as an actor began in 1913, when he was invited to Shanghai. There he performed at private parties and in the Tan-kuei theatre, perhaps the best known in the city. He was universally acclaimed and from that time onward went from strength to strength. He acted chiefly in Peking until the Japanese occupied

Manchuria in 1931. He then lived in Shanghai until 1937, when the outbreak of the war caused him to move to Hong Kong. When the colony fell to the Japanese in 1941, Mei Lan-fang went back to Shanghai, living there for some eight years. After the liberation in 1949 Peking again became his headquarters until his death in 1961.

From 1913 until his death, Mei was in great demand in all the leading cities of China and travelled widely in his own country. He was acting almost continuously throughout this period, only refusing to do so when he was in enemy-occupied cities during the war. Indeed, he grew a moustache as a protest against Japanese aggression, thus making the performance of *tan* roles an impossibility. Apart from his travels in China itself, Mei Lan-fang undertook many tours abroad; this enhanced his international prestige, making him the most popular and famous actor of the Peking Opera not merely in China itself but all over the world. In 1919, 1924 and 1956 he visited Japan, being acclaimed on all three occasions, and in 1930 he toured the United States, where he contributed greatly to American interest in the Chinese drama. In 1935 he travelled to Europe, where he played in the theatres of Moscow and London, and also visited Berlin and Paris. It was at this time that the great German dramatist Bertolt Brecht saw him act and was tremendously impressed. After witnessing a demonstration of Chinese acting techniques given by Mei, without theatrical paraphernalia or costumes, Brecht commented that 'by comparison with Asiatic acting our own art still seems hopelessly parsonical'.[13] He was particularly struck by the miming in the Chinese dramas, and it is well known that his works owe something to the theatre of China.

As befitted so greatly respected an artist, Mei Lan-fang could boast a wide repertoire and was expert in *K'un-ch'ü* as well as in Peking Opera. He was notable in various kinds of female roles and could perform, in addition to *ch'ing-i* parts, those of the fighting women (*wu-tan*) and the coquettish, lively 'flower' *tan*. When rendering all these types of characters he improved and reformed the techniques which he had inherited from his predecessors. He also took steps towards combining them, so that in his hands the sharp distinctions between the various kinds of *tan* tended to disappear. As for his skill in acrobatics, the famous dramatist Ou-yang Yü-ch'ien (1889–1962), himself an actor of no mean stature, once remarked, 'Not only is his footwork well disciplined, his rhythm precise, and his bearing magnificent, but he reveals a kind of inner overtone – as if the original acrobatics had been refined and tempered, and advanced to become a beautiful dance.'[14]

Despite his fame and popularity, Mei remained a modest man. Ou-yang Yü-ch'ien wrote about him, 'He is never proud and self-satisfied. If a secondary player apologizes to him for making a mistake, he always consoles him and gives him more instruction. He says, "If I spoke angrily to him, he would only lose his composure even more next time." '[15] Throughout his life Mei Lan-fang was an indefatigable worker. He himself used to say, in fact, that his success was due not to talent, but to his capacity for hard work. In his studio he kept an empty wine flagon, into which he used to practise singing (so that the sound, thus muffled, would not disturb the neighbours) and a large mirror, in front of which he learned to master gestures and facial expressions.

Mei had the reputation of unusual moral virtue, not only for his professional conscientiousness, but also for his relations with women. He did not follow the custom, quite usual among actors during the Republican period, of accepting the favours of his patrons' concubines or wives. When he visited Hong Kong in 1922 the local press reported that 'he has given out that it will be inconvenient for him to attend entertainments given in his honour in brothels in West Point'. This, the newspaper opined, 'presupposes some moral courage'.[16]

Mei was married twice. His first wife, Wang Ming-hua, was a capable woman with whom his family arranged a marriage for him when he was seventeen. In about 1919 he also took a concubine, an actress called Fu Chih-fang; Wang Ming-hua did not live long afterwards, and he then married Fu Chih-fang. By his first wife Mei had one son, who did not survive childhood. It was this misfortune which prompted the actor to marry Fu Chih-fang, by whom he had two children, a son and a daughter. It is striking that a man with such a good reputation should have taken a concubine at the very time when the May Fourth Movement was demonstrating that progressive opinion in China was fiercely hostile to this Confucian practice. We see here the continuing strength of the old patterns of thought in acting circles, even in a man such as Mei, who had supported the 1911 Revolution with great enthusiasm.

Besides his family Mei had numerous friends. For his work as an actor the most important was perhaps Ch'i Ju-shan (1877–1962), a voluminous writer on Chinese theatre and the author of many of the works on which I have depended in the present book. The two men first met in 1914 and remained on close terms until 1948, when Ch'i chose to move to Taiwan. Ch'i wrote or arranged many dramas specifically for performance by Mei. Another of Mei's friends was Ch'i Pai-shih (1863–1957), possibly modern China's best known painter and a great lover of flowers. It was this second characteristic that brought the two together, for Mei had always been interested in flowers and learned much from Ch'i about their cultivation.

But it was, above all, the ordinary Chinese population that adored Mei. Despite his modesty, he was a true star and was treated as such. The following newspaper report, which describes his reception when he visited Changsha in the spring of 1937, testifies vividly to his tremendous popularity:

> After Mr Mei got off the train, he was surrounded by a crowd of welcomers. He stood in the midst of a human mountain, a human sea, and could not move forward. Only after much manoevring among the crowd and with great difficulty could the friends who were looking after him find a way out and get Mr Mei into a car. . . . The Communications Bank was responsible for selling tickets [for his performances], but who would have thought that as soon as they started selling the tickets, those for ten days were sold out in one go? . . . Many people who came to Changsha and were unable to get tickets requested that a day session on Sunday be added, and Mr Mei agreed. On that occasion it was decided that seats in the [open-air] theatre square should all be priced at four *yüan* [a high price], yet people fought for them all. . . . Although the theatre square was bad and the audiences large [at all his performances], everyone would fall silent as soon as he came on the stage.[17]

The extraordinary magnetism of Mei Lan-fang's personality, both as an actor and as a man, is attested by these reactions.

Despite his overwhelming importance as China's foremost actor of modern times, I have decided not to discuss Mei Lan-fang at length, since so much has already been written about him, not only in Chinese but also in Western languages. I will therefore turn to another *ch'ing-i* player, Ch'eng Yen-ch'iu, who has received less attention from Western writers, although his stature falls little short of Mei's.

CH'ENG YEN-CH'IU

Ch'eng Yen-ch'iu was born on 4 January 1904. For several generations his ancestors, down to his father, had served the Ch'ing emperors as military officers; but with the Revolution of 1911 the family declined sharply, and Ch'eng's father died a poor man. Yen-ch'iu, the only one of his sons with any great talent, was much concerned at the plight of his widowed mother, who was now forced to sew for a living, and decided to get rich quickly by going on the stage.

At the time actors were a low class in society, and when Yen-ch'iu put his plan to his mother, she answered, 'You are a member of a clan of famous officials. Why do you want to throw yourself away on acting?' Ch'eng Yen-ch'iu replied, 'I have heard that it is very easy to learn singing and that you need only two or three years to become good at it. I may be able to do something about our poverty.'[18] His mother consented, pleading with him to avoid the corruptions of actors. He then became indentured as a disciple of the *tan* actor Jung Tieh-hsien, a step which probably led him to reverse his rash assumption that the theatrical arts were easy to learn. He certainly became successful and rich, and was also noted as a hard worker.

Some time after Ch'eng entered Jung's tutelage, the classical poet Lo Tun-jung saw him act and was greatly impressed. In 1918, Lo paid Jung a substantial sum of money to release Yen-ch'iu from his indenture. After that, the poet and the actor became close friends. Lo would go as often as possible to see his protégé on the stage and wrote or arranged a number of dramas in which he performed.

In 1919 Ch'eng went to Japan, where he performed with Mei Lan-fang and other actors. By this time he had received instruction from several famous actors, including Wang Yao-ch'ing and Mei himself, and his reputation as a *ch'ing-i* stood fairly high in Peking. In 1922 he visited Shanghai and was such a success that engagements in Hangchow and Canton followed. At the invitation of a French professor who had much admired him in Peking,[19] Ch'eng toured the Soviet Union, Germany, France and Italy in 1932 and 1933, his main aim being to learn about the European theatre. Another of his patrons was the senior Nationalist Government dignitary Li Shih-tseng, who took a keen interest in his career. Li Shih-tseng assisted Ch'eng in various ways, one of which was to arrange for him to become head of the Nanking Institute of Theatrical Music, a sinecure which carried with it some prestige.

As the 1930s progressed, Ch'eng, becoming stout and less fitted for work on the stage, increasingly took up teaching, in particular at the School of Chinese Drama in Peking. During the Sino-Japanese war he gave up acting for a time, but after 1945 he occasionally reappeared. Like most of China's best actors, he chose to remain in his country after the Communists came to power in 1949 (he had been sympathetic to the left wing for some time) and he continued his work under the new government. He remained actively engaged in teaching, writing and taking part in conferences on music and the drama right up to his death early in 1958.

One recent writer has described Ch'eng Yen-ch'iu's qualities as an actor thus: 'He was a tireless worker, and studied diligently and with a calm mind. He made up his own melodies, and did not plagiarize the stereotypes of his predecessors. His pronunciation was correct and . . . his intensity of feeling when performing in tragedies (for example, when weeping, accusing [those who had perpetrated injustices], or expressing resentment or longing) aroused deep emotion in his hearers. Those who learn *ch'ing-i* [roles] nowadays follow either Mei [Lan-fang's] style or that of Ch'eng'.[20] As this passage suggests, Ch'eng Yen-ch'iu was noted above all for his tragic roles. His voice was somewhat deeper than was usual for a *ch'ing-i*, and it was endowed with a touching quality that was unequalled by any of his contemporaries. His manner of performing was elegant and precise, and several observers remarked that this characteristic set him apart from Mei Lanfang, whose acting was marked by a more flowing beauty.

Ch'eng Yen-ch'iu was popular not only as an actor but also as a man. He was known for his willingness to help others and would frequently take part in performances given for charity, even contributing substantial sums from his own pocket. It is reported that after his friend Lo Tun-jung died, Ch'eng Yen-ch'iu experienced much trouble and difficulty as his executor. One of Lo's friends wrote: 'After Lo [Tun-jung] became sick and died, Yen-ch'iu managed all his affairs in a way found rarely even among gentlemen. After that I had an extremely high regard for him and did not look upon him as an [ordinary] actor.'[21]

Ch'eng's main failing was his excessive love of wine. Even though he could take a great deal without feeling the effects too severely, he would sometimes become drunk, even at the most inconvenient times. The story goes that once, in Shanghai, he drank a little too much when he was supposed to be preparing for a performance. When the time came for his entry, he was so intoxicated that he could hardly see where he was going. However, he followed the beats of the clapper and was able to perform his role without making too many mistakes. His audience was tolerant, and, far from being condemned, Ch'eng gained a reputation for great intelligence.

Ch'eng Yen-ch'iu was clearly able to accommodate himself to

circumstances. But his adaptability extended beyond making the most of a trivial mistake, and he kept in step with the wider and more important issues of his time. The most obvious example is his acceptance of the Communists when they came to power in 1949. But, much earlier than this, he had shown his interest in current trends by taking a prominent part in the performance of newly arranged pieces, or 'new dramas', a subject to which I shall now turn.

THE 'NEW DRAMAS'

During the Republican period, there was a marked increase in the practice of arranging what were called the 'new dramas' (*hsin-hsi*). An actor would ask a scholarly friend to adapt an already familiar story into a Peking Opera script, which then became more or less the performer's special property. He would devise its production and costumes and, in general, no other player would perform it. In this way an old and traditional story bore the imprint of a contemporary author and actor, thus giving the audiences some measure of variety. By contrast, it had rarely been possible to ascribe the Peking operas of the nineteenth century to individual authors.

Some of the 'new dramas' were very long, since their authors did not feel called upon to limit themselves to one brief scene. In a theatrical performance during the nineteenth century, it had been unusual to see more than three or four short scenes in succession devoted to developing a single plot, and sometimes a scene might tell a completely different story from the one that preceded or followed it. This scheme was altered in the 'new dramas', which frequently consisted of many scenes devoted to one plot, and sometimes required a day, or even several days, for their performance.

It is important to note that, despite their name, these dramas were new only in a limited sense. In the first place, the custom of presenting a new arrangement of a story in Peking Opera form had existed during the nineteenth century, even though it gathered momentum in the Republican period. Moreover, the music used in the 'new dramas' followed that of the traditional Peking Opera closely. These dramas were not spoken plays.

About half the total number of Peking operas performed during the years 1911–49 were newly arranged Peking operas. The actors who took the lead in popularizing the new works were mainly the greatest *tan* of the day, Mei Lan-fang, Ch'eng Yen-ch'iu, Shang

Hsiao-yün and Hsün Hui-sheng, though Yang Hsiao-lou also acted in them from time to time. One of the first 'new dramas' which Mei commissioned was *Ch'ang O Flees to the Moon* (*Ch'ang O pen-yüeh*), written by his friend, Ch'i Ju-shan, and first performed on 23 September 1915. This short drama tells the story of a mythical lady who steals the elixir of immortality and escapes to the palace of the moon. Despite the opposition of a few conservatives, *Ch'ang O Flees to the Moon* was a tremendous success and spurred Mei on to perform many more 'new dramas'. Between 1915 and 1936 he played in some twenty-five of them.

Of the other actors whom I have mentioned, Shang Hsiao-yün performed in forty-one new dramas, Hsün Hui-sheng in about forty and Ch'eng Yen-ch'iu in twenty-five from the 1920s onwards. The first of Ch'eng's was arranged for him by Lo Tun-jung and was first performed on 10 March 1923. Its title was *Hung-fu chuan* (*The Story of Hung-fu*), and it concerned the establishment of the great T'ang dynasty (618–907). Yang Su, an official of the wicked Emperor Yang (605–17) of the Sui dynasty (581–618), has in his mansion a concubine-actress called Hung-fu nü (the Red Duster Girl). She sees and falls in love with Li Ching, an ambitious man currently supporting the Sui against the future imperial family of the T'ang dynasty. The two elope to Shansi, where they become so impressed by Li Shih-min (597–649), later to become the second T'ang emperor, that they join his cause and help him to vanquish the Sui dynasty.

The theme of Ch'eng's first new drama was typical. The majority of the specially arranged pieces were based on old *K'un-ch'ü* dramas, novels, legends, historical events or love stories. If they contained a social message, this was generally indirect, and the costumes and techniques of acting followed tradition fairly closely. For a time Mei Lan-fang had considered embarking on a radical modernization of his art. In 1914 he had performed in a long drama called *Nieh-hai po-lan* (*Waves of the Sea of Sin*), which dealt with the evils of prostitution. The costumes were contemporary, the acting was realistic, and the social message was direct and clear. The piece won some popularity, but, although he produced similar dramas between 1914 and 1916, Mei eventually decided that he was not well fitted for such ventures and returned to the field where his genius really lay: the traditional theatre.

The modernization of the Peking Opera, as expressed in the 'new dramas', was not particularly radical, and Mei Lan-fang's attempts to make it so failed. The same cannot be said of the spoken plays. These were based partly on the Western theatrical tradition and used dialogue, scenery and realistic costumes. Their themes were in general directly related to the events and trends of the time. They brought out into the open controversial social issues like the changing structure of the family, and their authors did not hesitate to use them as vehicles for putting forward progressive ideas. Some of the leaders of the New Culture Movement, of which reform of the drama was but a part, were bitterly critical of the old Peking Opera and regarded it as a reactionary force. Dr Hu Shih, for instance, was doubtful about the value of the traditional conventions and was anxious to bring the Peking Opera into line with revolutionary trends in other branches of the arts. He believed that Mei Lan-fang's initial attempt should not have been abandoned, but developed.

Dr Hu Shih's new culture was an exclusively urban phenomenon. In fact, the greatest impact of the spoken play was felt in China's more Westernized industrial cities, particularly Shanghai, and for this reason I shall discuss it more fully in Chapter Seven (on Shanghai and the Lower Yangtze Valley). Spoken plays were given in Peking too, but Peking was only the focal point of their development during brief periods, such as shortly after the May Fourth Movement of 1919.

The spoken play had begun to lose its impact by that time. Many dramatists believed that the reason for this was because the revolutionary content had become too diluted and the methods of production, staging and advertising far too commercialized. The New Culture Movement (referred to at the beginning of this chapter) which developed at the time of the May Fourth Movement provoked a reaction against these trends. In 1921, following an initiative taken in Shanghai, the dramatist Ch'en Ta-pei began a campaign in Peking to encourage amateur actors (for whom the spoken play was by far the most important medium). He wrote, 'Our ideal is that the men of the theatre, who instruct society, should be amateurs. . . . They should not be managed or controlled by capitalists or capital. Amateur dramatists need not be students, but everyone must have received an education which can help him to develop the theatre.'[22]

Amateur theatre groups were established where members tried to remain completely aloof from commercialism. At first, many idealistic young people came forward who were willing to act, write or translate plays for these groups, in which great emphasis was placed on revolutionary content. But this movement survived for only three or four years after its inception in 1921. There were various reasons for this.

Many of the troupes were too loosely organized, and too short-lived; they also lacked permanent premises in which they could mount productions. More serious was a problem pointed out in September 1923 by Cheng Chen-to, one of the leaders of the movement: 'At present there are very many proponents of the drama, and student amateur dramatic groups are daily increasing. But the creation of plays seems unable to meet their needs. On all sides distress is felt at the dearth of plays; on all sides there are attempts to write all kinds of plays. Yet in the outcome very few are successful.'[23] A further weakness was that corrupt elements began to use the movement for their own ends. 'A few people engaged in amateur theatre work used the organization of troupes as a pretext for obtaining money by fraud or by plotting other activities; this happened frequently and turned off quite a few people who had supported amateur drama.'[24]

Yet, even though it failed in the long run, the movement did point to the need for play actors who were really devoted to their art and not just intent on making money. Not long after the movement's demise, Ch'en Ta-pei and his fellow dramatist P'u Po-ying won enough support to found in Peking China's first properly equipped school for actors of the spoken play. Standards of performance naturally rose greatly. A number of new spoken plays were written by famous playwrights, and interest in the form grew considerably in Peking's universities and among its intellectual population. Social comment continued to be a major element in the spoken drama.

The drama also became an important organ of propaganda, not only in Peking but everywhere in China, during the war against Japan. Actors made it their business to intensify hope and spread optimism among the populace, and they toured as widely as possible. Dramatists were also very active in the national cause, even though the requirements of propaganda, met in extremely difficult conditions, inevitably led to a lessening of subtlety in their work.

Although the drama had played an important role in maintaining the morale of the Chinese during the war against Japan and hence contributed to their victory, the years 1945–49 were not happy for the theatre. Both traditional and modern drama entered on an extremely bleak period which was only ended when stability was restored under the Communists. The aftermath of a catastrophic war which had cost the country dear, general demoralization and corrupt, oppressive government made conditions in China intolerable. And under such circumstances the arts cannot be expected to flourish.

4 Actors in Peking Society

One of the most important points to emerge from the discussion of the rise of the Peking Opera in Chapter One was the preponderance among the earliest great actors of the *tan*: the male actors who impersonated women. Indeed, throughout the Ch'ing dynasty none of the major public acting companies of Peking contained any women at all, and all female roles were played by men or boys. Their own history demonstrated to the Chinese that decent women did not appear on the stage.

One does not have to look far afield in theatrical history to find other countries where women were virtually excluded from the acting profession and where female roles were played by males. There were no women in the casts of ancient Greek or Roman dramas, actresses did not appear on the English stage until immediately before the Restoration; and the Japanese *kabuki* was invariably performed by all-male casts from the middle of the seventeenth century until very recent times. Apart from any social prejudice against the spectacle of women on the stage, many people have found it artistically satisfying to see a female role played by a man or a boy. After visiting Rome, Goethe wrote the following comments on its actors: 'We experience a double charm from the fact that these people are not women, but play the part of women. We see a youth who has studied the idiosyncrasies of the female sex in their character and behaviour; he has learned to know them, and reproduces them as artist. . . . We come to understand the female sex so much the better because some one has observed and meditated on their ways.'[1]

In China women's roles were normally played by men until after the Communists came to power, and mixed companies were more or less unknown during the Ch'ing era. Actresses, however, had always existed, and even in the late Ch'ing period there were two good companies in Peking which consisted solely of women. In general, these troupes performed only at private parties and were not seen in the main theatres. Ch'i Ju-shan saw several of their performances and was impressed by their high standards.[2] However, both troupes disbanded during the first decade of this century. In the early Republican years there were several female companies which enjoyed some popularity for a time, but from the mid-1920s onwards they went out of fashion and soon disbanded.

The first attempt to introduce a mixed company was made by the famous actor Yü Chen-t'ing, shortly after the Republican government was established. He was daring enough to perform in a Peking theatre together with the actress Sun I-ch'ing. The innovation was well received by the audience, but ended in disaster. According to Ch'i Ju-shan, Yüan Shih-k'ai's son fell in love with the actress and in a fit of jealousy had Yü Chen-t'ing imprisoned for several months. As a result, Sun I-ch'ing never acted again.[3]

Yü Chen-t'ing's experiment also met other obstacles. The actors' guild discussed the question of mixed companies at length and decided to resist the innovation. Its members pointed out, for instance, that great confusion would be caused in the allocation of costumes and in the dressing-rooms. However, the idea, once put into practice, did not die, and during the 1920s and 1930s a sufficient number of mixed troupes appeared to induce the authorities and the guild to abandon their opposition. Meanwhile, the all-male company did not die out, and it was not until after the Communists came to power that the practice of teaching boys to play female roles was suspended altogether.

It will be seen, therefore, that until 1949 the Peking stage was dominated by male actors, whether men or boys. It is to them, therefore, that I shall direct most of my attention in the remainder of this chapter. Let us consider the systems whereby they were recruited and trained, the treatment accorded to them, their morals and beliefs, their guilds, and their general status in the community.

ENTRY INTO THE ACTING PROFESSION

The early nineteenth-century sources contain notes and biographical information on some 150 *tan* players, and although this information is sketchy, we are in almost all cases told the age of the actor in question. According to my calculations, the average age of these performers was about seventeen.

The extreme youth of the famous *tan* actors of Peking is explained by a method of recruitment which developed in the 1790s, at the same time as Kao Lang-t'ing was establishing his reputation in Peking. Boys were bought in south China, taken to Peking and trained there as actors. The children were only seven or eight when indentured. In return for a small sum of money, their parents signed a contract which stipulated the boy's return after a period specified in years and months. It was possible to buy the boy out before the bond had expired, but only by paying two to three thousand taels of silver, a sum beyond the resources of any but a wealthy man. There was a reason why this trade in boys should have begun at this period. China's population had been growing steadily for many years and, according to Professor Ho Ping-ti, had reached the point at which it could yield the greatest economic welfare for the people at some time between 1750 and 1775.[4] After these years standards of living began to fall, and poverty caused by over-population became more severe. By the 1790s experts were warning that dire consequences would result if the trend continued. Under these circumstances it is not altogether surprising that poor people should have sought economic relief by selling a child for a given period.

At about the same time as the system of indenture was gaining momentum in China, the West was abandoning an even more inhuman practice connected with the recruiting of actors. Since the sixteenth century many European boys, especially in Italy, had been castrated to prevent their voices from breaking. The *castrati* often worked in church choirs but it was above all as opera-singers that they were admired. Audiences revelled in the power of their voices, which was combined with an exquisite falsetto timbre. For those, like the famous Caffarelli (1703–83), who were able to win success and prestige there were, no doubt, partial compensations for the loss of manhood. But the many who failed to make a name were in a much worse position than the Chinese singing boys, whose condition of slavery was only temporary. Though eunuchs were common in China before the Republic, the only actors among them were those who lived and worked permanently at the imperial court.

In Peking the boys either joined the training-schools (*k'o-pan*) attached to the major troupes or were resold to already established actors. Such men made a habit of gathering together two or three boys and adopting them as sons. The children were then regarded as both the sons and the private disciples of the older actors and were

71

referred to as *hsiang-kung*. They lived in their masters' houses, and such places came to occupy an important role in the Peking theatre; a distinguished actor often called himself by the name of his house.

The boy actors were on the whole well treated, and the more fortunate among them enjoyed a reasonably prosperous life, with many comforts and the attentions of servants. On the other hand, they worked very hard both before and after they started giving public performances. It was by no means uncommon for them to act two or even three times a day. They were well paid for their art, but most of their earnings were handed over to their master and the fact that they had been bought on contract made them virtual slaves. The majority gave up their careers on the stage as soon as they could, normally at the age of about twenty.

Acting was not the only function which these boys fulfilled. It was no secret in Peking that most of them soon became homosexuals. Indeed, the nineteenth-century sources which describe them were very often written by scholars who were themselves in love with the young actors. It was not unknown for a player to be invited to a party in the role of the wife of the host or of one of the guests. The boy actors were not too particular in their choice of patrons, and anybody with money could make friends with them. In fact, with the passage of time many people came to regard the *hsiang-kung* virtually as male prostitutes, and whether or not this is a valid comparison seems to me a semantic question. After finishing their day's work, these boys would stand about giggling, in the hope of attracting the attention of any interested members of the audience. In 1913 the new Republican government ordered their suppression on the grounds that they were harmful to public morals. Laws are not always fully effective, however, and the *hsiang-kung* did not disappear in Peking for about another decade. In some parts of China the practice of enslaving boys for theatrical training was not finally eliminated until the Communists came to power.

It is perhaps not surprising that homosexuality should have been widespread among the boy actors. They were, after all, deliberately trying to make themselves appear feminine, and it was part of their art to simulate beautiful women on the stage. It was not the fault of the children that they were coerced into sexual practices condemned by the society in which they lived. It was their owners who initiated them, and they must have felt terrified and defenceless when first approached.

Widespread homosexuality among actors is, of course, not a

Chinese monopoly. It occurred, for instance, in Japan in the fourth and fifth decades of the seventeenth century, when the *kabuki* theatre was dominated by pretty young men, known as *wakashū*, who portrayed women. It is said that some warriors became so attached to these boys that they fought over them in the theatres. The *wakashū* soon became such a subject of scandal that a series of edicts was issued against them. In 1652 they were formally banned, and before long were seen no more.

The *hsiang-kung* persisted much longer in China than did the *wakashū* in Japan. Moreover, slavery and homosexuality among Chinese actors were by no means new in the late eighteenth century, though the growth of population referred to above did lead indirectly to an increase in their incidence.

The system provides one explanation of the continued success of the Anhwei companies throughout the nineteenth century. For economic conditions did not improve, and the population continued to rise until the catastrophic carnage of the Taiping civil wars in the years 1850–64. The trade in boys continued throughout this period, and thereafter, though its scope was much changed by the great rebellion. Tremendous devastation was caused in the south, and the Grand Canal was affected, so that it became impossible to ship children from the southern districts to Peking. From this time, the *hsiang-kung* were mostly drawn from the capital itself, until this system of recruiting and training Peking's actors was completely superseded by another in the early years of this century.

This new system was embodied in the training-schools. These modernized establishments differed from the schools of the nineteenth century, in that they were not attached to specific companies. With a few exceptions, such as the school run during the early days of the Republic by Yü Chen-t'ing, the old dependent type of school now became obsolete.

The first and by far the most important of the new training-schools was founded in 1903 by Niu Tzu-hou, from Kirin, and in 1907 was named the Hsi-lien-ch'eng training-school. Niu was fortunate enough to find a deputy in an actor named Yeh Ch'un-shan, one of whose five sons, Sheng-lan, later became a famous exponent of the scholar-lover role (*hsiao-sheng*). Yeh's devotion to the school's interests and his expertise as a teacher continued undiminished until his death in 1935. After the Revolution of 1911 the Hsi-lien-ch'eng training-school was taken over by a man named Shen Jen-shan and was

73

renamed the Fu-lien-ch'eng. Shen had little interest in the theatre, but Yeh Ch'un-shan's hard work and ability ensured that the school's reputation did not suffer. After Yeh's death a decline set in which was hastened by the outbreak of war in 1937. The Fu-lien-ch'eng was forced to close down a few years later and never reopened.

Some of the greatest stars of the twentieth century received their basic training at the Fu-lien-ch'eng: for example, Mei Lan-fang, Chou Hsin-fang and T'an Fu-ying. Yet only a small minority of the thousand or more students who passed through the school ever rose to prominence. Many of the young actors succumbed beneath the pressures of life in the big Chinese cities, and not a few drifted into the underworld of corruption.

Life at a training-school was hard. It began at an early age: entrants ranged from about seven to thirteen. A boy had first to submit to an audition and to a trial period of training lasting about a month, designed to show whether or not he was a potentially good actor. If he was successful the school authorities and the parents signed a contract whereby the school guaranteed to provide seven years' training and keep, free of charge, in return for complete control over the child. This was hard for both the parents and the boy, but at least there was no question of the child being bought and sold.

In his autobiography Mei Lan-fang recalls that many boys were extremely unhappy when they first entered the training-school. He writes: 'There were some children too young to leave their parents and they were very homesick. Sometimes they wept noisily and incessantly for several days, and no amount of coaxing could stop them. [In these cases] there was no alternative but to ask the head of the family to take the child home and return him after giving him encouragement.'[5]

The boys' reluctance to stay at school is not hard to understand. Discipline was exceedingly rigid, and the daily routine was regulated according to a strict time-table. High standards and hard work were expected, and punishments for laziness or breaking the rules were severe. The boys were frequently flogged if they did not make the tremendously difficult and stylized movements of the Peking Opera in the proper way, and were very likely to be expelled if they did not behave themselves. Yet, for all its rigour the modernized training-school represented an advance on the system which it replaced. The instruction seems to have been more thorough than in the houses of the *hsiang-kung*, and schools such as the Fu-lien-ch'eng were not regarded as brothels.

Homosexuality had not died out, however, and many of the teachers continued to treat their charges as lovers. In the 1930s some of Peking's most distinguished actors and theatre enthusiasts founded a new institution called the School of Chinese Drama (Chung-hua hsi-ch'ü hsüeh-hsiao), in which they planned that homosexuality would find no place. The doors of the dormitories were left open all night, and at least one light was always kept on. A further inhibiting factor was that the students included girls as well as boys. The venture was successful, showing that it was possible to eliminate a practice which had always prevailed, not only in the houses of the *hsiang-kung*, but also in the training-schools which replaced them. The School of Chinese Drama was progressive, also, in that subjects other than drama were taught, so that the children could gain a broader education than had previously been available to actors undergoing training.

The schools did not furnish the only methods of entry into the acting profession. One other way was to take up acting as a *p'iao-yu*, or amateur, to attend one of the schools or clubs intended specifically for the non-professional, and then to join one of the accepted companies. There is no evidence of the presence of amateurs in the Peking Opera earlier than the 1840s, but in later times they grew considerably in number and importance. Indeed, some of the finest actors of the last hundred years first appeared on the stage as amateurs. It is true that such an actor began his training when already an adult, and that his teacher did not demand from him nearly the same degree of accomplishment as was expected from his counterpart in a training-school. On the other hand, the fact that the amateur voluntarily chose the theatre as his career meant that he normally possessed more natural talent, more zeal and more enthusiasm for acting than was usually found among the trainees.

ACTORS AS A PROFESSIONAL BODY

Despite the diversity of Chinese players, their differing backgrounds and the hierarchy (both social and professional) that divided the high from the low, there were certain factors which combined to form a strong group spirit among them. This cohesion extended far beyond the technical co-operation that is absolutely necessary for good performances on the stage. It affected many areas of the players' lives and was connected with their awareness that they constitued a professional body.

75

One aspect of the actors' unity of thinking lay in their religious life. Like the members of every trade or calling in China, they worshipped a pantheon of gods whom they regarded as their protectors, and relied on to bring them good fortune. The most important patron god of actors was the 'trade founder', also named Lao-lang shen, and many temples were dedicated to him. He was considered to be divine and to be endowed also with human qualities. It was he who was believed to look after the lives of actors, who did their best not to annoy him, fearing unpleasant consequences if they did so. Some said he was a manifestation of the Emperor Ming-huang (712–56), of the T'ang dynasty, others that he was a manifestation of the Emperor Chuang-tsung (923–6), of the Later T'ang dynasty (923–36), these two emperors having been famous early patrons of actors. In fact, Lao-lang shen was originally a deified star. Actors normally kept an image of this god in their house. One author wrote in 1842: 'Every time I have been into an actor's dwelling, I have scrutinized the image of Lao-lang shen to which they sacrifice. All are about one foot high, dazzling white and in the shape of a small child wrapped in a yellow robe. The actors sacrifice [to the image] with great reverence. The one who offers the incense is always the clown (*ch'ou*). They say that formerly Chuang-tsung would himself perform a *ch'ou* part with all his official actors.'[6]

There were many other gods in the pantheon of the actors. Among the most important were Hsi-shen, the God of Joy, and Kuan-kung, the God of War, who was the deified manifestation of the third-century hero Kuan Yü. Kuan-kung often appears on the stage in plays about the Three Kingdoms, and his appearance is highly awe-inspiring. Ch'i Ju-shan writes that, according to one actor, the Empress Dowager always used to 'make some excuse to leave her seat' when he entered.[7] Another god was Erh-lang shen, also a divine manifestation of an ancient historical personage.

I have mentioned only a few of the many divine patrons of the actors, though probably enough to show the complexity of the pantheon. The strength of religious belief in the acting profession remained little affected throughout the Ch'ing and Republican eras. It is true that the anti-religious movements of the Republican period made some impact on the better educated actors, but, in general, such influences did not permeate the acting population very deeply. Moreover, the practice of making sacrifices to the gods was continued even after the players had ceased to believe in it.

Another means by which actors expressed their group spirit was provided by their guilds (*hui-kuan*). These, too, existed in other trades and proliferated to such an extent during the Ch'ing period that no large commercial or professional group could afford to remain without its guild. The guilds were both social and religious organizations. They arranged dinners for members and sacrifices to the gods, and, as time went on, came increasingly to try to look after the interests of their members.

The actors' guild in Peking was originally called Li-yüan hui-kuan, or, the Guild of the Pear Garden. Its history began (it may even be much older) at least as early as the 1730s, for a stone inscription survives from that period which gives details of the guild. This inscription, and other similar examples, provide what little information we have about the guild during its early years.[8] The picture presented by these stelae is of an organization interested mainly in constructing cemeteries for dead actors and keeping its headquarters in repair. In fact, the guild was centred on a shrine near the Ching-chung Temple in the Outer City of Peking, and there sacrifices were offered at intervals to Lao-lang shen and to the other deities worshipped by the actors. In addition, parties were held to celebrate holidays, and a stage was maintained at the shrine, so that dramatic performances could accompany the festivities.

The head of the Guild of the Pear Garden was a government appointee, and the guild was responsible to the government from at least as early as the 1860s, and possibly even earlier. No company or actor could accept work in Peking before being registered by the guild. The leader of a proposed troupe had to report the names of the players under his care and the entire repertoire of the group. He also had to inform the guild when his company disbanded. All information on such matters was passed on to the government authorities. Ch'i Ju-shan claims to have had easy access to registration bills dating from 1863 to 1928.[9]

Some of the most famous men to occupy the post of head of the guild were Kao Lang-t'ing, Ch'eng Chang-keng and T'an Hsin-p'ei. All three were famous actors, and supremacy on the stage seems to have been the most important qualification for leadership of the Guild of the Pear Garden.

In the last years of the Ch'ing dynasty the players' guild fell into decline, and its headquarters was all but taken over by another body. With the establishment of the Republican government, however, the actors revitalized their association and in 1914 changed its name to the Cheng-yüeh yü-hua hui, or, the Rectifying Music and Educational Association. They took steps towards regaining the use of their old centre but were resisted. The matter was referred to the authorities, who recognized the temple as the property of the actors' guild but allowed the usurping association the right to occupy it permanently. In 1924 the actors therefore built a new centre nearby.

The Rectifying Music and Educational Association had certain features in common with its Ch'ing predecessor. The sacrifices to the gods were continued (even though they now held much less significance for the actors), burial of deceased members was still a matter of concern to the guild, registration was maintained and the qualifications demanded of the head of the guild were essentially unaltered. Officials were ideally 'the experienced, honest and aged, and the famous actors'.[10] On the other hand, the guild now enjoyed greater independence of the authorities. The head was no longer a government appointee, but was in theory chosen by the members, and in 1912 the guild successfully appealed to the new Republican government to relax some of the more stringent rules which affected the theatre (discussed in the next chapter). The association's functions had also widened in scope. Although it reserved the right to punish members who broke its rules, it showed some concern for their welfare and even arranged for the production of dramas in order to raise funds for general poor relief.

The collective organization of the actors seems, then, to have strengthened in the Republican period, and there was no longer any doubt about their ability to express their will or their views as a professional body.

THE SOCIAL STATUS OF ACTORS

As a social force, too, actors were by no means negligible, and far-reaching developments in Chinese society as a whole were reflected in the acting population. This was especially true of the changing social status of actors in Peking. At the time of the Opium War actors were, as a class, despised by the community. Possibly the main reason for this lay in the contempt with which actors were traditionally regarded in China, as, indeed, they have been regarded in most civilizations in the past. They were looked on as wanderers and vagabonds, shiftless and dishonest, and, worst of all, utterly immoral. There was very little reason why the popular attitude should have changed by the mid-nineteenth century. As I shall explain in Chapter Six, many players were still wanderers, and immorality was as rife among them as ever.

The attitudes of a community are reflected in its laws. In China, actors were bracketed with slaves and prostitutes as the lowest of the low, and edicts of 1313, 1369, 1652 and 1770 forbade them or their families to sit for the civil service examinations. This made it very difficult for them to rise in society, and, even though wealth became increasingly important as a gateway to the bureaucracy, very few actors, however rich and successful, advanced far enough to leave the stage and join China's social cream, the scholar-officialdom.

Legal discrimination against actors was, of course, not peculiar to China. In ancient Rome most players were branded as *infames* (slaves) and deprived of certain political rights. In the France of Louis XIV, too, actors were legally beyond the pale. Indeed, when François Hédélin, Abbé d'Aubignac, wrote his famous *La Pratique du Théâtre* (published in 1657), he concluded that one of the main reasons for the decline of the French theatre was 'the Infamy with which the Laws have noted those who make an open profession of being Players'.[11]

The restrictions imposed on players in China passed into oblivion with the abolition of the civil service examinations in 1905. This was one respect in which their position in society was changing. The process was, however, slow, and even in the Kuomintang period actors were not highly regarded socially. Writing in the 1930s, the sociologist P'an Kuang-tan could comment that 'to have a son who was an actor was equivalent to having no son at all'.[12] Yet their status was undoubtedly higher than it had been a century before, and some actors were considered very respectable people. Let us look at some of the causes of this improvement.

One cause was that, as the nineteenth century drew to its end, far larger numbers of popular actors performed for the aristocracy than had earlier been the case. During the eighteenth century and the early decades of the nineteenth, the court drama was normally performed by special companies which rarely ventured outside the palaces. But from the time of the Empress Dowager Tz'u-hsi onwards, the best actors of the day were frequently invited to the court to perform before the emperor or empress. This practice led to some extent to a blurring of the distinction between the popular actor and the court actor, with a consequent gain in prestige for the former. The establishment of the

Republic did not change this situation, even though the court was no longer important. The ministers of state, the rich, and other eminent citizens still invited good actors to perform for them, and the actors' image could not fail to improve.

Another factor which helped to elevate the actor from his lowly position in society was the rise of the amateur. Many amateur actors came from good families and had received a good education. Some had been in the government service, and there were even cases of Manchu imperial princes who took up amateur acting. The proportion of players from poor and illiterate families fell to some extent[13], and the profession as a whole derived a certain glory from its more blue-blooded members.

Possibly the theatre's greatest lustre came from the long series of famous actors who flourished in the late nineteenth century and in the early twentieth. This was definitely an age of 'stars', and, just as the great comic player Quintus Roscius (d. 62 BC) placed the Roman theatre in a new light by proving that a member of a notoriously low class could rise in the social scale, so, in China, Ch'eng Chang-keng, T'an Hsin-p'ei, Mei Lan-fang and Yü Shu-yen showed that actors could be as much respected as any other member of society. Unless he is notoriously immoral, a great actor cannot fail to enhance his profession's prestige, for there is a strong tendency for fame, superlative skill and social status to go hand in hand.

In any case, these outstanding Chinese actors were not always particularly immoral. Indeed, men like Ch'eng Chang-keng set a standard of 'theatrical virtue' which later actors strove to emulate. The disappearance of the *hsiang-kung* and the founding of the School of Chinese Drama improved the actors' reputation for morals to some extent, even though gossip about their private lives (often based on fact) continued to be spread.

The most important reason, however, for the lessening of the traditional contempt for actors lay in the changing fabric of Chinese society as a whole. The revolutions of Sun Yat-sen and Chiang Kai-shek failed in many of their basic aims, but both were initially progressive and helped to undermine stereotyped traditional values, and both were as much cultural as political. Generally speaking, the attitudes of young people in the 1930s were far more broad-minded than those of their fathers or grandfathers had been, and conventional viewpoints were no longer taken for granted. In these circumstances the old prejudices against 'the children of the Pear Garden' were bound to lose some of their force. In view of the extensive influence of the West, they were inevitably superseded to some extent by the more tolerant attitudes adopted by European peoples towards the theatrical profession.

Unfortunately, the very fact that the rise in social status of actors was part of the Republican revolutionary upsurge ensured that it could only be limited, since the successes of Sun Yat-sen and other leaders in the social sphere were so very incomplete. Yet the foundation had been laid for more radical improvements, and the 'children of the Pear Garden' had travelled some distance in their quest for social respect

5 The Theatre in Peking Society*

The English word 'theatre', in the sense of 'a place for dramatic performances', carries connotations of a construction which includes both a stage and arrangements for seating the spectators. Although the history of the Chinese drama began well before the time of Christ, public theatres do not appear to have been in widespread use until at least the T'ang period (618–907). Certainly they increased greatly in number and social importance during the Sung (960–1279). In the Peking of the Yüan dynasty (1280–1368), brothels commonly functioned as theatres also, but there is very little documentary evidence that buildings existed in that city for the public performance of drama before the Ch'ing period (1644–1911). The usual expedient was simply to erect a stage in front of a temple or in a market-place. The audiences stood around it or sat on the ground.

Legal documents attest to the existence in Peking of public theatres (called *hsi-kuan*) by the early Ch'ing period. Though some of these buildings may have been constructed specially as theatres, most seem to have been the private mansions of rich citizens which were then taken over for public performances of plays. The *hsi-kuan* were probably neither big nor numerous until the late eighteenth century.

The revival of interest in the drama which followed the arrival of Wei Ch'ang-sheng and his Clapper actors in 1779 resulted in an increase in the number and splendour of Peking's theatres, which were assured an important place in the lives of the populace from this time onwards. The trend recurred in the early years of the nineteenth century. As the Anhwei companies guaranteed the continuing popularity of the drama, the demand for playhouses grew until, by about the third decade of the century, there were enough theatres to cater for the needs of the people.

* See Ills. 15–16, p. 135.

From that time until the end of the Ch'ing dynasty no important new theatres were built. In 1900 many of the largest playhouses were destroyed or damaged by fire during the Boxer uprising. They were later rebuilt, and some were modernized, but theatres of the modern Western kind did not appear until the completion of the First Stage (*Ti-i wu-t'ai*; the first theatre of the Western type in Peking) in June 1914.

By the middle of the nineteenth century, contemporary writers were presenting a clear picture of the playhouses of Peking (their types, characteristics, sizes and audiences) and of the customs practised in them. In particular, the scholars Yang Mou-chien from Kwangtung and Chang Chi-liang from Fukien lived in the capital, took an avid interest in its theatres and wrote extensively on what they saw. A number of guide-books, written to point out to visitors the city's places of interest, also survive from this time and have much to say about the theatre.

THE PUBLIC THEATRES OF PEKING

During the nineteenth century there were two quite distinct kinds of theatre in Peking, the *hsi-chuang* and the *hsi-yüan*. They catered for different sections of the community and were dissimilar in their size, their nature and in the occasions which called for their use.

The *hsi-chuang* were, in the words of Yang Mou-chien, 'places where the gentry got together to celebrate a birthday or entertain guests'.[1] From the earliest times it has been customary in China to accompany a dinner party with music or drama and this practice was carried on in the *hsi-chuang*. Because of the exclusive character of these theatres, only the Anhwei companies (and usually only the five best) were invited to perform in them, while Clapper groups were generally excluded. The preliminaries to a gathering at a *hsi-chuang* were complex. Yang Mou-chien describes what happened: 'Somebody engages a musical group to be present and, after the arrangement has been made, he informs the host and has invitations drawn up. The host then sends them out to tell the guests the day and meeting-place and which company will be performing. On the appointed day, the gentry who come are always very sedate; fruits and dishes are laid out. As part of the ceremonial of the occasion, the guests and hosts bow many times to each other. They behave in this way, reverently and courteously, from the morning until the sun declines in the heavens.'[2]

The occasions which called for these private parties (*t'ang-hui*) were diverse. Every spring, people from the same province, or town, or in the same profession, or scholars who had passed examinations in the same year, would assemble, hold a banquet and watch drama. *T'ang-hui* also provided a means of celebrating an important family event, such as a birthday or marriage. Because these gatherings were much more intimate when held in a *hsi-chuang* than they could be if held in a large theatre, the guests were allowed to choose which dramas were to be performed. They were handed a list, on red paper, showing the repertoire of the company which had been invited. They then placed ticks beside the items which they wished to see. Normally they would leave a sum of money to reward the actors.

Though the *hsi-chuang* were open to the public, they were usually hired by private individuals for private purposes. But they were by no means the only places where *t'ang-hui* could take place. The private house of a rich person could be an appropriate rendezvous, and another possible location was a guild-hall. In Peking there were hundreds of such halls, where members of a particular trade or people from the same town or province could meet. As time went on, the *hsi-chuang* went out of fashion and *t'ang-hui* were held more and more in guild-halls or private houses.

The custom of the *t'ang-hui* survived until 1949. In Republican Peking, such famous actors as Mei Lan-fang or Yü Shu-yen were constantly to be seen performing at them. The rich could afford to pay the actors well, and merchants and other capitalists would invite eminent actors to a *t'ang-hui* to enhance their own prestige. After the national capital moved to Nanking in 1928 many of Peking's most prominent and wealthy citizens followed the government thither, with the result that in Peking the *t'ang-hui* declined in frequency and scale. Not surprisingly, the war hastened this decline, but it was not until the Communists came to power that the institution died out altogether, not only in Peking but throughout China. The *t'ang-hui* were the preserve of the rich and consequently quite unacceptable to China's new masters.

Probably the largest and most famous *t'ang-hui* in Chinese history was held by a man who stood for everything which the Communists opposed. This man was Tu Yüeh-sheng (1888–1951), one of the most influential men in Shanghai, a famous banker and the owner of many gambling dens. Tu gave the *t'ang-hui* to celebrate the completion of his ancestral temple, and the performances lasted three days, from 9

June to 11 June 1931. Virtually all the most famous actors of the day took part, and the programmes included displays by Mei Lan-fang, Ch'eng Yen-ch'iu, Shang Hsiao-yün, Hsün Hui-sheng (the four great *tan*), Yang Hsiao-lou, Ma Lien-liang and Chou Hsin-fang. There was a stage in the temple itself and some of the major items were given there. In these cases 'the main players were the great actors from Peking and the spectators naturally the top guests', among whom were some of the most famous men of the time. Tu also had 'a stage of coarse rush mats set up outside the temple where actors of the Shanghai style [of opera] performed, and he especially allowed the country people from P'u-tung [the area east of Shanghai's main river] to watch.'[3]

Such a concession was unusual at a *t'ang-hui*, and normally the common people had no choice but to patronize the ordinary theatres: the *hsi-yüan*. Although, unlike the *hsi-chuang*, these catered primarily for the man in the street, standards of acting in them were not necessarily low. In nineteenth-century Peking, the five major Anhwei companies constantly performed in the most important *hsi-yüan* and presented in them the most spectacular dramatic productions of the time. On the other hand, in the smaller *hsi-yüan* audiences were less well served and had to be satisfied with the minor Anhwei and Clapper companies.

In the guide-books of nineteenth-century Peking we find listed the names of fourteen *hsi-yüan*.[4] Of these, five were small, the others much larger and more important. The minor *hsi-yüan* lay outside the city walls, away from the main commercial centres; the major theatres were all concentrated in one area. This was in the central-northern sector of what was formerly called 'the Chinese City', or 'the Outer City', which was south of the famous Ch'ien-men, or Front Gate (also called the Cheng-yang Gate), itself not far to the south of the Imperial Palaces.

The concentration of Peking's theatres outside the Front Gate was due in part to Ch'ing law. Edicts of 1671, 1799 and later forbade the construction of *hsi-yüan* in the Inner City, where the Imperial Palaces were, and it was not until the very late years of the Ch'ing period that the proscription fell into disuse. This prohibition recalls the situation in Japan during the Tokugawa period (1603–1868), when Tokyo's theatres were by law all concentrated in one quarter, outside the city, so that the government could more easily keep an eye on them. One does not have to look far to find other examples of the 'theatre region'. In Elizabethan London, Finsbury Field to the north of the city and the Bankside to the south were famous for their playhouses, and even today most of the principal London theatres are located in one area: the West End. In Paris, too, the most important theatres were built in one sector of the city, and a similar situation prevails in other major European centres.

The *hsi-yüan* differed from the *hsi-chuang* in several ways. They were, in general, much larger and could hold far more people. They also tended to be very noisy. Yang Mou-chien writes, 'One can hear a constant noise of gongs, drums and people shouting approval. It is just like ten thousand crows vying in the noise they make cawing.'[5] One is reminded of the comments of the German, Prince Pückler-Muskau, who lived in England from 1826 to 1829 and made the following observations on the audiences in English theatres: 'The most striking thing to a foreigner in English theatres is the unheard-of coarseness and brutality of the audiences. The consequence of this is that the higher and more civilized classes go only to the Italian Opera, and very rarely visit their national theatre. . . . English freedom here degenerates into the rudest license, and it is not uncommon in the midst of the most affecting part of a tragedy . . . to hear some coarse expression shouted from the galleries in stentor voice. This is followed, according to the taste of the bystanders, either by loud laughter and approbation, or by the castigation and expulsion of the offender.'[6] The Chinese were by no means alone in considering silence unnecessary during theatrical performances.

To understand why the atmosphere of the Peking *hsi-yüan* was as Yang Mou-chien describes it, let us take a look at the structure of the larger ones. They were divided into various parts, each intended for people of different social and economic status. The auditorium was arranged in two layers and, just as in Elizabethan England, was built round three sides of the raised stage.

The most expensive seats were the 'official seats' (*kuan-tso*), reserved for rich people or officials. They were upstairs on a balcony to the right and left of the stage and near to it. They were cushioned, and were arranged in three or four groups, separated by movable screens. Behind the 'official seats' were the 'tables' (*cho-tzu*), which consisted of rows of short tables leading away from the stage. They also were expensive. People could sit at the tables and drink tea, facing each other rather than the stage, since the theatre was as much a place for chatting with friends as for watching drama.

The seats for the poor were also divided into categories. Chang

Chi-liang comments thus on the situation as he knew it: 'Downstairs, [the area to] the front on the left and right was called "scattered seats" (*san-tso*), that in the middle was called the "centre of the pond" (*ch'ih-hsin*). Those who sat in the *ch'ih-hsin* were all the lowly people of the market-places. One seat anywhere in the *san-tso* cost 100 cash [a very small sum] and this was called a "tea ticket". For children it was half-price, and this was called a "youth ticket". In the "centre of the pond" there were no seats for children. The regulations said, "No selling to the young in the centre of the pond." When the musical company had gone up on the stage, those seated were not allowed to leave. The regulations said, "Once the opera has begun, no tickets can be returned." A tea ticket for a seat in the "official seats" was seven times as much as in the "scattered seats".'[7]

The term 'tea ticket' is significant. Ch'i Ju-shan explains it by saying that 'one paid to drink tea, one did not pay to listen to opera'.[8] In fact, although seats could be booked in advance, tickets were not bought before the performance and then surrendered on admission to the theatre. This practice, normal in the West today, was unknown in China until the early years of the twentieth century. And even in the West, though it is now assumed that the passport for entry into a theatre should be in the form of a ticket, this has not always been the case. The system in Elizabethan England was in some ways strikingly similar to that in nineteenth-century Peking, as witness this comment from the diary of Thomas Platter from Basel, who visited England in 1599: 'There are, however, separate galleries and there one stands more comfortably and moreover can sit, but one pays more for it. Thus anyone who remains on the level standing pays only one English penny: but if he wants to sit, he is let in at a further door, and there he gives another penny. If he desires to sit on a cushion in the most comfortable place of all, where he not only sees everything well, but can also be seen, then he gives yet another English penny at another door.'[9]

Although the *hsi-yüan* of Peking functioned both as teahouses and as theatres, they differed from the *hsi-chuang* in that substantial meals were never provided. Those who wished to dine out before the performance, and could afford to do so, would select a good restaurant nearby and adjourn to the theatre after eating their fill. Nevertheless, in course of time, both the number of vendors in the playhouses, and the variety of the goods which they sold, steadily increased. Members of the audience bought what they wanted during the performance, and not, as in modern Europe or in Tokugawa Japan, during intervals. Therefore, the scope for the development of ancillary businesses in the theatre was virtually infinite. By paying a fixed price to the manager, any person was entitled to sell what he could in the theatre. Tea was of prime importance. In the big *hsi-yüan* tea-vendors began competing with each other. Some of them would obtain particularly good tea-leaves in a nearby shop and then take them to the theatre, where hot water and pots were readily available. By ensuring that the tea-leaves were better than any to be bought from other vendors at the playhouse itself, they frequently obtained the custom of the more discriminating members of the audience. Tea was not, however, the only form of refreshment sold in the *hsi-yüan*. The ubiquitous vendors also sold sweet fruit, peanuts and melons. Moreover, until the late nineteenth century, the purveyors of cigarette-holders, brush-racks, ear-rings and other small curios brought their wares to the *hsi-yüan* in the hope of selling them to people from outside Peking, who might want a memento of their stay in the city. Also available were the damp cloths with which Chinese mopped their brows on a hot day. These were often passed from one part of the theatre to another, and anyone who frequented Peking's playhouses in the 1930s will have seen the towels thrown through the air and invariably caught on descent.

Such a practice would have been considered most improper in a *hsi-chuang*. There was another very important difference between the two kinds of theatre. Whereas the guests at *t'ang-hui* chose the programme, no member of a *hsi-yüan* audience was allowed to select pieces to be performed. Not only the dramas, but also the actors of the individual roles, were chosen by the company itself. Since this was frequently done at short notice, and programmes were never advertised in advance, the audience rarely knew, when they entered the theatre, what dramas they were to see or which actors were to perform in them. In the late years of the nineteenth century the playbill (*hsi-tan*) was introduced. In nineteenth-century Peking, performances in the *hsi-yüan* began in the morning and finished at sunset. After the first few scenes of the day had been performed, sheets of paper, stating in handwriting what pieces were to follow, were passed around the audience. For a charge, one could look at this sheet, but not until the day's performances were well advanced could one buy a playbill which gave a record of all the pieces given. Moreover, the playbill did not inform the reader who would act in the various roles. When newspapers began to be widely circulated early in this century, however, full details of the dramas and the actors were published in them. Advertising techniques then developed, and the normal system with which we are familiar today became established: printed playbills, giving the titles of the dramas to be acted, and the casts, were sold at the theatre.

During the nineteenth century, actors believed that if they kept the programme a secret beforehand, many people would come to the theatre hoping to see the big names, and in this way less famous players also would gain the opportunity to act before large audiences and so to make their reputations. But this system could not last, since leakages of the vital information became increasingly common. Actors did not hesitate to tell their friends (though they were reluctant to tell anyone else) who was to perform and in which dramas. More significant was the growth of a class of people who sought to make money by selling such information to the public. Beggars would make it their business to find out which dramas were to be performed at each theatre, and the names of the actors. They would stand around the Front Gate and try to persuade theatre-goers to pay them a fee in return for details of programmes. When newspapers became generally available begging for this purpose died out.

Apart from such unofficial leakages, however, audiences were given some information about what they were to see. For instance, they could find out before the day which company was to perform. Every year the managers of the main theatres would arrange a roster with the troupes and advertise it at their theatres or in the streets. The lunar month of thirty days was divided into groups of three or four days. During one short period each company would perform at a pre-arranged theatre and then move on to a different one in a system of rotation. The major companies invariably performed in the main *hsi-yüan* outside the Front Gate. The less famous companies also acted in these large theatres when they could, but were in no position to refuse engagements elsewhere. This system proved satisfactory for several decades, but collapsed after most of the main *hsi-yüan* were burned down in 1900. By this time advertising was in much more general use, and the roster system had lost its point.

RESTRICTIONS ON THE DRAMA

Much of what I have written so far has probably created the impression that the atmosphere in a Peking theatre was rather free and easy. In some ways this would be a true impression. Just as in other times and countries (for example, in seventeenth- and eighteenth-century France), members of the audience frequently flooded the stage, to the inconvenience of the actors. There was little restraint on chatting to friends against a background of exhilarating singing, and nobody looked askance at people who ate and drank noisily, or spat, during the performance.

Yet restrictions on the drama were manifold, and the government never relaxed its suspicions about what went on in the theatres. This was especially the case during the Ch'ing period, when, well before the nineteenth century, regulations were introduced prohibiting certain classes of people from visiting *hsi-yüan*. The Bannermen of the Manchu army were excluded from them under several successive edicts. The government was afraid that they would plot dissension or rebellion there in the *hsi-yüan*, and that discipline in the ranks would therefore become relaxed. Notwithstanding these laws, soldiers were often to be found among the theatre audiences. Government officials, too, were forbidden by edicts of 1724, 1803 and 1811 to visit the *hsi-yüan*. These decrees also were frequently disobeyed and appear to have fallen into oblivion by the last years of the Ch'ing dynasty.

The largest section of the population to whom the *hsi-yüan* of the Ch'ing were closed was the women. The Ch'ing government was among the most rigorous in Chinese history in its insistence on the separation of the sexes, believing that the free mingling of men and women in the theatres would lead to a decline in public morals. Ch'i Ju-shan, writing from his personal experience of the late Ch'ing period, has listed the few occasions on which women were permitted to attend dramatic entertainments.

1. *T'ang-hui* dramas. One could mount dramas during birthdays for the old or young, during weddings, or a month after a confinement; [in such cases] the families of all relations and friends were naturally allowed to celebrate and look on. However, this kind of *t'ang-hui* was not very common, and it was only among the rich that they might take place. Not only were they very few, but also the performers were usually female companies. . . .

2. Dramas to honour the gods. . . . These were in character all appeals [for money or gifts] by monks or Taoist priests. In the Inner City there were a few temples with stages. Every year drama would be performed at set times, probably all on the feast-day of the relevant god, and so on. . . . I have been twice, but could only see the circumstances, I could not go in and sit down . . . because at this kind of drama there were only women watching and no men at all.

Ch'i goes on to remark that these 'dramas to honour the gods' for women were fairly expensive and were also rarely performed, perhaps only eight or ten times a year. Moreover, they were never performed in the Outer City.[10]

Women, then, had few chances to watch drama. This situation did not change until the early years of the Republican period. Even then, men and women were at first forced to sit in different parts of the theatre, and it was not until 1924 that the two sexes were allowed to sit together.

There were also rules prohibiting performances at certain times. When an emperor or empress died, all theatres were closed for a hundred days, and on the anniversaries of such imperial deaths they were closed for the day. Performances at *hsi-yüan* were also forbidden during periods when the emperor fasted in prayer for good rains. Yellow notices were put up on the door of the playhouse explaining why no dramas would be given that day. These customs and rules were abrogated in 1912 after an appeal to the new Republican government by the actors' guild.

Just as in Tudor England, drama was prohibited at night. Since the available forms of artificial lighting could easily lead to fire, this rule is not difficult to justify. In fact, no lamps were allowed during the day, so that when the sky was overcast it was practically impossible for the audiences to see what was happening on the stage. Under these circumstances the drama became an almost exclusively aural form of entertainment.

After 1900 the rules against lighting the theatre were relaxed, and performances were permitted at night. After the partial or complete destruction by fire of most of the *hsi-yüan* during the Boxer uprising in 1900, dramatic performances were held for a time in any available restaurants or guild-halls, including those in the Inner City. When the old theatres had been rebuilt, their managers began making efforts to improve the lighting system. They brought in oil-lamps, torches and eventually electric lights. With the introduction of these innovations the evening, which is after all when people normally take their leisure, became a practicable period for theatrical entertainment.

No treatment of restrictions on the drama would be complete without a reference to censorship, which, it is hardly necessary to point out, is by no means the monopoly of the Chinese. Throughout the entire Ch'ing and Republican periods (not to mention the Communist era), governments watched carefully for subversive or morally offensive material in the theatres. Censors could at any time attend the theatres, where 'official seats' were normally available to them, and order the closing of the theatre or the suspension of any drama from the stage. Successive governments have tried to rid themselves of those who sought to put forward hostile ideas through the drama. The Ch'ing arrested Republicans, the Nationalists left-wing critics, and the Japanese anybody who was unwilling to collaborate with them. All governments banned obscenity from the stage. Since time immemorial the Chinese authorities have viewed the drama as a means of propagating correct ethical values; hence both its content and the practices associated with its performance have been checked.

This attitude is clearly expressed in the edicts of the Ch'ing government. One, issued in Peking in 1834, stated that dramas (and novels) should defend such Confucian virtues as filial piety and loyalty, adding that they could 'correct the feelings of people and safeguard their customs'.[11] Another, of 1852, commented that 'each drama performed should encourage goodness and punish evil', but that bad pieces currently being shown in Peking would lead to sexual crimes and robbery.[12] A third edict, also issued in 1852, remarked on the harmful results of bad practices in the dramatic performances which took place in a temple just outside Peking. 'There have never been any prohibitions against the [practice whereby] the country people give thanks to the gods in the spring and autumn, and go to the temple to burn incense. . . . But robbers are going to such gatherings and using them as an excuse to dress up and perform various dramas, thereby causing men and women to mix together in disorder. This [practice] has a very strong bearing on public morals. So the head of the military police . . . and censors should first issue a proclamation, and if there should [still] be any of the aforementioned robbers, then they should arrest and punish them.'[13]

It may be illuminating to conclude this section by quoting by way of comparison an even more puritanical document, a letter (typical of its kind) written by the Lord Mayor and Aldermen of London to the Privy Council in 1597:

The inconveniences that grow by stage plays about the City of London.
1. They are a special cause of corrupting their youth, containing nothing but unchaste matters, lascivious devices, shifts of cozenage, and other lewd and ungodly practices, being so as that they impress the very quality and corruption of manners which they represent. . . .

2. They are the ordinary places for vagrant persons, masterless men, thieves, horse stealers, whoremongers . . . contrivers of treason, and other idle and dangerous persons to meet together and to make their matches to the great displeasure of Almighty God and the hurt and annoyance of Her Majesty's people. . . .
3. They maintain idleness in such persons as have no vocation and draw . . . all sorts of people from the resort unto sermons and other Christian exercises.[14]

The members of the Ch'ing government were not the only authorities who have feared and distrusted the theatre.

Possibly the most striking general point to emerge from this picture of the Peking theatre, and of the restrictions imposed on it, is that it is an institution much more closely welded into society than its counterpart in contemporary Europe or America. This is, indeed, true of the theatre everywhere in China. The general design of the traditional theatres of Peking, and the customs practised in them, show that they were not only places in which to enjoy the drama. They were just as important as places where one could meet friends in a relaxed and sociable atmosphere. The many laws restricting the theatre show that the government recognized the link between society and the playhouse. The Ch'ing authorities and their successors have tried to use the theatre to support their own rule and its underlying principles.

Despite these disadvantages, the close relationship between the theatre and everyday social life in China is in many ways a healthy sign, and many in the West today would like to imitate it as a step towards strengthening our own theatre. We are faced with a dilemma here, for since the early nineteenth century Western culture has tended increasingly to emphasize an individualistic attitude towards both the creation and the appreciation of all the arts. The tradition in China was much more one of group appreciation. When a Chinese was moved by a certain piece of music, this was probably as much because it reminded him of a particular social occasion as because the music was of good quality. During the first half of this century the impact of the West and of its individualistic notions weakened the importance of the group in the Chinese enjoyment of drama and music, and hence undermined the bond between the theatre and daily life. Since the accession of the Communists to power, this situation has been dramatically reversed in many respects, though, paradoxically, Western influence has been in some ways strengthened. The curious cultural mixture which has characterized the Chinese theatre over the last two decades is a subject which I shall treat (mainly) in Part Three.

6 The Theatre in Chinese Society*

Many Western observers of China, especially in the period before the Second World War, have remarked that the Chinese are an irreligious people. They have drawn attention to the rationalism of traditional Chinese philosophy and to the principles of humanistic ethics according to which emperors and officials endeavoured to govern the country. Recent scholarship has tended to discard this generalization and to dispel the myth of Chinese irreligiousness. It is true that there has always been a strongly rationalistic streak among educated Chinese. At the same time, religious rituals and sacrifices occupied an important place in the running of the state until recently: great clans regularly performed religious ceremonies in honour of their dead ancestors, and the life of the common people revolved around festivals at which requests, prayers or thanksgiving were addressed to the harvest, kitchen and fertility gods, among others.

Until very recent times the life of local village communities in China was centred on religious observances, and few activities were entirely divorced from these. This was particularly true of the theatre, which was, in the mind of the average villager, inseparably connected with religious festivals.

THE RURAL POPULAR THEATRE

Among the most important social and religious occasions of the poorer sectors of the community were the temple fairs. These were held everywhere, but especially in the rural districts of north China.[1] They were normally held in the late winter and early spring and symbolized the beginning of the cycle of life. They were, in fact, seasonal events

* See Ills. 17–21, pp. 136–37.

connected with the harvest. Sacrifices were offered to the gods in thanks for the good year just granted, and in prayer for a prosperous one to follow. Other activities were also arranged: merchants and pedlars were busy selling their wares, and actors mounted theatrical performances outside the temple.

Sacrifices and festivities in honour of the gods took place at intervals all over the country, and a stage for dramatic performances could be erected near the temple. Artistic standards were not always taken seriously and the performances were sometimes excessively noisy. This is borne out by the following description of theatrical festivities in and near Swatow, Kwangtung province, quoted from an administrative document of 1876:

> On festivals for the feastdays of the gods, the people usually bring in drama companies which sing on different stages but [at the same time and] in the same general area. They go all day and all night without rest, and call it a competition (*tou-hsi*). The organizers set up a large red woollen banner in advance and offer several dollars in prize money to be given to the victor. The main criterion is endurance, the winner being the one who lasts out the longest. All this tires the people and hurts their pockets, it wastes their time when they should be at work. Men and women mix together unrestrainedly, the whole country is as if mad and there are even quarrels and fights. . . . The actors from the companies outside the region are all young. Many do not like singing and few of them take part in the competition. But there is a kind of local company, the actors of which range in age from eleven to fifteen. These boys are not their own masters and during the competition they can neither eat nor sleep.[2]

The official who made this report was undoubtedly highly suspicious of the whole affair. He was not alone in this. In the administrative and legal documents of the Ch'ing period one constantly finds the complaint that 'men and women mix together unrestrainedly'. During the Republican period, too, it was known by all that temple fairs and other religious holidays offered the best opportunities for flirtation. For this reason many families forbade their womenfolk to attend such celebrations.

Undesirable practices were normal during performances given during religious festivities. The following extract from a Kiangsu administrative document printed in 1877 is quite typical: 'Every year on the 30th day of the second lunar month, when it is the feast-day of the temple god [that is, the City God of Lintsin county], gamblers come from all quarters and, on the pretext of giving thanks to the god, they hold theatrical performances and gamble for money. Over a hundred open-air sheds are set up for the purpose. . . . Loafers band together in various places and practise villainy, robbery and deceit. The whole business is the occasion of a great deal of trouble.'[3] It seems that the temple fairs and similar festivities were a major problem for the government. Gambling was widely practised in China under the Ch'ing dynasty and even more so under the Republic. Yet it was in theory frowned upon by those in authority and was actually forbidden by the Ch'ing penal code. But when the Kiangsu official wrote of villainy, he may have had in mind much more serious crimes than gambling. The law books give many examples of violence and murder committed during popular dramatic performances. Worse still, secret societies were wont to gather on these occasions to plot rebellion. Dramatic performances offered ideal opportunities for plotters to meet, outwardly for an innocent purpose but in fact for a subversive one. Normally, any large gathering of people would immediately create suspicion among officials, and the history of China from 1840 to 1949 demonstrates that successive governments had every reason to fear the secret societies and their motives.

It will be realized, then, that although the popular drama was founded on religious festivals, many highly irreligious practices became associated with it. One cannot therefore be surprised that the content of these 'religious' theatrical performances was mostly not sacred at all. Very often the first scene of a performance dealt with some Buddhist or mythological theme, but most pieces were either tales of the heroic warriors of the past or love stories. As usual, government officials fulminated against the 'lewdness' of the popular theatre. Why, they demanded, did not the people choose dramas about 'the loyal subjects and filial sons of the past and present, or the exemplary words and behaviour of wonderful men and women?'[4]

The moral and political nature of the local drama is quite clear from the preceding paragraphs. The landed gentry and officials believed that it should strengthen the Confucian moral attitudes, and hence their own power. But the economic and social power of the landlords had shrunk during the seventeenth and eighteenth centuries, and, partly because of this, the aristocratic K'un-ch'ü had declined seriously. Its place was being taken by the rising regional theatre of the masses, which reached its height in the eighteenth century. The peasantry were henceforth much more interested in the expression of their own counter-culture, which tended to be against Confucianism, against the landlords and against the officials. Actors frequently interspersed their performances with references to current events which were usually hostile to the Confucian *status quo*. The local theatre was a genuinely popular art form, and, no matter what the authorities did, they never succeeded in making it serve their own political or ideological ends.

Local officials might well worry when the time arrived for a temple fair, or some other occasion involving the performance of popular drama, to take place. For though in some respects they could perhaps be thought over-zealous in their attempts to restrain the people, in other matters one is bound to agree with their attitude. One of the consequences brought about by the popular drama was the practice of extorting money from the poor. In theory, temple fairs and theatrical performances were free. In practice, the organizers of the dramatic companies would frequently come round the village houses, asking for money; sometimes the sum demanded exceeded by far what the actors needed to cover the costs of the performances. No wonder the Swatow official quoted above could say that the popular theatre 'hurts their [the people's] pockets'.

Naturally there were other ways of financing these drama festivals. Merchants and others who sought profit paid actors to perform because the drama provided an excellent opportunity to draw crowds and, consequently, potential buyers of their goods. It is therefore not accidental that drama festivals almost always took place in conjunction with fairs held at local temples. As the modern Japanese scholar Tanaka Issei has shown, the rise and fall of the local drama in any given district was closely associated with the extent of the economic patronage that the local merchants and other controllers of finance were able to provide.[5]

Temple fairs and theatrical seasons connected with religious festivals rarely lasted for more than a few days. One reason for this was that dramatic companies had to be mobile; they travelled round the country, visiting even very small villages and seeking employment wherever they could find it. As a result, they were usually unknown to the people and acquired the reputation of being vagabonds – shiftless, untrustworthy people, with 'no fixed address'. Their status was therefore very lowly in the eyes of peasants and officials alike. Like the boys of the Anhwei companies, the actors of the strolling troupes were frequently recruited as virtual slaves. They were bought from their parents, who signed a contract giving the troupe leader complete control over the children for a specified period of time. The young members of these intinerant companies could expect harsh treatment from their masters and were sometimes even beaten to death. They had no legal rights whatever, and so it was useless for them to complain to the officials.

Apart from the dramas given by the lowly wandering actors, the rural folk could enjoy performances mounted by their own fellow villagers. Amateur dramatics were widespread throughout China. 'The peasants would themselves rehearse and perform, and when the time for the show came about the women and old ladies would dress up in new clothes, just as at New Year, to go and watch the drama',[6] and the men who were not acting could go as well. Like their professional counterparts, the peasant amateur actors usually chose the less busy times of year, in order not to interfere with the work of the harvest. Although they sometimes acted in their everyday clothes, it was also their standard practice in most parts of China to don the costumes of the traditional local drama in order to enhance the occasion.

One consequence of the fact that the performances of rural actors, both professional and amateur, were seasonal, was that the stages which they used were very often temporary. It is true that many temples were equipped with permanent stages, and examples may be found all over China to this day. On the other hand, most of the smaller temples lacked built-in stages, and so a company would erect a temporary stage and then dismantle it after the short dramatic season was over. The actors used whatever space was available outside the shrine, but if this proved inconvenient or inadequate, a nearby market-place or other area would serve. Lu Hsun, probably twentieth-century China's greatest prose-writer, recalls a play being given on a 'stage standing in a plot of empty ground by the river outside the village'.[7] The responsibility for erecting the stage rested entirely with the players, even if they did not actually carry out the physical labour themselves. One late nineteenth-century record from Shensi informs us bluntly that 'the performance of drama to honour the gods is not official business; [public officials] might provide wooden material for the stages, but it is certainly not their public duty [to do so].'[8] As in the Peking *hsi-yüan* the audience sat on three sides of the stage. Not surprisingly, seating arrangements were somewhat primitive, and spectators often simply sat on the ground. They were not protected from the elements, since the performance took place in the open air, but, despite the obvious disadvantages of possible disruption by rain and high wind, this system had the virtue of simplicity and made it easier for spectators to come and go as they pleased. Lu Hsun remarks that 'the Chinese opera is so full of gongs and cymbals, shouting and jumping, that it makes the onlookers' heads swim. It is quite unsuited for presentation in a theatre but, if performed in the country and watched from a distance, it has its charm.'[9]

The reader may well have been struck by the similarity between the conventions of the rural drama of China and those of popular theatres in other countries. Indeed, it has often been pointed out that the development of the theatre in general has tended to proceed on similar lines in many parts of the world. For instance, it is true not only of China but of many other civilizations that in its early phases the theatre was connected with religious festivals and was often seasonal. The sacred dances of ancient Japan and the medieval mystery plays of Europe are but two cases in point, and the temple or the church functioned as a site for theatrical performances in many countries in early times. In India, for instance, there were in the past innumerable temples with adjacent theatrical enclosures. Even today dramatic performances are given in such temples in Kerala and in a few other parts of the country. Rural fairs based on religious festivals have for centuries offered excellent opportunities for the drama in India. Companies would act on temporary platforms in the open air, where the congregated villagers could best see them. Temple fairs are still held in India. At the Sonepur fair in Bihar, one of the biggest of all the rural fairs, folk troupes still erect their own stages and perform popular pieces; even in Delhi the feast-days of certain saints call for similar theatrical activities.

Another feature of the popular drama's development in the world at large has been the gradual adoption of secular themes in pieces given during supposedly religious festivals. At first, the subject-matter of the plays would fit the occasion fairly well. But as time went on, the drama tended to lose its moral and didactic purpose and became much more a source of amusement, a mere adjunct to a festival whose main function was to bring together and entertain large numbers of people. This process occurred in many places, including India and medieval Europe.

In its religious festival stage, the drama was usually performed by itinerant companies. In the history of world drama we find many different kinds of such troupes, varying widely in size and competence.

In Europe they mostly included both men and women, in sharp contrast to the situation in China, where only men could belong to them. In almost every country, however, the actors attached to wandering companies were despised by society and regarded as dishonest vagabonds of low morals.

DRAMA IN THE CITIES

In China, as elsewhere, strolling companies were found not only in the countryside but also in the cities, and the rural theatre shared many characteristics with its urban counterpart. As in the countryside, so in the city religion was the basis of many types of drama, and religious festivals frequently provided the principal occasions for theatrical performances. Yet there were some fundamental differences between the urban and the rural theatres. The reason for this is that the city-dwellers were in general much richer and more sophisticated than the country folk, and their lives were not nearly so much dominated by the exigencies of the seasons. It is the seasonal factor which explains why strolling players visited the cities so often. For most of the year, especially in the summer, peasants worked hard in the fields and could spare no time to see the entertainment provided by touring companies. The companies therefore moved to the cities, where their members frequently disbanded and joined other troupes. Unless they could gain employment in large teahouse-theatres, these players continued to act at religious celebrations, but, even in this field alone, much more work was available in the cities than in the countryside.

There was a wide range of festivals in the cities. Apart from major dates like the Spring or Lantern Festivals (held on the first and fifteenth days of the first lunar month), many days were set aside for individual commercial or professional groups. All of these worshipped a protector in the natural hope that he would bring brisk business and good fortune. In the general gazetteer of Shansi we read that in one particular city of the province there were some 120 well known commercial societies, all of which 'had theatrical performances in honour of their god, so that there was not a single day in the year when [the actors] were idle'.[10]

If the cities' relative independence of the seasons made it possible for an actor to find work in them all the year round, the greater sophistication of the urban populace led to certain types of premises, rarely found in the villages, being used for theatrical performances.

These included the brothel, the teahouse and the winehouse. The performers were normally prostitutes; everybody assumed that a good courtesan would be able to act, sing and play musical instruments. Sometimes the girls would be formed into a company, and not only the female but also the male roles would be performed by the brothel's inmates.

Before the nineteenth century the quarters of the cities where the sing-song girls flourished provided the only public indoor theatres.[11] There were numerous grades. The courtesans at the top of the prostitutes' social scale were visited mainly by *literati*, and it is with these high-class girls that most surviving records deal. The more lowly 'sing-song girls' catered for less cultivated tastes and were not so refined in their artistry, but, as the name 'sing-song girl' indicates, they too could provide theatrical entertainment of one sort or another for their guests. Yet even after the rise of the large-scale teahouse-theatres in the nineteenth century (discussed below), acting continued to be one of the main activities of the prostitute. Wang Shu-nu tells us, in his scholarly work on Chinese prostitution, that in Republican Shanghai many such women were found in the ranks of 'actresses, female story-tellers, female fortune-tellers, film stars and dancing girls' and adds: 'It is said that there are altogether 120,000 public, private and disguised prostitutes in Shanghai. This estimate may not be exactly right, but is not too wide of the mark.'[12]

The precise combination of the prostitute and the actress is not found in many countries. On the other hand, in most countries, at any period in the past, actresses have had a reputation for low morals and have been linked in the popular mind with prostitution. In traditional India an actress was frequently, if not necessarily, also a prostitute, and actresses were condemned by society as a result. In seventeenth-century France, d'Aubignac hoped to improve the deplorable image of actresses and the theatre by recommending the king to order 'that no single Woman shall act, if they have not their Father or Mother in the Company, and that all Widdows shall be oblig'd to marry within six months after their year is out for mourning; and in that year shall not act except they are married again'.[13]

During the nineteenth century, the playhouse of the sing-song girls' quarters began to take second place to the teahouse-theatre in China's cities. Peking had assumed the lead in this development but in course of time these larger theatres were also established in Shanghai, Tientsin and elsewhere. One of the most important examples in

Shanghai was the Tan-kuei teahouse, opened in 1867. Many famous actors were invited from Peking and Tientsin to perform there, and in later years they were to include such well known stage artists as Mei Lan-fang and T'an Hsin-p'ei. A guidebook to Tientsin dated 1898 lists several teahouse-theatres in that city, among them the T'ien-hsien, T'ien-kuei and T'ien-fu.[14] These, too, were visited by many of Peking's best players and provided the springboard from which others launched themselves into fame.

The rise of great urban theatres is a natural stage in the development of the popular drama. All over the world we find that the stage at which wandering players performed during religious festivals has been succeeded by a more sophisticated and complex phase. The strollers do not necessarily cease their activities, but the new theatre is city-based and not so dependent on the seasons for its audiences. Performances are frequent and not confined to festivals. The secular element becomes predominant and the religious recedes. Drama is presented in permanent buildings designed for the purpose, and becomes an indoor rather than an outdoor entertainment. Troupes become centred on one place, and their need to be constantly on the move disappears.

In China this phase was succeeded by yet another one, which was heavily influenced by the Western theatre and followed European conventions. These demanded a greater concentration by the audience on what the actors were doing and a higher degree of organization in such matters as reservations and seating. Western-style theatres became common in China's big cities after the founding of the Republic. One example was of unusual interest in that it was founded by one man in a deliberate attempt to modernize the theatre in a 'model community'.

Chang Chien (1853–1926) was one of the most remarkable reformers of modern China. After a successful career under the Ch'ing he set out in the last years of his life to make his native town (Nantung, near Shanghai) an example of modernization which could be followed all over the country. He introduced or expanded industry, social welfare and modern medicine and went to great lengths to beautify his town. He also established a meteorological station, a water conservancy project and a museum. In the present context, his main achievements were to build, in 1919, a three-storied theatre designed to hold twelve hundred people and, soon afterwards, to found a school in which a permanent drama troupe could be trained. The seats in the theatre were numbered carefully and had to be booked in advance, and the older customs described in Chapter Five were abandoned. Chang Chien tried to inculcate modern habits in the audiences, who were expected to behave in a disciplined way and were encouraged to applaud, rather than shout, to show their approval.[15] Public reaction to the theatre was favourable, and the standards of performance were kept high. Mei Lan-fang visited Nantung and acted in its theatre three times (in 1919, 1920 and 1922), and other great actors, such as Yang Hsiao-lou, also appeared. Unfortunately, however, Chang's theatre was forced to close down, together with the school attached to it, in 1925.

The theatre of Nantung was built by Chang Chien for the specific purpose of providing the people with cultural entertainment and improvement. It may therefore be called a 'popular' theatre. So far in this chapter, I have considered only the drama performed mainly for the ordinary people. To complete the picture it will be necessary to discuss the social background of the drama which was acted primarily for the benefit of the rich.

THE DRAMA OF THE UPPER CLASSES

In almost every country, the court has been an important centre of the theatre. Whether in Cambodia, Japan or China, or in the old states of Italy or India, the monarch or ruling potentate has played an active part in patronizing the drama. Very often the royal theatre has functioned partly as an aspect of the state ritual. This was certainly so in China during the Ch'ing period, when drama was given at court not only for the amusement of the emperor but also as part of a religious celebration.

Some of the Ch'ing emperors took a particular interest in the drama. The Emperor Ch'ien-lung (1736–96) set up a special bureau, which functioned until 1910, to deal with the organization of court actors and dramas. At first the imperial players were all permanent residents at court. But this policy was later modified, and the Empress Dowager frequently invited great actors for individual performances. We have already seen that Sun Chü-hsien, T'an Hsin-p'ei and Yang Hsiao-lou were included in their number.

The imperial family naturally stood at the top of the social scale, and its theatrical entertainment was especially sumptuous. Yet since it numbered but a few persons, and in any case ceased to be significant after 1911, I shall devote more space to considering the part played by the drama in the life of the great families which ranked below the emperor's.

Like the ordinary people of the village communities, the members of great families were bound together by the performance of seasonal sacrifices. The gods in whose honour they conducted these celebrations were of two kinds. Firstly, the clans did not scorn to invoke the protection of the spirits worshipped by the ordinary people. They might even take the initiative in arranging for rituals to be offered to the popular deities, and ensure that a dramatic company was available to perform after the ceremony. Secondly, the members of important families worshipped their own ancestors as deities. A special shrine was set aside to honour forbears, and it was here that seasonal sacrifices were offered to them. In many parts of China, especially the southern coastal provinces, such as Chekiang, theatrical performances were a common feature of the ceremonies.

It was the members of the family itself who organized these quasi-religious performances, and the various branches of the family would take it in turns to fulfil this task. The following short extract, taken from the section on ceremonial in the register of a Ch'en clan in Shao-hing, Chekiang, provides a typical example: 'At the ancestral temple they would perform every spring equinox a complete session of drama (one drama for the local earth gods, another in honour of the ancestral spirits). Those whose turn it was in the [particular] year to make the arrangements would select and engage a company to perform, and they would also deal with other matters such as the financial aspects'.[16]

It is clear from this passage that the ancestral temple could be used as a site for performances. The stage was usually outside the shrine, in some cases being specially erected there for one occasion. Many clan elders had a vague, and occasionally very clear, feeling that there was something irreverent about the drama, and so preferred that performances should be given well away from the actual centre of sacrifice. Every now and then, however, we find that they make a concession, accompanied, of course, with reservations: 'When a dramatic performance takes place inside the temple – in the central hall – only honoured elders, guests from afar or men may sit [directly in front of the actors]. Women may sit only in the two wings and must watch from there. Disciplinary action will be taken against those who disobey.'[17] In this instance the number of spectators was severely limited, but if the stage was outside the temple the peasants could attend. In any case, they could normally expect to be asked to contribute in some form or another to the cost of the drama. This was mostly met through various forms of taxation. Some families designated certain areas of their land as 'theatre fields', which they hired out to villagers. At harvest time the peasant user was expected to hand over a portion of the yield to the family, and the money thus made from the fields was then used to pay for the drama. Other families taxed the use of fishing pools to cover the costs of the performances. In course of time a whole host of means was devised. The family might share in the expense itself, though, inevitably, the burden was felt most by the poorer villagers.

The peasants were often allowed to watch the sacrificial drama in return for their contribution. Indeed, this stimulated their interest in the theatre and was one of the factors leading to the growth of the regional drama. Yet despite the continuing importance of the quasi-religious drama of the gentry in the late Ch'ing and Republican periods, the landlord-sponsored theatre had actually declined by the eighteenth century in comparison with the preceding era, and the peasants sought entertainment much more in the temple fairs and market-places, as described earlier in this chapter.

One symptom of the downward trend of the gentry theatre lay in the disappearance of the private family troupe. In the eighteenth century and earlier, many great families maintained their own companies, which performed for guests when the lord of the house invited his friends for dinner. Families without a troupe could hire one for the occasion. During the nineteenth century, the custom of running privately owned companies gradually went out of fashion and by the Republican period survived only in a few families. Concurrently, the practice of hiring troupes flourished throughout China. Performances given in this way in private houses were known not only in Peking, but everywhere, as *t'ang-hui*. Since I have already discussed the *t'ang-hui* of Peking in the previous chapter, and since *t'ang-hui* held in other places did not differ significantly from those of Peking, I need say nothing further about them here.

Many of the social features of the Chinese theatre discussed above are of ancient origin. The basic connection between religion and the drama is recorded or implied in some extremely old sources, in particular the *Book of Odes* (*Shih-ching*), written between about 1100 and 600 BC. All the customs to which I have drawn attention reached maturity during the Ch'ing period, and almost all, except those related to the court, survived at least until the 1937–45 Sino-Japanese War.

Yet Chinese society was not completely static between the rise of the Ch'ing in the mid-seventeenth century and the middle of the twentieth. Sun Yat-sen's revolution may have failed to produce the immediate and radical social reforms for which its main supporters hoped. Nevertheless, the whole process of gradual change in attitude on the part of the poorer members of society from the seventeenth century onwards produced a cumulative effect of tremendous importance. What happened was that the poor were gradually turning away from Confucian morality, a process which the gentry and educated classes were unable to prevent. This trend was reflected in the growth of the popular regional theatre with its anti-official social framework and anti-Confucian content. Finally, the intellectuals also began to turn away from Confucianism, as is shown by the gradual decline of the *K'un-ch'ü* and, above all, by the New Culture Movement. The political implications of these processes are clear. When eventually a group of leaders, the Communists, arose who wished to overthrow the Confucian order altogether, they found much fertile and already partly prepared ground in the minds of the peasants and the poor. The victory of the Communists may not have been inevitable, but neither was it an unexpected result of the changing social attitudes of the preceding centuries.

7 Shanghai and the Lower Yangtze Valley*

Until the 1780s, when the actors of the Clapper Opera, led by Wei Ch'ang-sheng, made Peking China's foremost theatrical centre, the empire's greatest dramatic activities had been heavily concentrated in the districts along the lower reaches of the Yangtze River. The most important province was Kiangsu, but others, such as Kiangsi, Anhwei, Hupeh and Chekiang, could also boast a high level of theatrical achievement. The pre-eminence of these provinces in the theatrical arts was based both on economic and on cultural factors. The lower Yangtze region was by far the most advanced in the country in technology and production, and within it a vast range of inter-provincial trade was carried on. The number of people distinguished in the arts whom it produced was out of all proportion to its population, and the region also contributed to the government bureaucracy more officials per head than any other part of China except Fukien and Peking itself.

For the theatre the two principal cities were undoubtedly Soochow and Yangchow, both in Kiangsu province. Soochow had been the birth-place of the aristocratic *K'un-ch'ü* (discussed in the Introduction) in the sixteenth century and remained among its foremost centres until the Taiping uprising of the mid-nineteenth century. The city and its environs abounded in wealthy families who kept their own *K'un-ch'ü* companies, and its courtesans were famous throughout China not only for their beauty but also for their talent as dancers and actresses.

Yangchow was the centre of the region's important salt trade. The merchants who dealt in this commodity were fabulously rich. In his definitive study of these men, Professor Ho Ping-ti writes that 'prior to . . . the first half of the nineteenth century, the salt merchants of

---

* See Ills. 22–26, pp. 138–39.

Yang-chou [Yangchow] boasted of some large individual fortunes and certainly the largest aggregate capital possessed by any single commercial or industrial group in the empire.'[1] They also made it their business to patronize the arts, and, above all, the theatre. Owing to their efforts Yangchow could, until the 1780s, claim to have been the home of the finest actors, and of the widest variety of drama, of any city in all China.

During the nineteenth century, Soochow and Yangchow began to lose their economic importance in the face of the increasing wealth of Shanghai. Their significance as theatrical centres also waned, and was reduced to a fairly low ebb by the Taiping rebellion. Inevitably, troupes from all over the lower Yangtze region tended to drift to Shanghai in an attempt to make their fortunes there, and Shanghai replaced Yangchow as the most theatrically cosmopolitan city in the area.

The *K'un-ch'ü*, which had been so popular among the gentry of Soochow and Yangchow, became a *passé* art form, and it was left to the practitioners of the more 'rustic' styles to maintain the drama's vitality. Yet the 'elegant' drama did exercise considerable influence over the less exclusive forms, and a great many of China's styles of regional drama bear its imprint in one way or another. This is particularly true of the branch of folk drama in Kiangsu and Chekiang known as *T'an-huang*.

T'AN-HUANG

The principal characteristics of this kind of theatre were that its 'speech was colloquial and easy to understand ... its dialogue passages outweighed by far its sung sections and its tunes were extremely simple'.[2] The music was largely derived from the *K'un-ch'ü*, and was therefore melodious and not strident, but was based just as much, or even more, on local folk tunes. Moreover, the instruments used were not all the same as in the *K'un-ch'ü*. No flute was included in the orchestra, and stringed instruments, such as the *hu-ch'in* (or fiddle) and *p'i-p'a* (or lute) were dominant. There were normally only about five actors, including a *sheng*, a *tan*, a *ching* and a *ch'ou*.

The birth-place of this style was Soochow. The date of its origin, however, is uncertain, and scholars have put forward various theories. The most widely accepted nowadays is that the *T'an-huang* was first heard in the eighteenth century, and a few dramas printed during that period mention this form. As one writer puts it, 'Even Taoist priests and fortune-tellers [of the eighteenth century] wanted to sing *T'an-huang*, so we can see how generally accepted it was at that time'.[3] Some scholars believe that the style originated later, a theory which is supported by an oral tradition, handed down by actors: 'After the death of the Chia-ch'ing Emperor in 1820, there was a suspension of all drama to mourn the event, so no drama was allowed among the people and the livelihood of actors was interrupted. At that time a certain artist called Wang Tzu-hsiang, who had gone blind and could not perform, gathered together three or four sons and nephews into a company and changed [the existing *K'un-ch'ü*] into *T'an-huang*.'[4] Most of the *T'an-huang* scripts came from the hand of the *K'un-ch'ü* actor Ch'ien K'un-yüan, who favoured the new style and devoted much energy to ensuring its success.

Some actors maintain that the emperor whose death occasioned this growth was Tao-kuang (1820–50), not Chia-ch'ing, and that the *T'an-huang* consequently developed some years later, but, in any case, the story quoted above is not reliable. I mention it because there seems no reason to doubt that the already existing *T'an-huang* took on new strength as a result of the moratorium on the drama. This would have affected such major forms as the *K'un-chü* severely, and it would be natural for unemployed actors to turn in desperation to a little known type of drama which stood a good chance of evading the notice of the authorities.

The small scale of the early *T'an-huang* play was typical of the popular Chinese theatre. Like plays written in many other forms, it was originally often performed by only one or two actors, who merely told a story to the ordinary folk who constituted the audience and did not necessarily dress in spectacular costumes or practise the complex acting techniques characteristic of the established kinds of drama. Sometimes they did not even need a stage. Large-scale *T'an-huang* dramas were not written until later times.

The themes of the *T'an-huang* dramas were largely founded on the *K'un-ch'ü*, love stories, legends of the supernatural and tales of old heroes being extremely common. The popular drama of the lower Yangtze region drew material from the *T'an-huang*, supplementing it with pieces about peasant life or with stories based on local legend. After 1900 we also find examples of the *T'an-huang* being based on contemporary or revolutionary material. For instance, one *T'an-huang* actor, Lin Pu-ch'ing, became popular partly because of his skill in incorporating items of the day's news into the drama which he was performing. In 1919, during the May Fourth Movement, another actor (Fan Shao-shan, from Soochow) was invited to a *t'ang-hui* in Peking which was held by an eminent person from Soochow. He used the occasion to mock one of the guests, Ts'ao Ju-lin, the Minister of Communications, who was a major target of protest during the movement on account of his agreement that Japan should be allowed to succeed to Germany's former rights in Shantung. Ts'ao Ju-lin subsequently resigned his post.

The occasion which demanded the performance of Soochow *T'an-huang* in Peking was an isolated one, for few people in the north could appreciate the music. On the other hand, the style did spread from Soochow to many other cities of the lower Yangtze. In Yangchow, according to one account, popular artists would 'form themselves into companies and [play] pieces with scripts based on the dramas of the Yüan dynasty; their music and rhythm, costumes and stage properties were extremely coarse'.[5] The new music from nearby Soochow created an impression on these lowly actors, and a kind of regional drama evolved which has come to be known as *Yang-chü*, or Yangchow Opera. In Wusih, Kiangsu province, and Hangchow in Chekiang, among other places, similar processes took place and the most popular local styles of these two cities, *Hsi-chü* (Wusih Opera) and *Hang-chü* (Hangchow Opera), are based on the *T'an-huang*.

In about 1860 *T'an-huang* actors first brought their style from Soochow to Shanghai. They were led by Wang Li-sheng, originally a minor customs clerk, and Huang Mao-sheng, a former assistant in a seafood shop. At first they performed only at the *t'ang-hui* of scholars from Soochow who were interested in the folk theatre, but then they began performing for the ordinary people in small teahouses, or in the streets and alleys. In an effort to expand their influence they also took pupils. Because there were so many people in Shanghai from outlying regions where the *T'an-huang* was already known, the new music quickly aroused considerable enthusiasm and became permanently established in the city. What is now called Shanghai Opera (*Hu-chü*) is a development of the work of these two actors.

It was not until the 1920s that women first performed in *T'an-huang* either in Shanghai or in Soochow. In the former city this novelty was due to the initiative of a blind actor called Chin Ch'ao-tsung, who taught his wife and daughter to sing and had them perform in the Wing On Company, a department store which at the time included a stage in the canteen upstairs. Mixed troupes, and later a number of all-female companies, developed in the wake of Chin's enterprise.

During the 1930s, a number of people still took an interest in *T'an-huang* in Shanghai, and a scholarly society was founded to promote it. Yet performances took place mostly at *t'ang-hui* or on the temporary stages, and the style only rarely penetrated the major theatres, where Peking Opera and Shaohing Opera (discussed below) had greater prestige and could draw larger crowds. It is not surprising that the outbreak of the Sino-Japanese war dealt the *T'an-huang* a heavy blow, not only in Shanghai but elsewhere as well. The post-war years saw an even steeper decline, and by 1949 the *T'an-huang* was everywhere close to extinction.

SHAOHING OPERA

In Shanghai one of the main kinds of drama to supersede the *T'an-huang* was the Shaohing Opera, known in Chinese either as *Yüeh-chü* (Chekiang Opera) or, alternatively, as *Sheng-hsien hsi* (the Theatre of Sheng County).

Since the Shaohing Opera originated in the late years of the Ch'ing period, its history is much shorter than that of most major Chinese dramatic forms. It arose in Shaohing, in Sheng county, in Chekiang province, hence the various names by which it is known. At first it was small in scale; the plays were based entirely on folk tunes, accompanied by only a clapper (*pan*). Its progress can perhaps best be related in the words of an author (a native of Chekiang), whose pen-name is Tzu-o.

In 1913, two actors of the Village of the T'ung Family in western Sheng [county], Wang Kuei-lao and Huang Ta-pao, arranged suitable libretti for the songs and music [of the Shaohing Opera]. They staged trial performances, but these [proved to be] extremely bawdy.... The magistrate of the city, considering them to be harmful to public morals, issued a strict proscription against them. However, certain corrupt local elements emerged to protect [the *Sheng-hsien hsi*], and it became even more prosperous than before the prohibition, which eventually lapsed completely. Some lower members of the gentry then selected the famous actors from all the existing troupes and opened a theatre, called Chen-yeh, in the Kiangsi guild-hall of Sheng county. It was invariably booked out and in a very short time the opera had spread to Shanghai, Hangchow, Shaohing city and other places, in each of which theatres were opened to perform it.[6]

This is a typical story of the acceptance of small-scale folk drama, through the patronage of the gentry, by urban society and, consequently, of its establishment in permanent theatres.

The actor responsible for the introduction of Shaohing Opera into Shanghai was Wang Chin-shui, who arrived there in 1916. He performed principally outside houses where natives of Chekiang were known to be staying, since these people loved the familiar music of their province; but he attracted little attention elsewhere. The next year, other companies came to Shanghai from Chekiang. They were more successful, and many people became interested in the new music. In response, the actors enlarged the style's expressive range: they added more instruments to the orchestra (including gongs, drums, the *erh-hu*, the *pan-hu* and the *san-hsien*), and acting techniques were improved. Eventually, intellectuals became interested in the Shaohing Opera and it came under the influence of the Peking Opera, the spoken play and Western methods of stagecraft. In particular, scenery came to be widely used to enliven the stage spectacle – a procedure which became quite normal in Shanghai though it was still rare in the traditional Chinese theatre elsewhere.

With its introduction into Shanghai, a further important change took place in the Shaohing Opera. In the countryside, the plays had been acted by all-male companies, according to the usual Chinese practice. In 1923, however, an entirely female company acted Shaohing operas in Shanghai. They were not well received and returned to Chekiang, where some training-schools for student actresses were established. Actresses then joined previously all-male companies, and finally Shaohing Opera troupes came to include only women.

This, the best known feature of the Shaohing Opera, was the source of certain limitations, but also of certain assets. Heroic and military drama is necessarily excluded, and consequently acrobatics as well, since they are characteristic of the military pieces. This is a drawback, because the splendid gymnastic skill seen on the Chinese stage has long been one of its main attractions. On the other hand, the all-female casts of the Shaohing Opera endow it with a certain grace and gentleness not found in other Chinese dramatic forms. Love stories, in which the scholar-lover (*hsiao-sheng*) is played by a woman, are a particular favourite: the story of the elopement, death and transformation into butterflies of Liang Shan-po and his beloved, Chu Ying-t'ai, is possibly the most famous in the repertoire of the Shaohing Opera.[7] Moreover, there is great musical beauty in the Shaohing

Opera, which more than compensates for the limitations mentioned above. The Shaohing Opera became extremely popular in Shanghai, and in the West it is, after the Peking Opera, the most famous of all types of Chinese drama.

PEKING OPERA: THE SOUTHERN SCHOOL

In view of Shanghai's commercial and cultural importance and its status as China's largest city, it was inevitable that the Peking Opera should be introduced there. We have already seen that great actors from Peking, such as T'an Hsin-p'ei, Mei Lan-fang and Yü Shu-yen, visited Shanghai and could be assured of rapturous welcomes there. In the course of time, however, the city came to have its own troupes and developed its own style of Peking Opera. Called the Southern School, this was close in its musical and in its stage conventions to the Peking Opera in the north, but did not follow this rigidly. Some local musical conventions were used, and dramas were written especially for the Shanghai stage.

By far the most important exponent of the Southern School was Chou Hsin-fang, who was born in 1895 in a small town near Ningpo, in Chekiang province. His family prided themselves on their education, but were nevertheless very poor, and at the age of six Chou began learning to act. At seven, he started giving performances as a *lao-sheng* in Hangchow. His understanding of how to portray old men was so remarkable that he was affectionately called the Seven-year-old Boy (Ch'i-lin t'ung). At the age of eleven he had already acquired some recognition as an actor in his own province, and he was now called the Unicorn Boy (also Ch'i-lin t'ung in Chinese), a stage name which he retained throughout his career.

Chou was a quick learner and soon ventured to perform in Tientsin and Peking. He entered the Hsi-lien-ch'eng training-school in Peking and there became a close friend of Mei Lan-fang. In his autobiography Mei wrote of him: 'Our ages were identical. . . . and we were exactly the same in our personal characteristics in the Hsi-lien-ch'eng. We were there to study acting and became extremely intimate. . . . From the time we were together in the Hsi-lien-ch'eng until recently he was the only person with whom I often performed in partnership. This old comrade of more than forty years and I sometimes talk of former times together.'[8]

After graduating from the school where this friendship had begun,

Chou Hsin-fang left Peking and acted for a time in Chefoo (in Shantung province) and Tientsin. In Tientsin he belonged to the same company as an actress called Chin Yüeh-mei, who made a habit of commenting on the news of the day in her performances. After a short stay in Tientsin, he returned to Shanghai. Clearly under Chin's influence, Chou now began to take a deep interest in modern and political drama. He adapted many plays on traditional themes, incorporating a social message in numerous cases. He made no secret of his view that the theatre should sometimes propagate a certain viewpoint. At the time of the May Fourth Movement a drama in which he performed was immediately suspended by the authorities on the grounds that it was subversive. During the war he was active in reinforcing optimism, patriotism and anti-Japanese feeling through his art. He became an active supporter of the Communists and at first fared very well under their government. I shall return briefly to the last phase of his career, from 1949 onwards, in Chapter Twelve.

The Unicorn Boy was noted for his prowess in dialogue, which he enunciated with great power. The expressiveness of his acting, and his appearance, were also considered magnificent, and it was on them that his fame chiefly rested. There used to be a saying in Shanghai that 'he had expression even on his back'. As a singer he was not highly regarded. Hatano Kenichi comments unkindly: 'His voice is extremely gritty. However, there are those in Shanghai who like his gritty sounds.'[9] Indeed, most critics agreed that Chou was not at his best in sung passages, which he therefore tended to keep to the minimum. His performances were like those of stylized spoken plays with some singing included. He was, in fact, reacting against the tendency in some theatrical circles in China to emphasize the aural aspect of the Peking Opera at the expense of the others.

Though Chou was by far the most famous actor of Peking Opera in Shanghai, there were other good exponents of the style in the city. After Chou, the finest was Chang Ying-chieh, known on the stage as Kai Chiao-t'ien, the youngest in a family of five boys from Kaoyang, in Hopeh province. Three of the brothers became actors.[10] The fourth eldest, Ying-chün, was a *wu-sheng* and taught Kai the arts of this type of actor. It is said, however, that Ying-chün was jealous of his abler younger brother and tried to dissuade him from a career on the stage by disparaging his work. Kai, on the other hand, seems to have been blessed with a kindly disposition. After he had achieved success he became very popular with his fellow actors, who admired him for his filial piety and for the respect which he showed towards his elder brother.

In his professional life, Kai was a man of great determination. One incident, which occurred when he was forty-seven, shows this very clearly. During an acrobatic display he slipped and broke his leg. The doctor who treated him set the bone wrongly, and it seemed that Kai would have to give up his stage career, since physical fitness is absolutely essential for a *wu-sheng*. Kai, however, deliberately broke his leg again and told the doctor to reset the bone, which the doctor did, correctly this time. Kai's action was no doubt somewhat risky, but it succeeded. After a lengthy convalescence he re-appeared on the stage, and his performances were as fine as ever.

The significance of the episode lies in the source of Kai's fame as an actor. He was not a particularly good singer, and the style of his dialogue passages was no more than adequate. It was for his spectacular acrobatic skill that he was most admired. He thrilled his audiences with the perilous complexity and speed of his gymnastics and consequently chose roles in which he could exploit this talent to the full. He was best known as Wu Sung, one of the heroes of the classical novel *The Water Margin*.

Men such as Chou Hsin-fang and Kai Chiao-t'ien ensured the continuing popularity of the Peking Opera in Shanghai. No actor of the popular regional dramas approached them in fame.

THE SHAO-CHÜ

There is only one other branch of Shanghai's traditional theatre that I need mention, and this never achieved anything like the success of the Peking Opera or Shaohing Opera: namely, the *Shao-chü*, which, like the *Yüeh-chü*, originated in Shaohing.

The *Shao-chü* is based on Clapper Opera (whose derivative in Shaohing is called *luan-t'an*) and the music of the *Yiyang ch'iang*, to which I referred in the Introduction.

For centuries both Clapper Opera and *Yiyang ch'iang* had spread widely, becoming very popular in the provinces of the lower Yangtze, especially Kiangsi, Anhwei and Chekiang. Shaohing was an important commercial centre visited by traders from many places. It is therefore not surprising that it should have absorbed a variety of theatrical forms, since wandering companies made ample use of trade routes. In the *luan-t'an* the accompanying instruments include the fiddles (the *pan-hu* and *erh-hu*) and sometimes the flute (*ti-tzu*), as well as gongs and drums. The *Yiyang ch'iang* uses mainly percussion, large and small drums (*ta-ku, hsiao-ku*), gongs, cymbals and clappers (*pan*), and occasionally the double-reeded *so-na*. In both varieties the categorization of actors follows the norm of the Chinese drama: *sheng, tan, ching,* and so on.

Social and religious occasions reinforced the *Shao-chü* once it had emerged from a fusion of the *luan-t'an* and the *Yiyang ch'iang*. We also find Taoist priests making a contribution; some of them 'formed companies of Taoist priests performing the *luan-t'an* of Shaohing as a side-business, while some, although they did not organize troupes, sat and sang *luan-t'an* as a side-business'.[11]

Like the Peking Opera and some other theatrical forms, the *Shao-chü* included both military drama, in which acrobatics were important, and plays based on non-military themes, such as love stories. Until the late years of the Ch'ing period, separate companies performed each kind of drama, but in the first decade of the present century the diminishing supply of actors, and deteriorating economic and political conditions, led to a decline in the *Shao-chü*, especially in the military troupes. Actors specializing in one or other of the two types of drama were therefore forced to merge their groups.

It was at this time that a number of *Shao-chü* actors decided to try their luck in Shanghai. There were many natives of Shaohing in the great port, and since these were strongly concentrated in one area of the city, the players established themselves in a playhouse in that area. They were fairly successful at first, but then luck turned against them. Their theatre was destroyed, one of the best of their number died and another returned to Shaohing. Even though a new theatre was found, their patrons now tended to desert them in favour of the Peking Opera.

In 1923 a second wave of *Shao-chü* performers entered Shanghai. The best known of them was the *lao-sheng* Liang Yu-nung, who remained in the city until his death in 1935. He performed with considerable success in a number of Shanghai's theatres, including the famous amusement centre, The Great World. (Once considered a vulgar place, and notorious as the haunt of prostitutes, this has since been made respectable. It still provides a wide range of regional drama.) One contemporary scholar has described Liang Yu-nung as 'the T'an Hsin-p'ei of *Shao-chü*',[12] but this seems to me a false comparison. T'an developed the Peking Opera greatly, and after his death other actors continued his work. Liang Yu-nung, on the other hand, was not noted for the originality of his art; some people complained that he acted only old pieces, and at his death he left no successors. The *Shao-chü* lost its following, and the outbreak of war in 1937 saw its eclipse not only in Shanghai but elsewhere. A slight and unconvincing recovery took place after 1945, but this did not last long and by 1949 the *Shao-chü* was everywhere virtually extinct.

THE SPOKEN PLAY

The traditional forms of regional drama, of which the *Shao-chü* is a good example, represented in many minds a relic of the past. They stirred up relatively little enthusiasm among those sections of the population which, from about 1860, became interested in reforming Chinese society and in bringing the country up to date to meet the exigencies of the contemporary world. Such people found a far greater appeal in the spoken play (*hua-chü*), which in due course became an important force in the theatrical circles of twentieth-century Shanghai. Since that city has been the principal centre of the Chinese spoken play during most phases of its development, it is appropriate to discuss it at length here.

Apart from a few traditional pieces consisting entirely of stylized dialogue, the spoken play did not appear in China as an indigenous dramatic form until the late nineteenth century. At that time many Christian missionaries ran schools, and encouraged their pupils to produce plays to mark festivals such as Christmas. The response was good, but the scope of the performances remained very limited indeed and the standards were low. Although the idea of producing spoken plays was taken up in other sectors of society, it was not until 1907 that a real attempt was made to stage them on a larger scale. In that year a group of Overseas Chinese in Tokyo founded the Spring Willow Society (Ch'un-liu she). This group derived its main inspiration from the modern theatre of the West and performed some pieces based on the European literatures, the most notable one being *The Black Slave's Cry to Heaven* (*Hei-nu yü-t'ien lu*), which was dramatized from a translation of *Uncle Tom's Cabin*. Very soon the initiative in Tokyo was followed in China itself. Ou-yang Yü-ch'ien, a dramatist and actor of considerable importance and a member of the Spring Willow Society, sums up the origins of the spoken play in China as follows: 'Before 1907 this form of play did not exist, or [at least] only in a few informal amateur performances given at schools or private meetings. In 1907 Wang Chung-sheng organized in Shanghai the Spring (Ch'un-yang) Society which mounted *The Black Slave's Cry to Heaven*. This was the first time that a spoken play was acted which had been divided properly into acts, that scenery was used or that a full-scale performance was given in a theatre. Although the venture was not entirely successful and there were still many shortcomings, this performance must rank as the prologue in the Chinese *hua-chü*.'[13]

The new plays were known as *wen-ming hsi* (civilization dramas). Most were progressive in content, and in this respect contributed to some extent to the Revolution of 1911. Other societies followed the Spring Society, one of the most famous being the Enlightenment Society (K'ai-ming she), founded in May 1912. After 1911 spoken plays were often used as a propaganda weapon against Yüan Shih-k'ai, and were at first well received by audiences; but by 1916 a lack of leadership, the defection of many of the best actors to the new film industry and the growing commercialism in the running of the theatres had led, in Shanghai and other big cities, to a decline in public interest.

The New Culture and May Fourth movements did much to revive the spoken play. The stress on amateur theatricals, to which I referred in Chapter Three, was felt in Shanghai as well as in Peking. Certain dramatists, in particular T'ien Han (b. 1898), strove to revive enthusiasm for the spoken play in the south. T'ien, who ranks among twentieth-century China's most distinguished playwrights, also founded a periodical, a film society and an academy, none of which lasted long, and, in 1928, the South China Society (Nan-kuo she). A number of distinguished men of the theatre, including Ou-yang Yü-ch'ien and Chou Hsin-fang, took part in its activities. The society performed in Shanghai several of T'ien's own spoken plays, and also others translated from European languages or from Japanese. Early in 1929 they toured several other cities, including Soochow, Hangchow, Canton and Nanking. Conditions were not always easy. One of the leading actresses of the group, T'ang Shu-ming, makes these comments: 'We arrived in Nanking on a windy, snowy day and there stayed in an empty room in the People's Education Office. We had no beds and so slept on the floor and looked for a lot of straw to put on the ground. We did not have enough blankets – one for two or three people – so everyone huddled together to get over the severe cold. There was a charcoal fire brazier in our makeup room; our hands were cold, so we stood around it rubbing each other's hands.'[14]

In 1930 the South China Society was suspended by the government because of alleged subversive activities. There were many other similar groups at the time, such as the Shanghai Society of Arts and Drama (I-shu chü-she), led by Cheng Po-ch'i and Hsia Yen, which was extremely left-wing in its programme and sympathies. This did not endear it to the Nationalists, who quickly suppressed it. Cheng himself says that 'in the depth of the night of 29 April 1930, not long after our second public performance, the false [that is, Kuomintang] Public Security Bureau sent some hundred armed detectives to surround our premises. . . . Five of our members were arrested.'[15] Cheng adds that others later shared this fate, some being imprisoned and a few even killed.

This was a period of great literary activity in revolutionary circles, not merely in the field of the spoken play but in other forms as well. It was also a time of particularly savage repression by the Kuomintang, which had broken the united front with the Communists in 1927 and was trying to unite the country effectively under Chiang Kai-shek. The experience of the Society of Arts and Drama was in fact a microcosm of what was happening throughout Chinese society as a whole.

There were many societies devoted to the spoken play in the lower Yangtze region during the 1930s. Nearly all the plays of China's major dramatists were presented in Shanghai, and most of these received their first performances there. By far the most successful of these playwrights was Ts'ao Yü (b. 1910), the popularity of whose works in Shanghai led to the founding of several companies which acted spoken plays. Among his best known plays is *Thunderstorm* (*Lei-yü*), written in 1933. It is a tragedy concerning the hypocrisy of the rich and the evils of the old family system.[16] Ts'ao Yü was influenced by Western dramatists, including Ibsen, Chekhov and O'Neill, and used the theatre as a means of discussing social problems. I mention Ts'ao Yü because his attitude to the drama was typical of his time and because he contributed more towards winning popular appeal for the spoken play than did any of his contemporaries. His plays are still popular with amateur drama groups in Hong Kong. It is not, however, my intention to examine the literary careers of the playwrights of the 1930s, a subject which belongs more to the history of China's literature than to that of its theatre.

Though the Sino-Japanese war killed many of the traditional forms of regional theatre, the spoken play showed no signs of succumbing to this catastrophe. On the contrary, dramatic troupes devoted to this form became more active than ever and even toured the rural regions. As in virtually all countries occupied by the enemy during wartime, many of their productions might well be considered propaganda, although the escapist instinct inevitable in these circumstances is given expression in some pieces. Whatever its character, the entertainment which the plays provided was certainly welcomed and enjoyed by the people, and constituted a significant morale booster.

The way in which the spoken play was used during the war highlights one of its most important features: the flexibility of its themes. These were of all kinds: historical, social, political or mythological. There was, however, a strong tendency for the authors of spoken plays to draw their material from the major trends and events of the time. During the twentieth century China has undergone a series of upheavals and revolutions, each of which has affected the spoken play deeply and been in turn influenced by it. The Revolution of 1911, the May Fourth Movement, Chiang Kai-shek's Northern March of 1926–28, and the war against Japan are the main examples from the pre-Communist period.

One of the reasons for the intimate connection of the spoken play with politics and social issues may well be that this modern form of Chinese drama has always been dominated by intellectuals. During most phases of its development the spoken play has found its greatest appeal in the universities and among young students, from whose ranks many of its actors emerged. These factors have made it an almost exclusively urban phenomenon. Only during the war did it attain anything like a mass following or percolate into the countryside.

The progress of China's modern spoken drama has depended, even more than that of the traditional theatre, on the calibre of the men who have led the societies devoted to promoting it. This is normally so of arts which are foreign importations and initially fit none too comfortably into the culture onto which they are grafted. It was fortunate that the Chinese spoken play was fostered by such talented men as Wang Chung-sheng, T'ien Han and Ou-yang Yü-ch'ien. But any group which they founded invariably lost its impetus once they withdrew their leadership.

SHANGHAI ACTORS IN THE REVOLUTION OF 1911

The contribution of Chinese theatrical circles to the political history of the twentieth century has extended beyond their role as moulders of public opinion, and some stage artists have even participated, both politically and militarily, in revolutionary movements. Possibly the most prominent of them were the three Shanghai actors P'an Yüeh-ch'iao and the Hsia brothers, Yüeh-shan and Yüeh-jun, all of whom took part in the fighting which led to the overthrow of the Manchus. They arrived in Shanghai towards the end of the nineteenth century and were active in the reform of the Peking Opera. They tried to free the traditional drama from some of its old-style conventions. For example, the Hsia brothers managed a modern theatre on the Western model which had a circular instead of square stage and were the first to use a revolving stage and scenery for performances of the Shanghai classical drama. They also reduced the proportion of sung sections and expanded that of dialogue. Above all, the three actors collaborated to treat social themes, such as the harm caused by smoking opium, in the traditional dramas which they performed.

P'an Yüeh-ch'iao came originally from Yangchow. After the death of his father, who was a carpenter, he moved with his brothers to Tientsin, where he took up acting as a *lao-sheng*, at first learning Clapper music and later transferring his attention to Peking Opera. After moving to Shanghai, he acted in the T'ien-hsien teahouse theatre until its destruction by fire, after which he moved to a newly built theatre of the modern Western type.

The Hsia brothers differed from P'an in that they came from an acting family. Their father was a *wu-sheng*; from their earliest youth in Anhwei they moved in acting circles, and Hsia Yüeh-jun married the daughter of T'an Hsin-p'ei. Even before they moved to Shanghai the Hsia brothers showed a rebellious spirit. In their youth they performed for Tuan-fang (see page 42), whose retainers treated them with the contempt that actors could normally expect from such people at the time. Yüeh-jun started to complain vociferously about this, at which Tuan-fang's son gave the young actor a savage beating. The Hsia brothers were not prepared to take this insult and raised a great protest about it, with the result that Tuan-fang reprimanded his son severely. According to one contemporary writer, whose pen-name was K'an-wai jen (which means 'somebody outside the threshold') 'the courage of the oppressed in being bitter and daring against authority coloured their lives from then on' as a result of this incident.[17]

In Shanghai, the two brothers continued their interest not only in the theatre but also in politics and social work. For example, P'an Yüeh-ch'iao's experience showed the great danger of fire to the theatres of Shanghai. The Hsias duly took effective action to combat this by founding a fire brigade; but they increased their standing among the local people by placing the brigade at the service not only of the theatre managers but of everybody who might need it.

All these three men worked earnestly for the overthrow of the Ch'ing government and were delighted at the outbreak of the Revolution in Wuchang on 10 October 1911. Not long after this event most provinces declared their independence of the government. By the beginning of November only a few provinces remained loyal, but these included some of those along the lower Yangtze, and Shanghai was still in imperial hands. Ch'en Ch'i-mei, one of Sun Yat-sen's chief supporters, who was later to refuse a cabinet post under Yüan Shih-k'ai, organized the Revolution in Shanghai. He decided that the capture of the Kiangnan Arsenal, founded in 1865, was essential to his strategy, and he made his plans accordingly. Volunteers came forward from many walks of life, including the acting profession, and P'an Yüeh-ch'iao rallied many of his colleagues to join Ch'en in the attack on the all-important arsenal. On 3 November Ch'en Ch'i-mei, having tried without success to win over the guards, made an onslaught with two hundred followers. Though he was quickly taken prisoner, revolutionary strength was by no means exhausted. Mei Lan-fang continues the story: 'The Hsia brothers thought of attacking [the arsenal] with fire. They immediately sent their cousin . . . to buy two tins of kerosene, which Hsia Yüeh-jun himself then began pouring on a pile of shavings. In an instant a fire was blazing fiercely. To stop it from spreading [too far], they also got together some fire-fighters to extinguish it at the appropriate time. The volunteer corps saw the flames, and on all sides started shouting so loudly that their sounds shook heaven and earth.'[18] The fire and noise caused confusion among the arsenal's defenders. A volunteer soldier took advantage of this state of affairs to enter through a small opening in the walls and unlock the gates from the inside. The revolutionary force swept in, the arsenal fell, and soon afterwards Shanghai was under the banner of Sun Yat-sen's followers.

Within a very short time Soochow had declared allegiance to the Republic, and the combined forces of several cities of the lower Yangtze then advanced on Nanking. For his help in taking Shanghai, P'an Yüeh-ch'iao was given the rank of major-general and went to fight for the capture of Nanking, which surrendered on 12 December. The whole Yangtze valley was now in the hands of the revolutionaries.

P'an was later promoted by Ch'en Ch'i-mei and placed in charge of a research unit of the Shanghai army.

The actors of Shanghai seem to have been much more active in the Revolution of 1911, and to have taken a greater interest in the political trends of the period, than their colleagues in Peking. This is not surprising. Shanghai was more productive of new and unconventional ideas than Peking. It was a modern city, a great port and the most important economic centre in the country. In view of its larger foreign population and closer contacts with other countries, Shanghai might be expected to have a cultural life more influenced by the West and less tied to the past than almost any other city in China. Tradition certainly flourished there, but not to an overpowering extent, and it was inevitable that this situation should be reflected in the texture of Shanghai's theatrical life.

8 The South-eastern Provinces: Fukien and Kwangtung*

The provinces of Fukien and Kwangtung lie on the south-eastern coast of China. They were the first regions in China to be subjected to Western influence through the Portuguese maritime explorers, and the first provinces to trade with the major European nations. In fact, for over a century before its defeat in the Opium War forced China to open up several coastal cities, Canton, the capital of Kwangtung, was the only port through which the Ch'ing government allowed Europeans to trade with China. During the Ch'ing period, the two south-eastern provinces were also vitally important links with the outside world on account of their voluminous trade with South-east Asia. Many vessels plied every year between the ports of virtually all the countries of South-east Asia and Amoy or Canton. It was largely because of their prominence in overseas trade that the people of Fukien and Kwangtung acquired the reputation of being the most commercially minded in China.

Substantial emigration took place concurrently with this extensive trade; indeed, far more Chinese emigrated to South-east Asia and elsewhere from Fukien and Kwangtung than from any other provinces. This is of great relevance to the theatre, because these immigrants into South-east Asia aroused a demand for the regional styles of Fukien and Kwangtung. As a result, actors from the south-eastern coastal areas have been more prone to travel in South-east Asia and elsewhere than actors from other parts of China. Even to this day the theatrical traditions of Fukien and Kwangtung remain strong in many parts of South-east Asia.

The distance of the south-eastern provinces from Peking was also

* See Ills. 27–28, p. 140.

significant. Few provinces were less influenced by the Manchus than Kwangtung, and hostility to them was stronger there than in most other areas. The province saw an unusually large number of revolts against the central government. It spawned the Taiping 'Heavenly King', Hung Hsiu-ch'üan, and we shall see later in this chapter that the actors of the region played a part in the revolution which he led. Perhaps more important, Kwangtung was the home province of Sun Yat-sen, and Canton was the seat of the government of which he was the head from 1923 to 1925. Its distance from Peking and its proximity to the British colony of Hong Kong furnish two other reasons why Kwangtung played a vital role in the growth of modern Chinese nationalism.

At the same time, the south-east is important for the culture which it has inherited, especially its theatrical traditions. One of the oldest forms of Chinese regional drama for which records survive is the Southern Drama (*nan-hsi*) of the Sung period (960–1279), which I have discussed in the Introduction. Its place of origin was Wenchow in southern Chekiang, which is adjacent to Fukien, to the north-east, and in due course it spread to many parts of the empire. Though the Southern Drama had died out completely as an independent form by the late years of the Ming dynasty, many of its stage conventions were absorbed into virtually all types of later Chinese drama, and even today traces of its music can be heard in the local drama of southern Fukien. In two regions of this province, Chuanchow and Amoy, the influence of the Southern Drama is particularly evident, owing to its survival in the form of regional drama known as *Li-yüan hsi* (the Pear Garden Theatre).

FUKIEN

The name of the style of Fukienese drama known as the Pear Garden Theatre led its actors to assume that it was derived from the famous Pear Garden acting school of the Emperor Ming-huang (712–56). A legend arose that the Pear Garden Theatre was the creation of a certain Fukienese youth of the eighth century. According to the tradition, 'the boy was very intelligent from his earliest years and, although unable to speak, could play any wind or stringed instrument. Once he was sinking a well in a village and dug up some ancient musical scores which nobody [else] could understand. However, *he* could play according to the scores and his ability was noised far and wide.'[1] Ming-huang heard about him and summoned him to court, where he played in the imperial presence a special jade flute which nobody else had been able to play, and was granted the title of graduate of the highest official examinations (*chin-shih*).

There is no evidence in primary sources for this story, and the earliest known written drama of the Pear Garden Theatre dates from the sixteenth century. Yet even this later date indicates that the Pear Garden Theatre is much older than most other surviving regional forms, and many of its tunes are older still. For apart from remnants of the Southern Drama mentioned above, we find in this Fukienese theatre some melodies derived from the ancient puppet theatre of the area. Also, many folk songs have found their way into the Pear Garden Theatre, and some of these may well date from the eleventh or twelfth century.

The instruments which nowadays accompany this ancient music belong largely to the wind category, and the Chinese end-blown and transverse flutes (*hsiao* and *ti-tzu*) often predominate. Stringed instruments, such as the plucked lute (*p'i-p'a*) are also used. The percussion has a characteristic high-pitched flavour and is rarely obtrusive. This is in sharp contrast to the music of many forms of Chinese regional theatre and makes the Pear Garden Theatre among the gentlest musically of all. The structure of the orchestra, the beautiful voices of Fukienese singers and the quality of the melodies lend a rare poignancy to the dramas, and, to me at least, the music of the Pear Garden Theatre is among the most delightful and most moving to be heard in China.

The Pear Garden Theatre has been remarkably little influenced by such major forms as the Peking Opera. In the style of acting, it owes a great deal to the ancient puppet shows and to regional dances. The stage movements of the actors, and the stylized motions of the waist, shoulders and hands, have a strong local character. There are also local characteristics in the costumes and make-up, though in these respects the similarities with other types of Chinese theatre far outweigh the differences. The categories of actors (*sheng, tan, ch'ou*, and so on) are also much the same as in the theatres of other regions. This was already the case in the sixteenth century and can be confirmed from the text of the drama, mentioned above, which survives from that time.

The piece in question is called the *Li-ching chi* (*The Record of the Lichee and the Mirror*) and, since it is far the most famous example of the Pear Garden Theatre, it deserves some attention here. The story of the modern version, which is called *Ch'en San and Wu-niang*,[2] may be summarized as follows. The young scholar Ch'en San sees the rich young girl Huang Wu-niang during a festival in Swatow and falls in love with her. Not long afterwards he happens to pass beneath her window and she throws him a lichee as a sign of love. Ch'en San takes a job as a mirror-cleaner in order to gain entry into the Huang mansion and then deliberately breaks a precious mirror, with the object of offering to make good the damage by becoming a family slave. His plan succeeds and he is given employment in the house. After a long delay he brings himself to declare his love for Wu-niang, whose parents have unfortunately promised her in marriage to a wealthy local man. The two lovers therefore elope to Fukien province. This drama takes place entirely in the border areas of Kwangtung and Fukien and is filled with references to local customs. It is not surprising that a charming love story such as this should have become so popular in the region. It has been adapted to other styles of drama in the south-eastern provinces but has never been popular in the north.

The *Li-ching chi* is remarkable in that it is one of the very few texts of the Chinese regional drama to have survived from as early as the sixteenth century. Later editions of this piece date from the early and late Ch'ing periods. Apart from this one drama, very little is known about the history of the Pear Garden Theatre. For a long period it appears to have been performed mainly by the troupes of the landed gentry and not to have percolated deeply to the peasant masses until the nineteenth century. It had spread to Foochow and other cities of Fukien by 1900, but, even for the Republican period, interesting and reliable written material about it is very scanty indeed.

Another type of regional theatre popular in Foochow is the *Min-chü*, or Fukienese drama. This is in many respects more typical of the Chinese theatre in general than the Pear Garden Theatre. Its stage movements are closer to those of the Peking Opera, its tunes more influenced by the music of other regions, and its history is somewhat shorter and less isolated from the broad sweep of the Chinese theatre. Its orchestra includes several types of *hu-ch'in*, the *yüeh-ch'in*, the *ti-tzu* and the *so-na* (with the *erh-hu* and *ti-tzu* dominating most often), as well as various percussion instruments.

There are three main sources of the music, acting techniques, plots and texts of the *Min-chü*. The first is the rural drama of central Fukien. The tunes sung at puppet shows or by story-tellers were developed to form a kind of drama performed during festivals in honour of the gods. As in other regions, folk-songs formed the basis of the music, but they were less local in colour than those of the Pear Garden Theatre and, according to the contemporary scholar Chou I-pai, some bore the same names as melodies heard in the *T'an-huang* of Kiangsu and Chekiang or sung by story-tellers in eighteenth-century Yang-chow.[3] Following the pattern of folk theatre everywhere in China, there was a strong tendency for this rural drama to spread also to the cities, where some of the companies settled permanently.

The second source was the type of drama performed before the gentry by the privately run companies of Foochow and the surround-ing areas. This was known as *Ju-lin pan* ('Confucian writings com-panies'). There is a tradition that a high-ranking official of the late Ming period, Ts'ao Hsüeh-ch'üan, was one of the chief early pro-moters of the *Ju-lin pan*. Ts'ao established his own villa, where he relaxed and enjoyed the drama, but after the Manchus conquered China he committed suicide and his garden fell into disrepair. During the second half of the nineteenth century the villa was restored, and a certain P'u Chih-shan organized a company to perform and revitalize the *Ju-lin pan* in a temple beside the old garden.

The *Ju-lin pan* differed from the privately performed drama of most regions of China in that it was based on the *Yiyang ch'iang* music, which was normally considered vulgar. As in other regions, the Foo-chow *Yiyang ch'iang* was originally accompanied only by percussion and a chorus. Later, some wind instruments and the *hu-ch'in* were added for variety.

When the *Ju-lin pan* was at its height, some local people invited a few troupes from Anhwei, and these became the third source of the *Min-chü* art. The officials of Foochow would also engage fine actors from Peking or Shanghai to act with the Anhwei companies and might sometimes allow the common people to enjoy their performances. However, owing to dialect difficulties, the Anhwei companies were not particularly successful in Foochow and they declined sharply after the Manchu dynasty fell. By 1916 all had disbanded, and their best actors joined the folk troupes.

Over the next few years these companies absorbed the *Ju-lin pan* as well. With the amalgamation of the three distinct sources into one whole we may say that the *Min-chü* had come into being. At the same time, public theatres were built in Foochow, so that large numbers of people of all classes could gather together in one building to watch the drama. Training-schools, including one for girls, were also opened.

1 A performance of a drama during the Yüan period (1280–1368). The five men in the foreground are the actors. Behind them are the musicians. The bearded musician on the left is playing a drum; behind him, to his left, a musician is playing a *ti-tzu*; the second musician from the right is playing a clapper. Behind the stage there is a curtain. From a wall-painting in a temple in Shansi province, 1324.

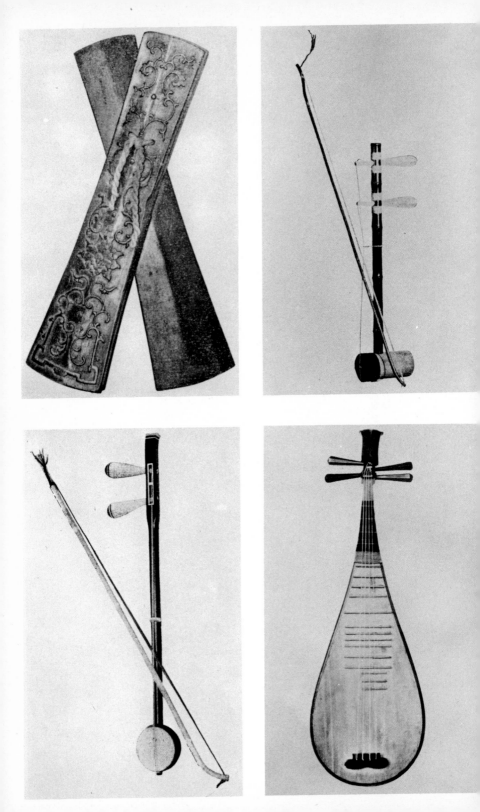

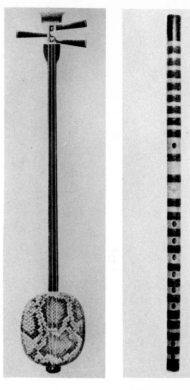

CHINESE MUSICAL INSTRUMENTS

2 The *pan* (clapper) consists of three pieces of wood, two of them fastened together (patterned surface visible), the other behind.

3 The *hu-ch'in*, the most important of the bowed stringed instruments.

4 The *pan-hu*, one of the *hu-ch'in* group of bowed stringed instruments.

5 The *p'i-p'a*, the most important of the plucked stringed instruments.

6, 7 The *yüeh-ch'in* and the *san-hsien*: after the *p'i-p'a*, the two principal plucked stringed instruments.

8 The *ti-tzu*, or transverse flute. The mouth-hole is about one-third of the distance from the base of the instrument as shown.

9 Three *so-na* of different compasses. The *so-na* is a double-reeded wind instrument similar to the Western oboe.

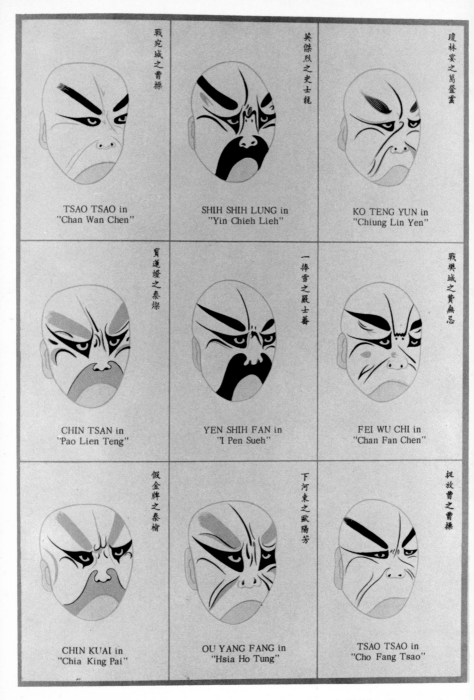

戰宛城之曹操	英傑烈之史士龍	瓊林宴之蔦登雲
TSAO TSAO in "Chan Wan Chen"	SHIH SHIH LUNG in "Yin Chieh Lieh"	KO TENG YUN in "Chiung Lin Yen"
賀蓮燈之泰燦	一捧雪之厰士蕃	戰樊城之費無忌
CHIN TSAN in "Pao Lien Teng"	YEN SHIH FAN in "I Pen Sueh"	FEI WU CHI in "Chan Fan Chen"
假金牌之泰檜	下河東之歐陽芳	捉放曹之曹操
CHIN KUAI in "Chia King Pai"	OU YANG FANG in "Hsia Ho Tung"	TSAO TSAO in "Cho Fang Tsao"

10 Examples of make-up worn by *ching* characters in Peking Opera and other forms of the *P'i-huang* system.

五花洞之吳大炮

WU TA PAO in
"Wu Hua Tung"

失印救火之金祥瑞

KING HSIANG SUE in
"Shih Yin Chiu Huo"

戲迷傳之伍六伴

WU LU LU in
"Hsi Mi Chuan"

大回朝之費仲

FEI CHUNG in
"Ta Hui Tsao"

小上坟之劉祿敬

LIU LU CHIN in
"Hsiao Shang Fen"

武松殺嫂之武大魂

WU TA HUN in
"Wu Sung Sha Shao"

黃金台之侯樂

HO LUAN in
"Huang King Tai"

刺湯之湯勤

TANG CHIN in
"Tzu Tang"

烏龍院之之張文遠

CHANG WEN YUAN in
"Wu Lung Yuan"

11 Examples of make-up worn by *ch'ou* characters in Peking Opera and
other forms of the *P'i-huang* system.

12 Mei Lan-fang, the greatest Chinese actor of modern times, as Tu Li-niang in a version of *Huan-hun chi* (*The Return of the Soul*), the masterpiece of T'ang Hsien-tsu (1550–1617).

13 Ch'eng Yen-ch'iu, a contemporary of Mei Lan-fang. Especially renowned as an actor of tragic parts, Ch'eng toured widely in Western Europe and the Soviet Union, as well as in China and Japan.

14 Ch'eng Yen-ch'iu with (right) Yü Chen-fei in a performance in 1931 of *Ch'un-kuei meng* (*Dream in the Ladies' Chamber*), arranged by Ch'eng. The plot of the drama concerns the dreams of a newly-wed bride (acted by Ch'eng), who has just learned that her husband (acted by Yü) has been killed in battle.

15 A representation of a seventeenth-century stage in Peking, probably in the grounds of a private mansion. The audience would have watched the performances from the courtyard or the halls, separate from the stage itself. Stages such as this still exist in the Summer Palace, Peking, and elsewhere, but are no longer used.

16 Theatrical performance given at a private house in Peking during the nineteenth century. The actors perform on a raised platform in the courtyard, while the members of the audience drink tea and smoke.

17 A temporary stage in front of a temple during the Ming period (1368–1644). Etching by Josephine Huang Hung, 1966.

18 A performance of *Ch'ien-chin chi* (*The Story of the Thousand Pieces of Gold*), by Shen Ts'ai, given on a traditional temple stage.

19 A late nineteenth-century teahouse-theatre. The audience watch the performance from tables, at which they sit, drink tea, and converse.

20 A theatrical performance in a private mansion. The actors perform on a carpet, and the musicians can be seen in the foreground. An illustration to a seventeenth-century edition of the anonymous novel *Chin P'ing Mei*, written during the Ming period.

21 A performance of a drama at a banquet during the Ming period. The actors perform on a rug between the two main rows of guests, and the musicians can be seen in the foreground. An illustration to the edition (first half of the seventeenth century) by Yang Ting-chien of the novel *Shui-hu chuan* (*The Water Margin*), by Lo Kuan-chung.

137

22 A scene from the Shaohing opera, *Liang Shan-po and Chu Ying-t'ai*, showing the two lovers and (on the right) their two servants.

23 Chou Hsin-fang, the most important actor of the Southern School of Peking Opera.

24 Ts'ao Yü, the leading author of spoken plays in China from the 1930s.

25 Chou Hsin-fang and (left) Liu Pin-k'un as the aged parents in *Ch'ing-feng t'ing* (*The Ch'ing-feng Pavilion*). The plot concerns the punishment of an unfilial adopted son, who is killed by thunder after the suicide of his parents. Ink sketch by Ch'eng Shih-fa, 1961.

26 The opening scene from one of Ts'ao Yü's best known plays, *Lei-yü* (*Thunderstorm*, 1933).

27 A scene from the Kwangtung opera *Sou-shu yüan* (*The Runaway Maid*), acted by the Cantonese Opera Company of Kwangtung in a revised version prepared by them. The plot concerns the love of a slave girl, Green Lotus (far right), and a young scholar, Chang I-min (second from right), who hides her after she has fled from the house of her master, a general.

28 Hung-hsien-nü (K'uang Chien-lien), wife of the actor Ma Shih-tseng and the most famous artist in Kwangtung Opera since 1949.

29 Chang Te-ch'eng, a leading actor of the Szechwanese Opera, as Kuan Yü in *Tan-tao hui* (literally, *The Meeting of the Single Knife*; sometimes translated as *Lord Kuan goes to the Feast*). The drama is based on the classical novel *San-kuo yen-i* (*The Romance of the Three Kingdoms*), by Lo Kuan-chung, Mao Tsung-kang and others, and the drama *Kuan ta-wang tan-tao hui* (*Lord Kuan goes to the Feast*), by Kuan Han-ch'ing (*c.* 1245–*c.* 1322), generally regarded as China's greatest playwright.

30 A scene from the Szechwanese opera *K'ung-ch'eng chi* (*The Ruse of the Empty City*), based on *San-kuo yen-i* (*Romance of the Three Kingdoms*). Chu-ko Liang, who has occupied West City with his forces, has opened the city gates and is sitting at the top of the walls with his *ch'in* (a musical instrument). He then deceives Ssu-ma I (left), who is about to attack, into thinking that his forces will themselves be attacked if he enters the city. Ssu-ma I accordingly withdraws, allowing Chu-ko Liang time in which to bring up reinforcements. Ink drawing.

31 A performance by amateur actors of a classical play, given in a street in Huang-kou, Northern Anhwei province, in *c.* 1962.

32, 33, 34 Three scenes from the 1970 version of *Hung-teng chi* (*The Story of the Red Lantern*)

Li Yü-ho (centre) refuses to yield to torture and adopts a heroic pose before the Japanese general (far right).

After Li T'ieh-mei is released by the Japanese she takes the code to the Chinese guerrillas in the mountains. The Japanese pursue her but are defeated by the guerrillas. The guerrilla with the sword (top) is adopting a strongly classical stance as he attacks his Japanese opponent.

35 A scene from *Tu-chüan shan* (*Azalea Mountain*). T'ien Ta-chiang (right, foreground), one of the partisans, has just been fatally shot by one of the civil guards. K'o Hsiang, the heroine of the drama, is standing behind T'ien Ta-chiang and two other partisans. The flowers in the foreground are azaleas.

During the 1920s, there were more than thirty *Min-chü* troupes based in Foochow. Since the city did not always need so many, some of them frequently travelled to other parts of Fukien, and even to Amoy or other places in the south. Initially, none of Foochow's troupes included both men and women. A few were entirely female, the great majority exclusively male. It was only in the late 1920s and the 1930s that mixed companies developed.

Like most other forms of traditional Chinese theatre, the *Min-chü* was badly affected by the war, and post-war recovery was only partial. A great many of the actors produced by the training-schools had apparently fallen by the wayside, and by 1949 only six companies were still performing. All these companies were large, however, and the Fukienese theatre was far from defunct.

The *Min-chü* was not the only drama in the south-eastern region to develop from the *Yiyang ch'iang*. Another was the *Ch'ao-chü* (Swatow Opera), which has been popular in northern Kwangtung since the sixteenth century. In some ways the Swatow Opera forms a link between the theatres of the two provinces under discussion in this chapter. Though its home is Kwangtung, its music has more similarities with the drama of Fukien than with most other theatrical styles in Kwangtung. Certainly it has very little in common with the most important kind of theatre in Kwangtung, the Kwangtung Opera, about which a considerable amount of information is available and which I shall now consider in detail.

THE KWANGTUNG OPERA

The drama best loved by the people of Kwangtung and Canton is called *Yüeh-chü*,[4] or Kwangtung Opera. Despite the region's relative isolation from the capital during the Ch'ing dynasty, this type of local theatre has much in common with the Peking Opera, especially its domination by the two tunes *Erh-huang* and *Hsi-p'i*. On the other hand, its orchestral accompaniment is more varied, and wind instruments such as the *so-na* and end-blown flute are more often used. In addition, there is a certain mellifluousness in the texture of the actors' voices in sung passages which can be very affecting. It is a pity that low standards of performance in Hong Kong, and the failure on the part of foreigners to attune their ear to the music, have combined to give the Kwangtung Opera a poor reputation outside China.

The companies of the Kwangtung Opera regard as the founder of

145

their style of drama an eighteenth-century actor from Hupeh called Chang Wu. There is a tradition, whose foundation in fact there seems no reason to doubt, that Chang performed for a while in Peking in the 1720s or 1730s, but was then exiled from the capital because the Ch'ing government considered his acting subversive. He travelled to Kwangtung and settled in Foshan, a city near Canton. By that time Foshan was already the very important commercial centre which it was to remain for some time; during the nineteenth century an Englishman was to describe it as 'the Birmingham of China'.[5] In Foshan, Chang Wu adopted a number of pupils and established a theatrical company which became popular among the local people. He also founded a guild-hall for actors, known as the Ch'iung-hua, which lasted until the Taiping rebellion. Yang Mou-chien, writing in 1842, tells us a few interesting details about this institution:

> The Ch'iung-hua guild-hall of Foshan near Canton is where actors honour their gods. One finds much incense and paper money there. Every year at the time of the sacrifices, the members of each troupe collectively choose one *sheng* player [as their leader]. He must be a life-long actor who has never been a servant or menial. [His duty is] to take the image of the god out of its niche and put it into a coloured pavilion. For the past few decades the only man to hold the image of the god has been the military *hsiao-sheng* A-hua, and up till now there has been no change in this. A-hua's voice, appearance and acting ability are really magnificent and he would earn an annual salary of more than 1,000 taels.[6]

This was a fairly large sum for an actor to earn, and A-hua seems to have been regarded as a worthy successor to Chang Wu.

During the late eighteenth century and the nineteenth, the companies centred on Chang's guild-hall became influenced by the influx of theatrical groups from other provinces. In particular, many actors came from Anhwei, where *Erh-huang* and *Hsi-p'i* were already very popular, and it was because of this that the Kwangtung Opera became so closely linked with the Peking Opera. Unlike the Anhwei companies of Foochow, those of Kwangtung were able to adapt their art to the local dialects. Another province to supply Kwangtung with actors was neighbouring Hunan. In 1953 Ou-yang Yü-ch'ien, one of the foremost modern authorities on the Chinese theatre, wrote of the companies from Hunan as follows: 'They came mostly from Hengyang and Kiyang [both on the Siang River in southern Hunan]. The Hengyang troupes sang mostly *K'un-ch'ü*; and even now there are still a great many *K'un-ch'ü* pieces [in Kwangtung Opera] and the ways of performing them have not changed. As for the Kiyang companies, they stressed *Nan-pei lu* [that is, *Erh-huang* and *Hsi-p'i*], but also performed *Kao-ch'iang* [*Yiyang-ch'iang*]. Twenty years ago I met an aged Kwangtung actor and an old Hunanese living in Canton, both of whom confirmed how many Kiyang troupes there had been in Kwangtung.'[7]

By the time of the Taiping rebellion, the dramatic companies of Kwangtung were classified by the population in two distinct categories: the *wai-chiang pan* ('companies from other provinces') and the *pen-ti pan* ('local companies'). The differences between these categories came in time to depend not on their provenance (as their names suggest), but on their social status. The 'companies from other provinces' were attached to wealthy people and performed at official banquets. One recorded example was that of a salt merchant named Li, 'whose family raised a company of fledgling actors [among their servants] and then engaged a teacher from Kiangsu to instruct them'.[8]

The 'local companies' differed in that they performed popular drama for the benefit of the ordinary people. A regional gazetteer of Canton describes them thus: 'Those that were taught by teachers from Kwangtung and performed mostly in the cities and villages were called local companies. They were particularly good at *Erh-huang*, *Hsi-p'i*, Clapper Opera and dramas with wrestling. There were a great many actors of this kind and their stage properties and costumes were very splendid and beautiful. The actors whose appearance, voice and skill were finest earned an income of up to 2,000 or 3,000 taels each year. . . . The actors lived the whole year in large barges and would accept the invitations of every village. They were rarely able to rest, and their music ceased only in the hottest month.'[9]

One of the most important turning-points in the history of the Kwangtung Opera was the outbreak of the Taiping uprising in 1850. The acting population of the province played a significant part in this, and the gazetteer quoted above admits that 'many players led each other off in bands to become robbers'.[10] One of the most important of the Taiping leaders in the south-east was an actor called Li Wen-mao, who came from Hoshan county in Kwangtung. Li gathered together a large army of actors and tried to take Canton for the Taipings. He was repelled by the forces of Yeh Ming-ch'en (1807–59), the governor-general of Kwangtung and Kwangsi, and withdrew to the latter province, where he captured several cities and set up an independent kingdom based on Liuchow. Ou-yang Yü-ch'ien says that 'the officials under Li Wen-mao would go barefooted on the streets every day carrying baskets to sell vegetables, and the masses called Wen-mao's wife "sister-in-law"; so we can see how well grounded in popular affection his government was'.[11] Be that as it may, Li's attempt to take the city of Kweilin in 1858 failed, and he was wounded. Liuchow was later recaptured by the Ch'ing armies, and Li died in 1861.

The support of the acting population for the Taipings naturally provoked Yeh Ming-ch'en into taking repressive measures, and he banned the 'local companies'. All kinds of accusations were brought against them by the authorities, such as that 'they harmed public morals', that they were 'impious brigands who used the [practice of] honouring the gods as a pretext for making money by going from door to door, exacting contributions',[12] and so forth. In response, the members of the 'local companies' either styled themselves Peking Opera troupes or sought admittance into the 'companies from other provinces'. The proscription did not last long, however, and was revoked as a result of the following charming incident.

In 1868 the new governor-general of Kwangtung and Kwangsi, Jui-lin, invited some actors to his mansion to give performances in honour of his mother's birthday. They included the well-known *wu-sheng* K'uang Tien-ch'ing, whose stage name was Hsin-hua, and a *tan* whose surname was Ho (his stage name was Kou-pi-chang). When Ho started acting, Jui-lin's mother burst into tears and left the room. She ordered the performance to cease, summoned Ho to her presence and then detained him in the mansion after the other actors had left. The next day, Hsin-hua and a few others came to enquire what was happening and found to their astonishment that Ho had changed into a 'young lady of the family'.

> The governor-general had had a younger sister who had died young and who looked just the same as Chang [Ho]. When the governor-general's mother saw Chang, she was reminded of her daughter and so adopted Chang. She made him dress in women's clothes and become her daughter in order to comfort her old breast. From then on he sat enjoying wealth and high position. . . . Hsin-hua's long-cherished ambition was to revive the Kwangtung [Opera] troupes, so he asked Kou-pi-chang to request the governor-general to revoke the prohibition, and Chang agreed. After that Jui-lin did indeed send in a memorial to the Ch'ing court recommending that the Kwangtung [Opera] companies be allowed to resume their profession.[13]

Another effect of the Taiping uprising was the destruction of the Ch'iung-hua guild-hall in Foshan. After the ban on the Kwangtung (or Cantonese) Opera had been relaxed Hsin-hua set up a new organization called the Pa-ho Society and was himself elected as its head. Its headquarters were in the Chi-ch'ing guild in Canton, and, as a result, the city became recognized as the theatrical centre of the province. The building of public theatres in Canton had begun during the reign of Tao-kuang (1820–50), but these now increased in number and importance.

At the same time the influence of *K'un-ch'ü* declined sharply, and the 'companies from other provinces' were forced to disband through lack of audiences. The rich no longer ran their own companies, but, instead, either patronized the 'local companies' or went to the public theatres. One result was that more members of the literary class made friends with popular actors and could therefore help them to compose new dramas or rearrange the old ones. The standards of the texts for the Kwangtung Opera therefore rose.

The themes of the popular Kwangtung drama during the nineteenth century were not very different from those of the Peking Opera. Tales of ancient heroes (based largely on such novels as *The Water Margin*, by Lo Kuan-chung) would always be appreciated and gentler stories (such as those which relate the loves of scholars of old times, and excerpts based on *The Dream of the Red Chamber*, by Ts'ao Chan), were also used. Naturally the actors sang or spoke in local dialect. In contrast to the practice in Peking, a company would perform a single drama over a whole day.

The content of the Kwangtung Opera was further influenced by the development from 1907 of the spoken play. Not only were political and social themes now introduced, but many of the old conventions were discarded in favour of Western practices. Actors began to wear contemporary and Western costumes on the stage, and for the first time scenery was used. Moreover, naturalistic movement to some extent replaced the stylized gestures which characterize all forms of traditional Chinese theatre. After a time, companies began to adapt spoken plays to the music of the traditional Kwangtung Opera, thereby creating a somewhat strange mixture of cultures. During the Republican period, the Kwangtung Opera was probably more heavily influenced by Western patterns than any other type of Chinese regional theatre. This was partly because Canton was very close to Hong Kong, and partly because actors who visited great ports outside China, such as Singapore, to cater for the demands of their numerous inhabitants of Cantonese extraction, could hardly escape foreign influences.

In general, the influence of the West upon the Kwangtung Opera was unfavourable. Many good actors and actresses were drawn into the growing film industry, in which they could earn far higher sums than in the traditional theatre. Artistically, too, the Kwangtung Opera suffered from the ever-increasing Western-inspired demand for novelty, with the result that the plays performed were more notable for their quantity than for their quality. During the Republican period more than a thousand new pieces were composed. They were of four kinds. Some were arranged from old Chinese dramas, others from old novels; others derived their inspiration from foreign novels or plays, and yet others were adapted from American films. Some of these plays aroused great interest, but most were poor, and consequently few of them ran for more than a few days.

The music of the Kwangtung Opera underwent certain changes during those years. The famous actors Hsüeh Chüeh-hsien and Ma Shih-tseng introduced such Western instruments as the violin, electric guitar and saxophone into the orchestra. While the violin blended perfectly well with the traditional Chinese instruments, it is doubtful if the same can be said of the electric guitar and the saxophone, which tended to give the Kwangtung Opera an unfortunately commercialized flavour.

Although the Republican period was not a glorious one in the history of the Kwangtung Opera, it did produce a few very fine actors. The most famous of them was the *ch'ou* Ma Shih-tseng, whose story is interesting not only in itself but also for what it tells us about the Kwangtung Opera in his time.

Ma Shih-tseng was born in 1900 of Cantonese parents. His family had had some education, and his great-great-uncle Ma Chen-yü ran an academy in Wuchang. Ma spent many of his childhood years in Wuchang, returning to Canton when the Republican revolution broke out. He received a high-school education and was then sent by his parents to Hong Kong to learn a business trade. Ma hated the work and escaped back to Canton, but, fearing his parents' anger, did not return home. All his life he had been fascinated by the Kwangtung Opera, so he went to the district where artists gathered in search of work and joined their ranks.

The life of unemployed actors was scarcely an appealing one. If they were lucky, they were taken up by the leader of a company and made to do menial work. Their status was much lower than that of graduates of the training-schools. Ma Shih-tseng was fortunate enough to find a job, and he signed a contract with his new master. He soon tired of this life, however, and looked for a way in which to improve his position.

His chance came when a Cantonese actor working in Singapore returned home in search of new actors. According to Ma's biographer, this man 'ought by rights to have looked for talent in the [formal] companies of Canton, but the price of players with a training-school education was too high and he could not afford it'.[14] He therefore searched in the more lowly troupes, found Ma Shih-tseng and agreed to take him to Singapore, where Ma hoped to find better prospects.

The young actor worked hard in his new environment. He travelled in various parts of the Malay peninsula and took various kinds of jobs, not only in theatre companies. For instance, for a while he was a teacher in a private Chinese school in Singapore. Finally he was offered employment as an actor in the troupe of the famous Kwangtung Opera actor, Ling Yüan-heng.[15] Not long after this an even better opportunity arose. Nieh Yao-ch'ing, the leader of the New China (Hsin Chung-hua) troupe, at that time among the most famous in Kwangtung, happened to be in Singapore and invited Ma to return to Canton to join his company. Ling did not want to let his protégé go, succeeded in making him postpone his departure, and when Ma eventually left, developed a lasting dislike for him. Some time later, a hooligan picked a fight with Shih-tseng and forced him to hand over a substantial sum of money. Many people believed Ling Yüan-heng to have been responsible for the incident, though he denied it.

By the time Ma Shih-tseng returned to China Nieh Yao-ch'ing no longer wanted to take him into the New China company, and instead obtained a place for him in the Jen-shou-nien, also a leading Canton troupe. Ma continued to act in Canton for four years, until 1929, consolidating his reputation and improving his art.

From 1929 to 1933 Ma Shih-tseng spent most of his time abroad. He first toured Vietnam, where he was welcomed especially by Saigon's Overseas Chinese population. In 1931 he went to California. His biographer comments that 'this was not only a great event in Ma Shih-tseng's theatrical career, but was also one of the most important in the last three decades in *Yüeh-chü* circles. It symbolized the Kwangtung Opera's development and wafted it across the seas to a new continent.'[16] Though the Chinese people of San Francisco were naturally thrilled to see this fine actor, Ma himself was somewhat disappointed by the tour. Life in the United States did not match his expectations, and he suffered a personal setback when arrangements which he had made to act in a Kwangtung Opera film came to nothing.

In 1933 Ma Shih-tseng went to Hong Kong, where he was invited to help organize the T'ai-p'ing troupe based on the theatre of the same name. He remained in the company for nearly a decade and was immensely successful. He made further tours, including one to Manila in 1941. Above all, he realized his ambition to make films. The outbreak of the war in 1937 had not disrupted his career and he played his role in the Chinese resistance by performing anti-Japanese dramas. Not until the eve of the occupation of Hong Kong in December 1941 did he finally return to Kwangtung.

Ma now organized a new company, the first of which he was actually the leader, called the War of Resistance (K'ang-chan) troupe. The company worked hard to live up to its name through the pieces which it performed and also toured widely in Kwangsi province, trying to intensify patriotic feeling. Later on the company's name was changed to Victory (Sheng-li). Apart from Ma Shih-tseng himself, the most important performer in this troupe was the young actress K'uang Chien-lien, who was to become (mainly after 1949) the most famous of all Kwangtung Opera artists under the stage name Hung-hsien-nü. Her relations with Ma extended well beyond cultural co-operation, for she became his wife. Ma had been married twice before, but neither partnership had been successful. (The first was an arranged marriage of the traditional kind.)

Ma Shih-tseng was an extremely versatile and creative actor. Though he performed most often as a *ch'ou*, he could handle virtually any type of role. He was a keen observer of human nature, and many critics commented on the acuteness with which he portrayed a wide variety of characters. He was an outstanding innovator and made extensive changes in the art of the Kwangtung Opera. For instance, Ou-yang Yü-ch'ien claims that 'the T'ai-p'ing troupe which he organized after returning from America used entirely Western instruments apart from percussion'.[17] Ma arranged a great many new dramas and wrote music for them; he also introduced changes in costume and staging.

In some ways Ma was an actor typical of his age, since not all his innovations were in good taste. Though he did not succeed by himself in bringing prestige to the Kwangtung Opera, the style would probably have become more highly regarded if all its reformers had been as talented as Ma Shih-tseng.

9 The Middle Yangtze Region: Hupeh and Szechwan*

The three cities of Wuchang, Hankow and Hanyang, collectively called Wuhan, stand together in Hupeh, in central China, at the junction of two great rivers, the Han and the Yangtze. Communications between them and other provinces have always been good. The Han has served to link the triple city with southern Shensi and the northwest, while the Yangtze has greatly facilitated trade and cultural relations with such eastern regions as Anhwei and Kiangsu. In more recent times Wuhan's geographical position was rendered even more important by the construction of the great north–south railway which passes through the city and links Peking with Canton.

Inter-regional contacts have not been so easy for the great southwestern province of Szechwan, the most populous and fertile in China. It is true that the Yangtze flows right through Szechwan and directly into Hupeh, but the river's value as a link between the two provinces is reduced by a long stretch of gorges which make the water turbulent and difficult to navigate. Szechwan's relative isolation has given it a tradition of political independence which has been a source of worry to many a Chinese government, including the present one. Another consequence of this isolation was that the province remained comparatively free from foreign influence during the decades of imperialist penetration of China.

Despite the differing efficiency of their communications with other provinces, both Szechwan and Hupeh show marked outside influences in their regional theatres. Furthermore, as we saw in Chapter One, both have contributed greatly to the development of the Peking Opera, especially Hupeh, where many of its finest actors, including Yü

* See Ills. 29–30, p. 141.

San-sheng and T'an Hsin-p'ei, have been born. The main type of regional theatre in Hupeh (*Han-chü*, or Hupeh Opera) is strikingly similar in its music to the Peking Opera.

THE HUPEH OPERA

The Hupeh Opera is a branch of the *P'i-huang* system (based on the melodies *Erh-huang* and *Hsi-p'i*) which flourishes in so many regions of China, and its orchestra is similar to that of the most important branch of the *P'i-huang*: the Peking Opera. *Erh-huang* seems to have been introduced from the east by companies wandering along the Yangtze, and *Hsi-p'i* by actors from Shensi moving down the Han. The two tunes had become popular in Hupeh by the end of the eighteenth century at the very latest, and many dramatic pieces already popular in the province were adapted to the new music.

Very little is known about the early period of the Hupeh Opera. It is mentioned in few primary sources and the surviving references only describe the influence of visiting Hupeh actors in Peking. This influence appears from the sources to have been substantial, which indicates the existence of a flourishing theatre in the home province, especially in Wuhan. Specific details, however, are lacking.

The Taiping uprising caused some disruption in the functioning of the Hupeh Opera, which was followed by a gradual revival. According to the actor Fu Hsin-i, a certain defeated military leader of the uprising 'took the name of Liu Chü-hui and escaped to the Siangyang-Fancheng region [on the middle Han in north-western Hupeh]. His former nature had not changed, and he was quick-tempered and enjoyed quarrels.' Despite these traits, he was apparently interested in the local theatre and upset at 'its rapid decline due to the war, so . . . contributed some capital towards the establishment of a training-school'.[1] This produced a great many fine actors, including Fu Hsin-i's own father, and in this way Liu's aim of revitalizing the Hupeh Opera was achieved.

The Hupeh companies continued to be active throughout the rest of the Ch'ing dynasty, assisted by the constant influx of artists from other regions. Though the province lost some of its finest actors to Peking, it benefited from the many visits paid to Wuhan by players from the capital. In fact, by the Republican period the Hupeh Opera, which had earlier influenced the Peking Opera so greatly, was beginning to feel its influence in turn.

Some plays were products of the Hupeh Opera and were not adapted from Peking Opera. Moreover, the theatre of the capital continued to some extent to absorb the Hupeh repertoire. Perhaps the most famous example was *Kuei-fei tsui-chiu* (*The Drunken Beauty*), which relates how the famous concubine of the Emperor Ming-huang, Yang Kuei-fei, drowns her sorrows in drink when her imperial lover fails to attend a banquet at which she is present. This play, originally a *K'un-ch'ü* piece, had been adapted to the Hupeh Opera by the Tao-kuang period (1820–50). It was introduced to Peking by Wu Hung-hsi, the famous *tan* of the Hupeh Opera, early in the twentieth century, and remained popular in the capital until very recently; it was, in fact, one of Mei Lan-fang's showpieces.

Despite their mutual influence, neither the Hupeh Opera nor the Peking Opera lost its identity, its musical character, or its special style of singing. The Hupeh Opera continued to use many of its own conventions, and even today no Chinese theatre-goer would confuse the Hupeh and Peking styles. By the 1920s there was a large guild for Hupeh actors. Its leader was Fu Hsin-i and it contained as many as seven thousand registered members, including a number of women.

As early as 1911 there had been all-female Hupeh Opera troupes in Wuhan. As in other cities, mixed companies were forbidden, and it was a long time before the prejudice against them was broken down. A school for actresses was established in about 1930; at first, it trained girls only for female companies and only later trained them for mixed troupes. The school was called Hsin-hua and, in accordance with the custom prevailing in Wuhan, its graduates included the school's name in their own stage names. Hsin-hua Ch'ai was among the most famous actresses in the city during the 1930s.

The Hupeh Opera produced a number of distinguished actors, the most popular of whom was the *lao-sheng* Yü Hung-yüan, and it became so strong in the affections of the people that it was able to resist the fate which overtook so many branches of the Chinese theatre: that of being submerged by the war. Instead it was used as a propaganda weapon against the Japanese. The reader will recall that Wuhan was Chiang Kai-shek's capital during the early stages of the war. Chou I-pai described how the Hupeh players reacted to the situation:

The patriots concentrated in the Wuhan region carried on anti-Japanese propaganda in different ways. Helped by them the artists of the *Han-chü* organized themselves and established ten *Han-chü* anti-Japanese propaganda teams, which split up and devoted themselves to propaganda work everywhere. After the fall of Wuhan, some of these ten teams went to Szechwan [where Chungking became the wartime capital] and some to the base areas of the border regions of Hunan and Hupeh. At this time, the items performed in the *Han-chü* were mostly old pieces, which expressed the upright feelings of the people, or new contemporary dramas which took their material from the struggle in hand. The costumes and actions of the Hupeh Opera were very stylized and most pieces were based on historical stories, so the sudden change to contemporary costumes [required by the new dramas] was at the time only regarded as a propaganda duty. There was no time for proper study and the results were therefore somewhat stiff.[2]

The exigencies of war may not have reduced the numbers of plays performed, but standards apparently suffered.

These propaganda teams included actors of another type of local drama as well as the Hupeh Opera. This was the *Ch'u-chü*, a kind of folk drama into which the music of Yiyang had been absorbed at a fairly early date. The famous Szechwanese scholar-official Li T'iao-yüan (1734–1803) records that in his time *Yiyang ch'iang* was popular in Hupeh under the name *Ch'ing-hsi*,[3] and it may have spread there even earlier. Despite the impact of this style from Kiangsi on the folk theatre of Hupeh, the Hupeh Opera remained in general surprisingly free from its influence, and it was not until the war that, to a large extent, actors specializing in one style acted in the same companies as actors specializing in the other.

SZECHWAN

The pattern whereby the various styles of regional theatre remained fairly independent of one another did not extend to the neighbouring province of Szechwan. There the *Ch'uan-chü*, or Szechwanese Opera, was formed through the amalgamation of five distinct types, each with its own history and characteristics. These were the *Kao-ch'iang*, *Hu-ch'in ch'iang*, *T'an-ch'iang*, *Teng-hsi* and *K'un-ch'ü*.

The *Kao-ch'iang* is a variant of the *Yiyang ch'iang*, whose main features it shares. The singing of the principal actors is accompanied only by percussion instruments, and a chorus comments on or repeats their observations. In the past, the members of the chorus also functioned as the percussion players and sat in full view of the audience, even though they wore their ordinary everyday clothes.

It is not exactly clear how the *Kao-ch'iang* came from Kiangsi to

Szechwan, and scholars have put forward various theories by way of explanation. The one point on which all are in agreement is that the introduction of the *Kao-ch'iang* into the south-west was roughly concurrent with the civil wars which brought about the fall of the Ming dynasty (1368–1644). At that time the rebel Chang Hsien-chung (c. 1605–1647) invaded Szechwan and set up an independent kingdom based on Chengtu. Chang's campaigns are said to have been 'marked by indescribable cruelty and under his regime the province of Szechwan endured untold suffering'.[4] So great was the extent of depopulation caused by his devastation that many people were ordered to migrate from eastern provinces, including Hunan and Kiangsi, to fill the gap. It is probable that they included some *Kao-ch'iang* companies, and such writers as the modern scholar Hsi Ming-chen have even claimed that the first professional troupes arrived in Szechwan at this time.[5]

The period at which the *Hu-ch'in ch'iang* style arrived in the west is also uncertain, though it appears to have become known there later than the *Kao-ch'iang*. The *Hu-ch'in ch'iang* is very similar to the Hupeh Opera and the Peking Opera in its stringed accompaniment and in its domination by the two tunes *Erh-huang* and *Hsi-p'i*. Some authors have surmised that the great Szechwanese actor Wei Ch'ang-sheng brought it back to his native province when he returned from Peking in about 1790, or that the credit may be given to Li T'iao-yüan, who fell from favour in the capital in 1783 and went the following year to live his remaining years in Szechwan. Both theories strike me as unconvincing. The Anhwei companies which popularized this music in Peking did not arrive there until 1790 – that is, after Wei and Li had departed. It is more likely that the introduction of the *Hu-ch'in ch'iang* must be ascribed to a later date, possibly to the time of the Taiping uprising, when several troupes journeyed from eastern provinces, such as Anhwei, to the south-west.

Li T'iao-yüan has also been credited with having familiarized his native province with the *T'an-ch'iang*, which is a form of Clapper Opera. It is true that Li was interested in Clapper Opera and was a friend of Wei Ch'ang-sheng, possibly its greatest exponent. On the other hand, Li himself, though a prolific writer and famous patron of the theatre, limits himself to recording that the Clapper Opera was accompanied by the clapper (*pang-tzu*) and stringed *yüeh-ch'in* and was extremely widespread in Szechwan by about 1775.[6] He lays no claim to any credit for its popularity. Moreover, we saw in Chapter One that by 1779 Szechwan could boast so many splendid Clapper actors that they were able to take Peking by storm with the magnificence of their art. Since it must have taken several decades to build up a tradition strong enough for such an achievement, the year of Li's birth (1734) indicates that he could not have been the father of Clapper Opera in Szechwan. The *T'an-ch'iang* was probably known there by the early eighteenth century, and the most plausible theory of its origin in the province must be that wandering companies brought it from neighbouring Shensi at about that time or earlier.

The only source of the Szechwanese Opera truly native to Szechwan was the *Teng-hsi*, or lantern theatre. Like the three styles discussed above, it was real folk theatre and probably grew from the mask dances of village shamans, who had performed exorcizing ceremonies in the villages from time immemorial. The music was simple, based on folk tunes and accompanied by an orchestra consisting only of the small drum, gong and fiddle (*hu-ch'in*). Dialogue sections predominated throughout, which explains why the sung melodies were never developed very far. The lantern theatre was a natural concomitant of the popular festivals and was frequently presented at weddings or funerals. Moreover, shamanistic performances persisted in the remoter regions until the last years of the Ch'ing dynasty, and the lantern theatre remained confined to the countryside until then. Even today, it arouses little response in the cities and is only rarely performed by urban professional companies.

Unlike the dramatic forms mentioned so far, the *K'un-ch'ü* began not as folk but as gentry theatre. Several early writers of the 'elegant drama' were born and lived much of their lives in Szechwan, and they almost certainly maintained private companies to perform their own works and those of others. Possibly the best known patron of the *K'un-ch'ü* was Wu T'ang (d. 1876), for a time the governor-general of Szechwan. Wu invited a group of good actors from Soochow, where the style originated (see page 16), set them up as his private *K'un-ch'ü* troupe, and named them the Shu-i company. They would perform whenever scholars and officials gathered at Wu's mansion for a party, and he also loved to listen to them when by himself. The company thrived so well under Wu T'ang that it was able to survive his death, and even perform not only for the rich but for the ordinary people as well. It did not disband until the founding of the Republic.

Possibly the main reason why the Shu-i troupe eventually became redundant lay in the movement towards modernizing the Szechwanese theatre which arose in the first decade of the present century. One of the movement's main achievements was to establish the traditional drama in urban playhouses. The first theatre of this kind was the Yüeh-lai, built in 1905 in Chengtu. The capital for this venture was contributed by the scholar Chou Hsiao-huai, and the theatre proved to be immensely successful. From now onwards in Szechwan, troupes were no longer required to hold performances only in temples and guild-halls, or on temporary stages. It became more practicable to manage permanent companies, and, not surprisingly, good actors were attracted from all over the province as a result. It was at this time that actors specializing in the five dramatic styles which I have been discussing began to work together in the same troupes, and attempts were made to produce a unified style: the Szechwanese Opera.

Following the pattern of Peking and other cities, Chengtu's theatres were also teahouses where the people could gather and sip tea as they watched the performances. They did not, however, sit at tables, but on long benches set out in rows. Some of the theatrical institutions of modern Peking were introduced, such as the sale of tickets. These consisted of copper tokens inscribed with numbers.

Since they were now able to perform in permanent public theatres, dramatic companies became independent of the local warlords or officials. They were still not free, however, since from the early 1900s they came under the control of a newly risen class of businessmen. Some old actors of Szechwan, interviewed during the Communist period, describe the position of such people as follows: 'This owner, *pan-chu*, owned the costumes, properties and other equipment, which gave him complete power over the fate of the company. Only the most famous actors would sometimes own their costumes; this made them less dependent on the owner and they might even change to another company. Every company paid regular sums to the owner.'[7]

At the same time, the new movement was given a literary basis through the collaboration of scholars with the actors. Chou Hsiao-huai, for instance, studied in Japan and, on his return to Szechwan, founded the Society for the Reform of the Theatre (Hsi-ch'ü kai-liang kung-hui), which not only helped carry out the changes already discussed but also encouraged dramatists to rewrite and modernize old pieces to suit contemporary tastes. The authors then helped the actors to understand their parts and analysed for them the characters whom they were to represent.

One of the most noted playwrights of the time was Chao Hsi, the teacher of Chou Hsiao-huai. Originally from a poor family, he had gained an education through the efforts of his elder brother and in 1890 passed the highest official examination. This opened up to him a career in the civil service, and in due course he held various posts in the government. Nevertheless, he was sympathetic to such reformers as K'ang Yu-wei and a close personal friend of several of them. He was also a poet of some distinction and assisted greatly in the work of the modern Szechwanese theatre.

Perhaps his most famous piece is *Ch'ing-t'an*, which is based on an ancient story which had been dramatized many times before this century. It concerns the scholar Wang K'uei, who marries a prostitute called Chiao Kuei-ying. The two swear eternal love for one another, but Wang then goes to the capital, where he is successful in the official examinations and marries the daughter of the prime minister. When Kuei-ying learns that she has been betrayed she commits suicide, and her spirit punishes her faithless lover.

This story had an obvious relevance to a society in which questions were being asked about concubinage and the old system of arranged marriages. But Chao had a special personal reason for writing the play. One writer of the People's Republic comments on it as follows:

> It was not without cause that Chao Hsi, an author of the ruling classes, could write *Ch'ing-t'an*, which belongs so thoroughly to the people. On the one hand, he could still be considered a comparatively upright person. On the other hand, the composition of *Ch'ing-t'an* was [inspired by the fact that] his daughter was very badly treated by her husband after her marriage. . . . Twenty or thirty years after the play's arrangement, when he saw a performance again, he wrote a poem called 'An Inscription on the Wang K'uei Drama'. . . . If his emotions about it were still so alive after such a long time [as the poem shows], one can imagine even more what he was feeling at the time he took up his brush to arrange the drama.[8]

Ch'ing-t'an was enthusiastically taken up in Chengtu and frequently performed. But it owed its greatest successes to the outstanding artistry of the San-ch'ing company and its leader K'ang Chih-lin (or K'ang Tzu-lin), a brilliant exponent of the part of Wang K'uei.

The San-ch'ing company was founded in 1912 in the Yüeh-lai teahouse theatre and was to dominate the Chengtu stage for several decades. It broke sharply with the tradition of earlier troupes in that it was managed entirely by the artists themselves and owed nothing to any owner. This naturally imposed financial restrictions but, at the same time, guaranteed a far greater freedom of action for the members and wider scope for the development of their talents.

The actors of the San-ch'ing company were truly dedicated men, anxious to improve their techniques even if their popular appeal should decline in consequence. They also tried to ensure that their high standards were carried on, and to this end established a training-school which was attached to their company. The school seems to have been in many respects rather different from actors' training-schools in other cities. Chou Mu-lien, one of the most famous *tan* actors of the Szechwanese Opera, remarked of it in 1958 as follows:

> The San-ch'ing company ran a training-school called Sheng-p'ing, where the students were all the younger brothers, sons or nephews of the company's artists. The choice of students at the time was of course not as strict as today and was aimed mainly at taking care of the responsibility of the artists' families; for this reason there were some students below standard. On the other hand, it produced quite a few good artists like T'ang Yin-fu, Yu-tse-ku, Yü-fei-ch'iung and others. The San-ch'ing company was very strict in its management of students, yet had no supervisors specially [hired to make sure they behaved properly]. Because there were a great many teachers in the San-ch'ing company, the actors of each different category [*tan*, *sheng*, and so on] were instructed by a teacher of the same category. The teachers loved their disciples as if they were sons and did not curse or beat them. K'ang Chih-lin often used to say: 'If I beat you and you changed, would there really have been any point in thrashing you; and if you did not change when I beat you, what use would the beating have been?'[9]

The actor with the extraordinarily progressive outlook revealed at the end of this excerpt was probably the best known exponent of the Szechwanese Opera to have appeared yet during this century. He was born on 13 February 1870 in a small town not far from Chengtu. His elder brother was also an actor, and his younger brother ran a pharmaceutical shop. K'ang Chih-lin started his career on the stage at the age of about ten and learned to master both *sheng* and *tan* roles. This training gave him the basis for a wide repertoire, and throughout his life he always insisted on the need for a broad range of skills. Although he himself certainly practised what he preached, it is as a *hsiao-sheng* (scholar-lover) that he is chiefly remembered.

By 1912, when the San-ch'ing troupe was founded, K'ang Chih-lin had already been a member of several Chengtu companies, and helped greatly in the work of combining the various strands of the Szechwanese Opera into a meaningful unity. He was, however, noted above all as a teacher. The standards which he demanded were extremely high, yet he was never too biting in his criticism. This made him popular with his students, especially since he expected even higher standards of himself and was never ostentatious. Chou Mu-lien, who studied under him, recalls that 'he lived very simply and was singularly free of addictions'.[10]

Being in agreement with the generally progressive policy of the San-ch'ing company, K'ang Chih-lin was also concerned about the low social status of actors. He wanted the theatrical profession itself to take the initiative by improving their education. He believed, too, that the greater an actor's learning, the finer his performances would be. 'We artists,' he said, 'are too lacking in culture, therefore we make far too many mistakes and are too often funny [without intending it]. We must learn culture and read more.'[11]

K'ang Chih-lin remained in the San-ch'ing company as an actor and teacher until his death in 1931. Early in that year, he and the company paid a visit to Chungking, whither they had been invited by Feng Shih-chu, the owner of the Yüeh-ho theatre. Feng proved a hard task-master and greatly overworked the visiting troupe. K'ang, in particular, was not in good health and under the strain of the tour began to lose his appetite. But it was the summer that finally broke the ailing actor, for the hot season is particularly oppressive in Chungking and the city has even been named 'China's furnace'. Chou Mu-lien records that Feng continued to drive K'ang Chih-lin, despite everything. One day, after he had finished his scene, 'he came backstage and [we found that] he was completely paralysed. Four or five days later his illness was still becoming more and more serious and he died soon after.'[12] In recognition of the work of this distinguished actor, the local newspaper published a special edition in his honour.

Actors as gifted and popular as K'ang Chih-lin have not been uncommon in the Chinese regional theatre, and it will be obvious that I have been highly selective in my discussion not only of actors, but also of provinces, in Part Two of this book. The northern provinces of Shansi and Shensi, to take but two examples, have received virtually no mention, despite their importance for the Clapper Opera. There is, however, a certain similarity in the pattern of development of the provincial theatrical styles in China, and, in any case, detailed and interesting historical material is available for only a few of them. Field study is the best potential source of information, and, although Chinese scholars devoted a great deal of effort to research in the local drama in the first years after 1949, very little further work has been carried out since the mid-1960s.

10 Government Policy towards the Theatre

The triumph in 1949 of Mao Tse-tung and the Communist Party which he led brought to the Chinese people a period of peace and stability which they had not previously enjoyed in modern times. This in itself created conditions favourable to the progress not only of the drama but of all forms of art. The new government encouraged painters, musicians and actors to revive the creativity which had been largely lost owing to the war and the succeeding years of civil conflict and disillusionment. The drama was particularly favoured by the Communists, for it had always been a popular art, to a great extent created for and enjoyed by the poorer sections of the community. Unlike, for example, the seven-stringed zither, the *ku-ch'in*, it had never been the monopoly of the educated and was rightly regarded as part of 'the people's culture'. The status of the drama as an art therefore rose. New books about it were published in large numbers, new theatres and companies were established, and the training of the next generation of actors was taken in hand.

In accordance with their general attitude of discouraging private enterprise, the Communists strove to bring the theatres and dramatic companies under state control. Their policy in this was, however, extremely cautious. Private business enterprises were not all nationalized immediately by the new government, and until the Cultural Revolution joint state/private shops and factories were permitted. In the same way, many theatres remained partly under private management until 1966. Some theatre-managers drew substantial incomes. They were given an official salary, retained ownership of their playhouses and were allowed to keep some of the profits derived from business. Existing dramatic companies, too, continued at first to be privately run, and no large-scale attempt was made to nationalize them until 1956. In January of that year fifteen of Tientsin's main troupes and some seventy of Shanghai's were nationalized. In the following months a similar process took place in China's other major cities. Not until the Cultural Revolution, however, did privately run companies disappear altogether. For example, the famous *tan* Shang Hsiao-yün and Hsün Hui-sheng, and the great *lao-sheng* Ma Lien-liang, were still leading their own troupes in Peking long after 1956, and in most parts of China many privately managed troupes continued to flourish for some years.

DRAMA REFORM

The nationalization of many of the dramatic companies was but one of the many radical changes in Chinese theatrical life brought about by the Communist government. The ways in which the reforms which were now to be carried out affected the actors and theatre-goers will be discussed in the following chapters. Here it is my concern to examine the impact of Communist policy on the dramas themselves.

Virtually all contemporary Chinese attitudes are based upon the thought of Mao Tse-tung, whose influence over the Chinese people has been of the greatest importance. Mao's views on the arts were outlined in 1942 in 'Talks at the Yenan Forum on Literature and Art', and this article is now the basic source of the correct Communist Chinese view of drama. Possibly the most important point stated by Mao is that art and politics are indivisible. He writes:

All culture, all literature and art belong to definite classes and are geared to definite political lines. There is in fact no such thing as art for art's sake, art that stands above classes or art that is detached from or independent of politics. Proletarian literature and art are part of the whole proletarian revolutionary cause; they are, as Lenin said, cogs and wheels in the whole revolutionary machine. Therefore, Party work in literature and art occupies a definite and assigned position in Party revolutionary work as a whole and is subordinated to the revolutionary tasks set by the Party in a given revolutionary period.[1]

Mao is saying in effect that all art propagates a certain viewpoint, whether it claims to do so or not. To maintain, as is frequently done in the West, that art can be devoid of political content is to him sheer nonsense and merely a ruse intended to deceive people into thinking that there are many aspects of life from which political opinions can be divorced. Art, then, is propaganda, and this means that the Chinese theatre must express the correct Party line on ethical and all other matters. Art is part of the superstructure of society; it is affected by the economic base, which it can influence in turn. On artists falls the duty of ensuring that their work benefits the broad mass of the people, and not of the bourgeoisie. This does not mean that Mao favours works which are inferior from an aesthetic point of view. He writes, 'What we demand is the unity of politics and art . . . and the highest possible perfection of artistic form. Works of art which lack artistic quality have no force, however progressive they are politically.'[2]

Art must be both stimulating aesthetically and correct politically. Moreover, Mao's emphasis on art as propaganda does not imply that he considers the culture of the past to be necessarily bad. He is quite explicit on this point: 'A splendid old culture was created during the long period of Chinese feudal society. To study the development of this old culture, to reject its feudal dross and assimilate its democratic essence is a necessary condition for developing our new national culture and increasing our national self-confidence, but we should never swallow anything and everything uncritically. It is imperative to separate the fine old culture of the people which had a more or less democratic and revolutionary character from all the decadence of the old feudal ruling class.'[3]

All three of these propositions have come close to being universally accepted in China. Yet they are open to various interpretations, and much controversy has raged over how best to put them into effect. In the field of drama, Communist policies and attitudes have changed greatly over the last thirty years, even though almost everybody concerned has claimed to be following the concepts of Chairman Mao.

Seven distinct phases can be discerned in the development of the Communist attitude towards the theatre. The first lasted from the time when Mao wrote his 'Talks at the Yenan Forum' down to 1949 and was characterized by an emphasis on the local peasant drama of the Communist base area in northern Shensi (in particular, the small-scale song-and-dance form called *yang-ko*). Historical dramas were written or revived, but the attention of artists was directed primarily towards current political aims, such as the prosecution of the war against Japan, the abolition of corruption and the extension of Communist influence among the people. The organization of the theatre was carried out by literary groups. In 1948, for the first time, a committee was set up for the specific purpose of revising old pieces to conform with Communist doctrine.

165

The liberation of the entire Chinese mainland in 1948–49 signalled the beginning of the second phase (1949–56). It became clear that the unsophisticated approach adopted during the earlier phase was inadequate, since the urban population was not satisfied with the peasant drama of Shensi. A complex hierarchy of committees (under the leadership of the Bureau of Drama Reform, headed by the famous playwright T'ien Han) was set up all over China to guide the work of assessing, revising and editing dramas. Efforts were made to re-educate actors and to encourage them to perform plays with modern, realistic, revolutionary themes. A favourite topic was the reform of the marriage system. Many pieces attacked child marriage, arranged marriages, and concubinage. The traditional theatre also remained extremely popular, and it was not difficult to give revolutionary interpretations to many of the most popular plays.

In the first years after 1949, a great deal of attention was devoted by leaders in the theatrical field to deciding exactly what was reactionary and what was progressive in the classical drama. Many plays were either banned or effectively driven from the stage by criticism in the press. But a more difficult problem lay in deciding how to rearrange or edit pieces which, though considered patriotic or beneficial to the people, contained feudal elements. Several high-level conferences were convened to discuss these matters. One of the most important was held in November 1954 and attended by a number of eminent dramatists, actors and dramatic critics, including such famous men as Ou-yang Yü-ch'ien, T'ien Han, Mei Lan-fang and Ch'eng Yen-ch'iu.

Various viewpoints were put forward at the conference, but most of the delegates agreed that it was unnecessary to tamper greatly with the technical features of the Peking Opera. For instance, it was decided that almost all the facial masks should remain in use. Mei Lan-fang rightly commented that 'certain set faces . . . have already become familiar to the masses of the people, and do not need to be changed now. When these characters appear on the stage, they do not have to announce themselves yet the audience knows who they are.'[4] Traditional stage mannerisms and costumes were also, for the most part, retained. On the other hand, a limited number of gestures, such as kow-towing, and a few items of costume, like the 'false feet' which enabled the actor to walk as though his feet were bound, had previously been banned as backward or unhealthy, and the conference maintained the prohibition on them. It also confirmed the practice of using scenery and curtains for some pieces and supported an earlier decision to seat the orchestra in the wings instead of on the stage.

The major task of reform, however, concerned the content and texts of the plays. The reformers eradicated numerous phrases in the dialogue and sung sections which seemed to them reactionary. Any passage which showed a popular hero in a humiliating position was deleted, since the heroic character prefers death to submission. Sentences showing a sympathetic person as superstitious, or even religious, were removed and replaced by others endowing him with a more progressive outlook. In many cases the plot was altered to show monks or other reactionary people in a bad light, and to bring out the courage of the hero more sharply.

At the time of this meeting there was a good deal of talk in theatrical circles about the 'socialist realism' of Stanislavsky (1863–1938), whose system of acting had long been officially accepted in the Soviet Union. In China his influence was naturally much more pronounced in the field of the spoken play than in that of the traditional play. All actors, including Mei Lan-fang, paid lip service to Stanislavsky's ideas, but to introduce Stanislavsky's realism into the acting methods of the traditional Peking Opera was a task which few artists were willing to undertake except to a very limited extent.

The stage conventions and plots of the classical theatre were not radically changed. The old dramas continued to attract a great following, especially after a conference held in June 1956 by the Ministry of Culture ushered in the third of the seven phases which we are considering. In accordance with the aims of the Hundred Flowers programme, the delegates decided to relax the bans on 'unhealthy' dramas and to seek out and edit large numbers of forgotten classical pieces. Theatre-goers were enthusiastic, for it was now possible to see dramas which had not been staged for several years, or, in some cases, for a much longer period. Many famous actors took part in the performances of these newly revived pieces, and the newspapers printed leading articles which favoured the trend.

This liberal phase did not last long. In 1957 the government changed its policy of intellectual and artistic freedom to one of restriction, and the theatre was naturally affected. On 21 July several famous actors, including Mei Lan-fang, Ch'eng Yen-ch'iu and Chou Hsin-fang, published an announcement urging that a halt should be called to the indiscriminate revival of old plays. 'The government does not suppress bad plays through administrative laws,' they wrote, 'but we must recognize that this is not equivalent to claiming that there are no standards of good and bad art.'[5] Gradually, dramas banned before 1956, and since revived, again disappeared from the stage.

The fourth phase began in 1958 as an adjunct of the Great Leap Forward. Since a stress on ideological motivation was an essential feature of this movement, it is not surprising that the government should now regard the promotion of the modern revolutionary theatre as its chief concern. Yet the classical drama was still encouraged. At an important conference of theatrical workers held in June and July 1958 Chou Yang, of the Party Propaganda Department in Peking, said: 'There should be a leap forward in drama expressing modern life. There should also be a leap forward in arranging and editing superior traditional items. From now on, pieces with material reflecting modern life should be greatly developed, and we should not demand excessive conditions. But for the traditional operas, we should strictly select the best among them, arrange and edit them more and thus in all respects raise and enrich the art of the stage.'[6]

This policy of 'walking on two legs' lasted in theory until 1963. But, in fact, as the Great Leap Forward waned, theatrical companies gave more of their attention to the old and less to the new dramas. In 1960, classical pieces constituted 97 per cent of all those produced, in 1961, 83 per cent, and in 1962 all the plays shown in Peking were classical.[7] The relaxation of ideological pressure in the wake of the intensity characteristic of 1958 and 1959 seems to have made the actors and people lose interest in the revolutionary theatre, while the growing antagonism towards the Soviet Union led the Chinese to value more highly a kind of theatre which showed no foreign influence of any sort.

It was not until 1963 that the government decided to push ahead more strongly with its programme to revolutionize the theatre. We now enter the fifth of the seven phases, when, for the first time, the government's intention to move towards the abolition of the traditional theatre becomes clear.

This change in policy was the result of a fierce debate within the Chinese leadership. The main proponent of the revolutionizing of the theatre and the virtual elimination of traditional themes was Chiang Ch'ing, the wife of Mao Tse-tung, who was supported by Mao himself and several eminent figures in Shanghai. On the opposing side were many of the leaders of the Party Propaganda Department in Peking, especially is Chou Yang, P'eng Chen and Lu Ting-i. The struggle undoubtedly signalled the rise of Chiang Ch'ing and was a prelude to the Cultural Revolution, which began two years later.

During the latter half of 1963, the press began to urge more forcefully that art in a socialist society should reflect reality and propagate socialist principles. Newspapers encouraged theatrical workers to 'distinguish the feudal dross from the democratic essence', and described dramas which portrayed heroes with Confucian virtues like filial piety as 'a method by which the ruling class poisons the people'.[8] There was of course nothing new in these propositions, but it quickly became clear that they were to be interpreted far more rigidly than before. Dramas which had earlier been thought to contain progressive elements, despite their 'feudal' overtones, were now to be condemned as reactionary, and far greater stress was laid on contemporary revolutionary themes:

> Because of historical and other aspects, old dramas about emperors, kings, generals and ministers, slave-girls and beauties, occupied the main position on the stage of the first period. But this is not appropriate for a socialist economic base. The economic base has changed, the times have changed, the theatre-going masses have changed, so the drama must also change. . . . The economic base stubbornly serves the function of determining the laws of the superstructure. Therefore, modern dramas must replace the old on the stage, and this is an irresistible historical impulse. . . . We advocate the revolutionary modern drama which alone must occupy the major position on the stage.[9]

Possibly the most important sign of the ascendancy of Chiang Ch'ing's view was the Festival of Peking Operas on Contemporary Themes, held in the capital from 5 June to 31 July 1964. From that time onwards, traditional dramas were performed in Peking only on a few special occasions, such as the National Day holidays (the first three days of October), New Year's Day and the Spring Festival (Lunar New Year). Other cities soon followed Peking's example. In February 1965, T'ao Chu, the First Secretary of the Party Central-South Bureau, told cultural workers in Canton that 'for the time being production of traditional plays will be disallowed. Only revolutionary modern plays will now be allowed to be written and produced. . . . A little bit of coercion will do some good. It may push everyone to do things better and faster.'[10]

By the time T'ao Chu made his remarks, all leaders were prepared to pay lip service, at least in public, to the idea that revolutionary drama should be fostered at the expense of classical. Chiang Ch'ing,

169

however, was still not satisfied. She felt that, both in characterization and music, the modern dramas were too heavily influenced by 'feudal' works and not nearly heroic enough in sentiment. P'eng Chen, who actually made the principal speech at the 1964 Festival and praised the theatrical reforms which the festival embodied, continued to resist many of Chiang Ch'ing's suggestions, and opposition persisted among other cultural leaders as well.

Considering Mao's clear statement on the critical inheritance of tradition, the new policy seems surprising, and even contrary to Mao's ideas. I was living in Peking during the period when it was taking effect, and when I raised the question with Chinese acquaintances, they told me that the revolutionary pieces still retained the music and other formal aspects of the classical theatre, and that consequently Mao's dictum was still being followed. While this is a tenable position, the extent to which tradition was rejected in the middle and late 1960s surely went a good deal beyond what the Chinese leaders had envisaged at any time before then.

The Cultural Revolution, which may be taken as the sixth phase, greatly reinforced the storm of hostility towards the past. This movement began late in 1965 with a denunciation of certain dramas on historical themes and of their authors. As it gathered momentum, especially with the appearance of Mao's youthful Red Guards in the streets of China's cities in mid-1966, the traditional theatre was subjected to ever fiercer condemnation. Chiang Ch'ing's primacy in cultural affairs became stronger. At the same time, most figures previously influential in artistic matters, even those who had seemed progressive, came under sharp criticism. Stanislavsky was condemned as a bourgeois, while, among Chinese leaders, Chou Yang, P'eng Chen and T'ao Chu were among the first to fall. Another was Lu Ting-i, who was described as 'the great "demon king" . . . [who] served as the No. 1 agent of China's Khrushchev [Liu Shao-ch'i, the President of the People's Republic of China, the chief target of the Cultural Revolution and to be dismissed in 1968] in literary and art circles'.[11] He was dubbed 'dictatorial and arrogant', and his part in the Festival of Peking Operas on Contemporary Themes of 1964 was bitterly attacked. In particular, his accusers claimed that he 'schemed to stage 40 percent of the traditional plays after the festival to impede the great onflow of the revolution of Peking opera.'[12]

During the Cultural Revolution the Maoist factions considered this a great crime. They held that drama should serve the interests not of the whole people, and certainly not of the rich, but of 'the masses of workers, peasants and soldiers'. Any encouragement of the traditional theatre, which they saw as part of the propaganda machinery of the old 'feudal' classes, seemed to them to be incompatible with this aim. They carried Mao's emphasis on art as propaganda to unprecedented lengths. Not only did they see the theatre as a medium for educating people in the thought of Mao Tse-tung; they also condemned Chou Yang because he had 'advocated "entertaining" literature and art', and attacked as harmful 'plays and operas which give the spectators relaxation and pleasure'.[13] Unless such dramas were primarily educative for revolutionary ends, they would tend to favour a return to pre-liberation ways of thinking.

The motive of the Maoist factions' total rejection of traditional approaches to the drama lies in their tremendous urge to eradicate both the physical and the spiritual vestiges of pre-1949 society. The advocates of the Cultural Revolution believe intensely in the power of the arts to influence the way in which people think and behave. To encourage the performance of plays about 'kings and emperors, ministers and generals, scholars and beauties' is to them equivalent to supporting the system of morality from which dramas of this kind developed; and such a code of ethics belongs to a past society which they wish to replace. Considering the injustices which were prevalent in imperial and Republican China, the desire of today's Maoists for change is extremely praiseworthy. However, the same cannot be said of the censorship which they deem necessary to bring about their aims, and in this respect they are, ironically, intensifying a form of injustice which they have inherited from the past.

It is interesting to find that in the views of Chiang Ch'ing and her followers there are implicit two attitudes which they share with many of their opponents, and with earlier Chinese governments. One is the realization of the overwhelming power of tradition. To uproot the influence of the past in a nation unused to radical change is a difficult and painful process. Earlier reformers have failed, but the Maoists are determined not to succumb to the pressures inherited from history. The other is the appreciation of the tight link between the theatre and society. I have noted several times that this relationship was particularly striking in the past, and it is not surprising to find that it still prevails in China. Communist ideology has evidently demanded that the link be maintained and used to further the government's ends. The alternative followed in the West – that the drama be allowed to become

171

divorced from the life of the people – has been rejected by the Chinese as unrealistic.

During the Cultural Revolution, the professional theatre in China had almost ceased to function, apart from the performance of a few 'model' revolutionary dramas. Towards the end of 1969, the authorities began to promote revised versions of the model revolutionary Peking operas. The entire texts of certain pieces were printed in *Red Flag* and other journals, and it became clear that the government was determined to begin a programme of reviving the Chinese theatre from the inactivity from which it had suffered during the Cultural Revolution. This was the beginning of the seventh phase. The revision of texts appears to have centred almost entirely on ideological matters. Heroes must now radiate revolutionary optimism and faith in Mao's concept of communism. Due emphasis must be laid upon their 'flesh-and-blood relationship with the masses' and on their willingness to devote their whole lives to the service of the people. Playwrights must portray villains as brutal, hypocritical, and without gentleness or other redeeming features. In other words, the class struggle, or 'struggle between the two lines', must be expressed sharply and intensely. The current concept of characterization in China, which is due largely to Chiang Ch'ing, differs widely from that predominant in the West. Most Westerners prefer a less black-and-white approach and would feel that the characters in modern revolutionary Chinese drama lack subtlety.

The first task in the revival of the drama after the Cultural Revolution was to ensure that the revised versions of the model items were accepted by the people. Reports came in from most of China's provinces that propaganda troupes were active in popularizing them. At first the emphasis was placed on the Peking Opera – and especially on several of their special model pieces – but more recently the troupes specializing in the regional styles have also revived. Although the efforts of these companies were at first concentrated on adapting the model Peking operas to the local styles, there has been plenty of scope for the re-emergence of other themes in the regional drama, provided that they are revolutionary in character and accord with the principles laid down by Chiang Ch'ing during the Cultural Revolution.

At about the time of the Tenth Congress of the Chinese Communist Party in August 1973, China entered a new political phase with the beginning of the Campaign to Criticize Lin Piao and Confucius. Lin was the former Minister of Defence who in 1969 was designated Mao

Tse-tung's successor as Party Chairman, but died in an air crash in September 1971 while trying to escape from China after plotting to assassinate Mao. Confucius (551–479 BC), once revered in China as a sage, was now seen as the symbol of reaction, the man who tried to hold back the wheel of history and restore the power of the slave-owning classes against the rising land-owning classes. Both men, in fact, symbolized reaction, and it was with this concept that the Campaign was primarily concerned, because the Chinese were determined not to give up the gains of their revolution and revert to old attitudes. The Campaign was thus in a very real sense a continuation of the Cultural Revolution.

The period of the Campaign against Lin Piao and Confucius has seen the continuing revival of the regional theatre, which was given prominence in the North China Theatrical Festival held in Peking from 22 January to 18 February 1974. It has also witnessed a series of strong attacks against one of the dramas performed at the Festival, a Shansi opera (*Chin-chü*) called *San-shang T'ao-feng* (*Going Up Peach Peak Three Times*), the producers of which were accused of trying to negate class struggle and to restore the pre-Cultural Revolutionary order through their work. This was the first time since the Cultural Revolution that such attacks had been directed against a drama being currently performed in a festival of note.

It would be possible to see the period of the Campaign against Lin Piao and Confucius as a further (eighth) phase in the history of Communist policy towards the theatre in China. Yet the most important features of the theatre during the Campaign have been the persistence of the ideals and approaches which had been followed from 1969 onwards. There has been little change in the tone of articles on artistic theory in the Chinese press. The same attitudes to the portrayal of characters in dramas, and the same attention to class struggle, have been evident. At the same time, there has been a continuing emphasis on expanding the number and variety of theatrical productions available to audiences. In view of these factors, it is surely more reasonable to see the period of the Campaign against Lin Piao and Confucius merely as a continuation of the last of the seven phases, which began in 1969.

At the time of writing (June 1974) the traditional drama was still banned to the public, and it may be interesting to speculate on its future. When I visited China in May and June 1973, I was struck by the regrowth of interest in traditional forms and themes in art. Indeed,

173

in one exhibition of the industrial arts which I saw in Peking, classical themes outweighed revolutionary by a considerable margin. In this context, the revival of traditional theatre seems a logical step. During an interview with Li Hsi-fan, a high-level cadre for the section on literature in the *People's Daily*, I was told that some classical pieces had already been shown to selected visiting dignitaries and would probably be performed publicly again in due course.

Has the Campaign to Criticize Lin Piao and Confucius forced the Chinese cultural authorities to change their minds about the apparently proposed revival of classical dramas? In mid-1974 it certainly seemed so. But there is one curious feature of the Campaign which would suggest that this change of mind may not be permanent. No campaign in the history of post-1949 China has focussed so consciously on the past as this one. It was based on an attack on Confucius for trying to hold back history, but more striking is the fact that it has seen positive and not merely negative features in China's ancient history, being in this respect strikingly different from the Cultural Revolution. Ch'in Shih-huang, an emperor condemned in Confucian historiography, was held up as a good example because he completed the overthrow of the slave-owning classes and the rise to power of the new land-owners. Some space has been given in the Chinese press to analyses of the 'struggle between the two lines' in Ch'in Shih-huang's court. If there is virtue in looking to an ancient emperor for a positive lesson, the way is surely open to transpose the same trend to the stage in the form of traditional dramas.

Such dramas, should they return, will almost certainly be different in emphasis from those seen before 1964. Although they will probably retain most of the costumes and stage movements of the past, they will probably emphasise peasant revolution and the heroism of the masses more strongly, and Ch'in Shih-huang's struggle to change society will be one likely theme. There seems no possibility of resuscitating drama based on fairy stories, and it is probable that the scholars and beauties so popular in former times will give place to the leaders of the struggle against feudal oppression.

THE POPULAR REACTION TO REVOLUTIONARY DRAMA

Even allowing for the return of interest in tradition in recent years, the fact remains that the Chinese theatre has undergone deep change, and this was bound to provoke opposition, as the Communists themselves recognize, and even stress, in their constant references to the 'struggle between the two lines'. On the other hand, in their organs of propaganda they usually try to give the impression of widespread – and sometimes almost universal – support for their policies. Chinese sources, while admitting that there has been some hostility to the drama reforms, have stressed that the majority of the population have supported them. Many foreign commentators, however, have emphasized the opposition and represented the affirmations of support as propaganda. It is, therefore, worth attempting an assessment of how actors and the people at large have reacted to the revolutionizing of the theatre.

On 18 July 1964 the New China News Agency claimed that certain veteran Peking Opera actors, including Ma Lien-liang, Shang Hsiao-yün, Hsün Hui-sheng, Chou Hsin-fang and Kai Chiao-t'ien, supported the modern plays. But there is ample evidence that not all actors favoured the new trends. In June 1963 the *Canton Evening News* (*Yang-ch'eng wan-pao*) wrote of the revolutionary dramas that 'the troupes spare no effort to avoid such plays and try not to perform them often'.[14] One member of a company in Canton is quoted as saying that 'the staging of modern plays is just like a gust of wind that blows for a while and then passes away'. Such remarks led one Western journalist to write in 1964, in an influential Hong Kong weekly, that 'strong resistance to the modern plays is coming, as might be expected, from the professional actors themselves'.[15]

In June 1965 the problem was stated in a Shanghai newspaper as follows:

The socialist remoulding of our theatrical teams is still incomplete. From the political point of view, the great majority of our theatrical workers are willing to be revolutionized, but it is still only the minority that have a thoroughly proletarian world view. Quite a number are still burdened in their brains with confused individual-istic notions which prevent them from serving the workers, peasants, soldiers and socialism wholeheartedly. . . . A few have not made their decision to fight for the revolutionary modern plays, or have made their decision but are still not wholly reliable.[16]

When the Cultural Revolution started the press claimed that 'bourgeois authorities' had tried to prevent actors from performing modern plays, that only old-fashioned actors preferred the classical pieces, and that the main thrust of the profession was in favour of the revolutionary drama. Chiang Ch'ing was given the credit for having persuaded the artists to resist 'counter-revolutionary revisionists' like P'eng Chen, who, it was claimed, wanted them to perform traditional dramas. A New China News Agency report of 30 September 1968 informed its readers that P'eng Chen had invited some actors, including T'an Hsin-p'ei's great-grandson T'an Yüan-shou, to his house to discuss their efforts at performing revolutionary drama. It said that he 'pretended to show "sympathy" with their attempts, but he urged them to put on old operas since this is what they were "expert" in. Tan Yuan-shou dared to object to Peng Chen's face: "No. From now on I will work one hundred per cent on revolutionary operas on contemporary themes." '

One gains the impression that many actors initially hostile to the revolutionary theatre saw no point in continuing their opposition once it became clear that the 'gust of wind' was to continue blowing. After all, few people can resist constant pressure, and, to the average actor, there is little that can be more important than the feeling that he is playing a vital part in society. It is not difficult to imagine an artist, who has been trained to perform traditional pieces, moving from dismay at the new plays to being 'willing to be revolutionized', though he is 'still burdened with confused individualistic notions'. Probably most actors came to enjoy playing revolutionary roles. Acting standards certainly remained high, as I can testify after seeing many modern plays performed in China, and most of the greatest traditional actors have taken up the revolutionary theatre. A good example is the 'painted face' actor Yüan Shih-hai. I have seen him perform in modern dramas and have heard him lecture about them; both as actor and as expositor he left me in little doubt that he favoured the new dramas.

On the other hand, support for the new is quite different from approval of the total ban on the old drama. Resentment against the prohibition has certainly remained in some acting circles, as is clear from the fact that so many traditional actors were criticized or physically attacked during the Cultural Revolution. Chou Hsin-fang and Ma Lien-liang, both claimed earlier as supporters of the revolutionary theatre, were among their number, and it was reported in Hong Kong that both died during the upheaval. Moreover, Li Hsi-fan told me during an interview with him in June 1973 that 'individualistic notions' were far from extinct in the minds of actors, especially those of the older generation, even though they were substantially less prevalent than before the Cultural Revolution.

In assessing the reaction of the people at large to the drama reforms one is faced with similarly conflicting evidence. One can cite the case of the young postal worker, mentioned in the *People's Daily* of 26 February 1964, who preferred attending performances of classical drama to taking part in the activities of his collective group. Or one can quote an actor who claimed in Hong Kong that the troupe to which he had belonged, which performed modern plays, had found no welcome in the Hunanese countryside in the winter of 1963-64. Similar stories appeared in the Chinese press, especially in that of the Yangtze Valley regions. One newspaper reported that when Shanghai's Shaohing Opera company went into the countryside and performed the modern drama *To-yin* ('Stealing the Seal'), the audience threw stones at the actors and drove them away.[17] Such reports led one Western commentator to remark in 1964 that 'the socialist revolution in China may have captured the lives of the Chinese populace, but the millions choosing to stay away from the revolutionary theatre suggest that it has yet to capture their imaginations'.[18]

Opposition to the suppression of the classical theatre has persisted. In mid-1968 many wall posters complained that the traditional culture was being destroyed, and in late 1969 the theoretical journal of the Communist Party's Central Committee, *Red Flag* (*Hung-ch'i*), admitted that certain elements were still trying to disparage the modern revolutionary dramas.[19] The fact that in 1973 there should have been talk of reviving selected classical pieces suggests that the traditional theatre still enjoys a certain following.

On the other hand, one does not have to look far for evidence that many people have responded enthusiastically to the new drama and prefer it to the old. The same article in the Shanghai newspaper, quoted earlier,[20] which acknowledged the lack of interest in revolution displayed by many actors, also stated flatly that 'the masses of workers, peasants and soldiers not only want to watch modern revolutionary operas, they also want to arrange and perform them themselves'. The well known Szechwanese Opera actress Ch'en Shu-fang reported that when she had performed in a modern revolutionary opera in May 1971 a poor peasant of about seventy said: 'I've lived through several dynasties and seen quite a few Szechwanese operas, but they were nothing but emperors, kings, generals, and ministers. But today's Szechwanese Opera can portray the heroic images among us labouring people, and that's really marvellous.' Other people told her: 'We can understand this kind of Szechwanese Opera, and we enjoy watching it.'[21]

The truth is that there are Chinese who welcome the modern drama and are unconcerned at the decline of the old, and those who resent the suppression of the traditional drama, even though they might, in many cases, also enjoy the new. To determine which group is the larger is very difficult, if not impossible. I have certainly formed the impression, however, that the revolutionary theatre has struck very deep roots in the imagination of the Chinese populace.

My reasons for this conclusion are based on personal experience in China over the years 1964–66. I remember discussing the problem of the classical theatre with a middle-aged Chinese friend of mine who had been brought up under the Kuomintang. I told him that I myself regretted the passing of an art which seemed to me one of the most perfect ever devised. He replied: 'China has embarked on a revolution, and there will always be cultural casualties under these circumstances. A glance at any of history's revolutionary movements will show this to be true. I myself was brought up to love the traditional theatre, but I do not miss it now. And, more important, my children have no use for those old dramas. What relation do they have to the lives and interests of China's youth?'

Several of my Chinese friends, especially among the young, confirmed to me that they had given up attending the classical theatre because they found it boring. I do not discount the possibility that some of them were motivated by political expediency, but I doubt whether this was so of the majority. I have found that the same attitude prevails among the younger generation of my Chinese friends from Taiwan, Hong Kong and Singapore, who point out that where there is radical social change there are likely to be profound changes in cultural tastes.

Finally, my experience does not confirm the contention that the people are staying away from the modern plays. During my stay in China I made it my business to go to the modern theatre as often as possible. I went not only at the invitation of my hosts to large theatres where capacity audiences could easily have been arranged in advance, but also, alone and on my own initiative, visited small playhouses in the back alleys of Peking; here I saw modern plays, as, indeed, I did in virtually all the twenty cities which I visited. On every occasion the theatre was nearly or completely full, and the audience invariably seemed to be enjoying the play. It is surely fair to conclude that most Chinese are patronizing the revolutionary drama from choice rather than from compulsion.

Although I did not enjoy nearly as much freedom of movement during a second much shorter visit to China in May and June 1973, and my impressions may therefore not be reliable, everything I saw and heard suggested that modern revolutionary art is still popular, even though traditional styles are simultaneously returning to favour. All the performances which I attended were packed out and well received. At one open-air performance which I saw in Canton the audience of several thousand included children, and even babies; they reacted to a shower of rain not by leaving, but by hoisting umbrellas.

It is no more surprising that the revolutionary society of China should produce and enjoy revolutionary art than that the ideals of the non-revolutionary Western peoples should be reflected in their art. China may be bound by its traditions to some extent, but it is neither unchangeable nor unwilling to change. If the impressions which I have formed are valid, and the taste of the Chinese population as a whole is indeed becoming adapted to the new theatre and to new art in general, then it is unlikely that the classical theatre will ever again enjoy the overwhelming popularity of former times. Possibly it will finally occupy a position not unlike that held by the ancient arts in the West today: strong, yet secondary in appeal to art which portrays the life of the present or of the recent past.

11 The Theatre and the Actor*

In China, where serious differences in riches and status are part of the legacy of the past, intensive and persistent education has been necessary to make even a start towards achieving the Communist objective of social equality, and the drama has been one of the main vehicles of propaganda. Naturally, the authorities have tried to make the drama available to all citizens, not only because the poor should enjoy any right granted to the rich, but also because the educative powers of the drama must be made to permeate the whole of society. The government has also attempted to eradicate the most glaring instances of the social stratification inherent in China's traditional theatrical life. Actors should be universally respected by society, whether they be young or old, experienced or inexperienced, famous or unknown; the theatres, likewise, should be constructed so as to give equal opportunities to all members of the audience.

THEATRES IN THE CITIES

Despite some significant reservations to be discussed later, it can be said that theatres in Chinese cities today reflect the Communist rejection of privilege and social stratification. Theatres built since 1949 are uniform in architectural style, and their designers appear to have followed the unimaginative standard modern Russian model. Building costs have been kept to the minimum, and comfort and beauty have consequently been of secondary importance. Carpets, for instance, are not usually found either in the foyer or in the auditorium, and decoration is very meagre both inside and outside.

The auditorium of contemporary Chinese theatres (whether newly

* See Ill. 31, p. 142.

built, or merely refurbished) is very similar to the pattern found in Western cinemas. Seats are arranged simply in rows and are usually all identical. In the biggest houses there might be two or even three tiers, but the differences between the various sections of the theatre lie solely in their positions and not in the physical comfort of the seats themselves. We no longer find areas of a theatre in which people pay to stand, nor private boxes which the poor can enter only as the servants of the rich.

Many of the habits connected with theatre-going in the past have now disappeared. The arrangement of the seats in rows precludes the custom whereby people sipped tea and sat around tables, chatting. Nowadays, the audience is expected to give its whole attention to what is happening on the stage. Theatres are no longer teahouses. Refreshments are now taken only during the interval, just as in a Western theatre, and the once ubiquitous vendors have virtually disappeared. To find a man selling food, drinks or souvenirs during the performance itself would be unthinkable nowadays, at least in the main cities. Those who require sustenance buy it from small stores just outside the auditorium, or, if there are no such stalls, as is frequently the case in small theatres, they go to a nearby market or shop.

One result of these changes has been that the noisiness which once characterized Chinese audiences has largely vanished. People rarely shout approval during the play itself and generally reserve their display of enthusiasm for the end. They then applaud, just as in the West, but the actors show their appreciation not by bowing but by clapping also. This charming practice of performers applauding their audiences is Russian in origin, and, indeed, with a few exceptions, the changes just described show clearly the Western influence which has in the main resulted from the Russian presence in the 1950s. This situation is ironic: the Chinese Communists have based their policy in theatrical matters on the desirability of maintaining a close link between the people's life and attitudes on the one hand and the drama on the other, yet have discarded many of the customs which formerly helped to strengthen this link. The present government is surely right to try to eliminate social stratification from the theatres, but it seems to me that the Chinese have not altogether served their own interests by rejecting the traditional structure and layout of their own theatres and adopting those of the West.

In the use of programmes, similarly, the trend has also been in the direction of conformity with the West. The bills which were prevalent in the past are still sometimes issued, but it has become increasingly common to print pamphlets or folded sheets which are sold for a small sum. These relate the story of the drama or, if several one-act plays are to be shown, the stories of all the pieces. They list the cast and often include pictures of scenes from the dramas. If the regional style announced is foreign to the audience, its history and characteristics are described. This ensures that the audience will always have some idea of what it is to see and hear. One effective method of explaining the play to the audience is to project the text of the sung passages on to a small screen beside the stage, so that everybody can read the words as they are being sung by the actors. The problem of differences of dialect is thereby overcome, since the written characters are uniform throughout China. This practice (followed at every professional performance which I attended in a Chinese theatre) seems to me an excellent one which might well be adopted in the West.

The desire of the authorities to maintain the people's interest in the drama is apparent in other respects also. Tickets are cheap, and even the poorest citizen can afford to go to the theatre. Prices vary according to the positions of seats, but the range is very small by comparison with European or American practice. Organizations frequently encourage theatre-going among their members by buying blocks of seats. This is done especially after a particular drama has been praised in the press, and one sometimes sees busloads of people arriving at a theatre from a factory or institute not long before the performance is due to start. Theatre-goers are also aided, as in other countries, by the extensive advertising of performances both at the theatres themselves and in the local press. The circulation figures of the newspapers are small by Western standards, but most people have access to newspapers, because the main dailies are posted on public notice-boards. This practice is made possible by the fact that few papers consist of more than six or eight pages, since the most important of them carry no commercial advertising matter.

Although the drama is, then, readily available to most urban Chinese, it would be a mistake to claim that the socialist objective of complete equality has been achieved in this field. For example, there is considerable competition to buy tickets for the best performances, and organizations are invariably given priority over individuals, with the result that many people either have to be content with the poorer seats, or may even fail to obtain seats at all. A letter written in March 1955 by an ordinary citizen of Peking to the monthly *Hsi-chü pao*

(*Theatre News*) raises complaints which are no doubt harboured by many Chinese enthusiasts for the drama. He writes: 'I am a theatre-lover, but over the last year I have encountered difficulties and have been unable to go to the theatre. Whenever I open a Peking newspaper I see that there are indeed many theatres and troupes. . . . But if I chance to notice one or two outstanding pieces, they are invariably shown as "booked out, booked out". If I really want to see them, I have to stand day and night in a queue to buy tickets. In Peking it is very usual to have to queue all day and night for seats.'[1] The writer goes on to complain that the most famous actors performed too rarely. He cites specific cases of lengthy absences from the stage for unexplained reasons. It is perhaps even more significant that the editors of the journal add that they have been receiving a number of similar letters.

Complaints of the kind raised in the letter just quoted are not without foundation. Privilege certainly persists in Chinese theatres. In 1956 one correspondent in *Theatre News* was very angry because some senior officials in a town in Kansu had taken it upon themselves to choose the programme for the evening at a local theatre. What was worse, they had one rather indecent play performed, and 'the masses were highly indignant at the drama company and those who had selected the piece'.[2] Occurrences of this sort are probably infrequent, and other kinds of privilege are more widespread. Many big Chinese theatres have special rooms in which foreigners or senior cadres can sit comfortably and drink tea during the interval. I have myself sometimes been ushered into such places, both before and after the Cultural Revolution. A more obvious temptation for someone in authority is to take the best seats for himself. Even as late as 1969 the New China News Agency felt obliged to berate cadres because 'when watching an opera they "need" to occupy seats in the first three rows'.[3] This sort of privilege is commonplace in most countries, and it is an interesting comment on the idealism of the Chinese that they should still be trying to stamp it out.

PROFESSIONAL DRAMA IN RURAL AREAS

If there are serious obstacles in the way of democratizing the practices of theatre-going in the cities, the problems involved in bringing drama to the millions of Chinese peasants in the rural areas are even greater. The wandering companies of the past, in their traditional form, would clearly be unacceptable in a society such as that of contemporary

China. The actors in these troupes did not stay together permanently, had no roots and were extremely difficult to control. Nowadays, every Chinese must belong to an organization and be based on some kind of residence; he cannot simply wander around the country independently and remain accountable to nobody. Although many itinerant companies of the old kind still existed during the 1950s, government pressure appears to have led to their disappearance since then.

Yet itinerant companies still flourish, though transformed in nature and administration. The practice today is for Party authorities and theatre managements to send troupes based on the towns and cities to the country areas, where they move from place to place performing for the peasants. In this way it has been possible to retain the function of the earlier strolling companies (namely, to bring drama to the rural population) and eliminate the disadvantages. The actors are no longer rootless or independent, and some control can be exerted over them.

Contemporary strolling companies naturally have much in common with those of the past. They can perform almost anywhere: on a temporary stage in a market-place or by a river, on a level strip of ground in the fields, or in a meeting-hall or teahouse. There have, however, been changes. The temple stage has fallen from favour, since the rural theatre is no longer based on religious festivals. Another modern development is the prevalence of rural club-houses, many of which include a permanent stage.

Since 1949 the organs of Chinese propaganda have persistently encouraged the urban theatrical companies periodically to abandon their settled life in the cities and give open-air performances in the countryside. The Party has extolled many 'model' troupes, whose members have made real efforts to bring their art to the maximum number of peasants. One example is the Shanghai Opera (*Hu-chü*) Company of Sungkiang, near Shanghai:

> This troupe had often gone on tour to the rural areas in recent years, but owing to the size of their casts and bulky stage sets, they had to limit their performances to the towns, so thousands of peasants never got a chance to see them. . . . To reach more peasants therefore the . . . Troupe in May last year divided itself into several small working teams. Carrying light stage props on shoulder poles, these 12-man teams can go anywhere and quickly stage a show upon arrival. Where a regular play can't be given, two or three can stage an entertainment in a tea house, during a work break, or for old commune members right there in their homes. When needed, two or three teams can be called together to give a bigger show.[4]

Members of the new kind of itinerant company are expected not only to perform for the peasants but to help them in other ways too, and generally to share their life. A typical newspaper report claimed that a group of Peking actors, music teachers and students, which toured the countryside at the end of 1963, had 'carried buckets of water for the peasants of the communes, mended their clothes, knitted them woollen jumpers, laid brick walls and cleaned the lavatories'.[5] An actor of a company attached to a small town in Kiangsu records that 'during the busy season members of the troupe often help with agricultural work, performing during rest breaks'.[6] A charming picture indeed! Naturally it is the government's hope and claim that the peasants appreciate the players' efforts and help them in return. The Kiangsu actor just cited remarks that the villagers did everything they could for the visiting company, 'from setting up the stage and providing living quarters to lending the actors stoves and pots, and bringing water for them'.

One particular kind of travelling company is the 'caravan troupe', which originated in Inner Mongolia in 1957. This differs from the normal professional theatre group in that its prime task is to tour the countryside, especially in the areas of the National Minorities, where the vast expanses of land and relatively sparse population require the troupes to travel constantly. Whereas the standard city-based companies spend about eight months acting in the cities, and four touring the rural areas, for the caravan troupes these proportions are reversed. Most caravan troupes are small and usually perform a widely varied repertoire of short and simple pieces. Since they rarely stay in one place for long, it follows that their members must be young and without family commitments. After marriage they either take it in turns to tour or else leave the company altogether. The responsibilities of the caravan troupes are otherwise similar to those of the standard touring professionals: they help the herdsmen or peasants in their daily tasks and expect assistance in return.

This system, however, has not always worked well in practice. In 1956 the editors of *Theatre News* commented that during rural tours 'quite a few professional companies . . . have not only not been helped everywhere, but have been obstructed in all kinds of ways'.[7] Yet it is probably the villagers who regard the touring companies with enthusiasm, rather than *vice versa*. For the peasants the troupes provide not only entertainment, but a change from their normal routine. For many of the urban drama groups, on the other hand, the prospect of touring the rural areas may be unappealing. The constant appearance of articles in the press urging city actors to embark on these tours suggests that the response has not been entirely satisfactory to the Party. Moreover, complaints from the actors have sometimes been published in Chinese newspapers. A particularly serious complaint was expressed in 1956 by an actor called Huang Chen-yüan, who belonged to a Hupeh Opera company based on Hwangkang, near Wuhan. His troupe roamed around the countryside not because it had been sent there, but because theatre facilities in the city were insufficient to keep the company in work there all the year round. The picture Huang gives of his life as a touring actor is far from rosy. He complains of overwork and inadequate food; and 'in the peasant villages and mountain regions it is not uncommon for us to hurry as many as twenty miles in wind, hail, rain or snow'.[8]

The most important difference between Huang Chen-yüan's troupe and the standard strolling companies in socialist China is ideological: in theory, actors should tour the countryside not for economic advantage, but in order to educate the peasants and themselves. It has been one of Chairman Mao's chief aims to break down the barriers between the urban and the rural areas, and this has involved persuading town- and city-dwellers to try to get to know their rural counterparts. Actors are by no means the only members of the urban population who have been encouraged to visit the countryside. In recent years the same course has been urged, for instance, on doctors and young intellectuals. Indeed, since the Cultural Revolution, many millions of students have left their city homes for the country and, unlike the touring actors, have in many cases been persuaded to live there for a long time.

These ideas have been even more prevalent since the Cultural Revolution than before it. It has been stressed even more powerfully that professional actors should tour the countryside, and the more remote the areas visited, the better. No peasant, it has been insisted, should be denied the opportunity to watch professional performances. The emphasis on rural tours has consequently become so strong that it is common to find that no plays at all are to be seen in the cities, even in the largest, at certain periods. During a nine-day stay in Peking in 1973 I saw not a single play advertised in the press – only one ballet.

THE AMATEUR THEATRE

The encouraging of city-dwellers to live in the countryside is but one of the many aspects of life in contemporary China which demonstrates the paramount place held in it by ideology. Another aspect is the stress laid by the government on the amateur theatre. The Party hopes that if the ordinary people are encouraged to act in plays themselves, they will absorb Maoist thinking more directly and completely than would ever be possible for them merely through watching plays performed by professional actors.

The Communists set about promoting amateur acting as soon as they came to power, and it was officially reported that by the end of 1950 no fewer than seven thousand amateur peasant troupes flourished in the north-eastern provinces alone.[9] The authorities encouraged the founding of cultural associations, including dramatic companies, in all sections of the community. In the cities the trade unions sponsor and subsidize workers' amateur theatrical groups, and there are similar activities in the universities and in the schools, as well as among the peasantry. Funds for recreational purposes have not always been easy to acquire in the Chinese countryside, and there are curious echoes from the past in the means employed there to raise money for amateur troupes. The following note (published in 1953) on a theatre association in a Chekiang village is particularly striking: 'Recently a decision was made to give the club an acre or so of land, the crops from which would finance its activities. And the peasants, into whose lives it has brought joy and new ideas, are volunteering to do a day's work on "our club's fields".'[10]

This group arranged its own dramas, laying heavy emphasis on such contemporary social themes as the suppression of the former activities of match-makers. Right from the start, the government expressed the wish that the modern drama should take root among amateur companies. Some amateurs resisted this pressure, and articles in the press, urging that more attention should be paid to contemporary themes, are not difficult to find. One typical article, printed early in 1959, deplored that Szechwanese amateurs were too keen on performing traditional pieces and suggested reasons why they should change their attitude:

It costs a great deal of money for amateur troupes to prepare and perform old-fashioned pieces like historical dramas, whereas there are no such difficulties in the way of performing modern plays. The costumes and stage properties are relatively easy to find – at the most only a little work is required – and do not cost much. In particular, it is possible to fit [the themes of the plays] in with the main activities of the time, material can be found locally and dramas can be arranged and performed by the people themselves. In this way we can give expression to the creativity of the masses on a large scale and strengthen the concrete functions of political service in literature and art. This is the most important point.[11]

It was to be expected that the writer should stress the ideological aspect of the matter. But he was also right to pay attention to the practical circumstances of amateur drama. The highly colourful costumes of the traditional Chinese theatre are not easily available to the average citizen, and the stylized movements are extremely difficult to master. It is therefore natural that amateurs should take more easily to the modern than to the classical drama, and that they should be far more willing to follow the Party's lead than their professional brothers. This was amply shown when, in 1963, the government moved towards the total elimination of the traditional theatre. We saw in the last chapter that the government was willing to admit that there was resistance to this policy among professional actors. On the other hand, glowing reports appeared about the response of the amateurs:

> In our East Chinese factories, peasant villages and army units, there are amateur dramatic troupes run by the workers, peasants and fighters themselves. They always insist on performing revolutionary modern plays. They sing the praises of the people they themselves really favour and perform the stories they themselves really want. They have been supported by the broad masses, and no number of perverse gusts can blow them down. In the last two years [since 1963], spurred on by the whole revolution in the theatre, the amateur theatrical movement among the workers, peasants and soldiers has widened, and produced many good plays and much talent.[12]

Nevertheless, the amateur theatre has presented some problems – above all, the trend towards professionalization. Many newspaper reports, especially before the Cultural Revolution, have complained that some amateur actors devote so much time and effort to the theatre that their normal work suffers. Since amateur drama is intended to heighten the political consciousness of the people and hence actually to increase production, such a fault must clearly be condemned severely. It has been partly to overcome the danger of professionalization that the government has always urged that plays performed by amateurs should be short and simple.

Since the beginning of the Cultural Revolution the amateur has assumed a new importance in the Chinese theatre. One reason for this is that the professional actors were virtually in abeyance during the movement and have been slow to return to their normal level of activity. But a more significant reason is that the protagonists of the Cultural Revolution strongly opposed the notion that an elite of professionals was desirable, on the grounds that such people tended to be city-bound and that their services did not benefit the majority of the people. Despite the previous policy of sending urban actors on tours of the rural areas, professional performers were as much exposed to this criticism as experts in other fields.

Both practical and ideological factors, then, have encouraged the expansion of amateur drama since 1966. Amateurs remained active even at the height of the Cultural Revolution and have become even more active since. I have elsewhere estimated the number of peasant amateur actors in China in 1960 at about seven million.[13] In June 1973 Li Hsi-fan, of the *People's Daily*, told me that by then the total number of amateur actors in China was 'several tens of millions'. In almost every factory, school, university and commune brigade that I visited at that time, I was told that amateur troupes were active there. In many factories, every workshop supports its own theatre group and the workers often write their own plays. Productions are cheap to mount, and any necessary funds are supplied by the clubs, trade unions, or similar bodies. Contrary to the practice prevailing before the Cultural Revolution, there is nowadays no charge for admittance to amateur performances.

To judge from those productions that I have seen, the performers act and sing with great verve and enthusiasm. Admittedly, the plays presented tend to be too moralistic in tone to appeal to the taste of most Westerners, and the plots still tend to lack variety. It must be recognized, however, that the fostering of the amateur theatre in China cannot help but bring the drama to ever larger sections of the community, and is bound to reveal a great deal of latent talent and creativity among the people.

One group of actors which should be mentioned separately are those of the People's Liberation Army (P.L.A.). These form a bridge between this section of the chapter and the next, because although the majority are amateurs, the P.L.A. also runs some professional companies whose full-time job is to ensure the ideological correctness and morale of the troops through their dramatic performances. The Chinese Communist army has been active in both the amateur and the professional theatre since its beginning in 1927 and its actors played a significant propaganda role in winning success for the revolution. It

189

was also of vital importance in the propagation of the modern revolutionary drama during the period leading up to the Cultural Revolution. Its role is no less important today, and no visitor to China can help being struck by the large number of public performances given by the P.L.A. theatre groups.

THE PROFESSIONAL ACTOR IN CONTEMPORARY CHINA

According to Li Hsi-fan, the number of professional actors in China in mid-1973 was 'several hundred thousand'. They are thus far less numerous than the amateurs. Nevertheless, as full-time workers in the theatre, they are still the leaders in the field. It is important to consider how they have fared under Communist administration and what status they are accorded by society.

The reader will recall that actors suffered various kinds of legal and social discrimination in the past. The Communists, believing in the need for social equality, have made it their business to try to improve the position of the actor in the community. Their claim, right from the time when their revolution triumphed, has been that 'theatre workers are accorded the same respect as writers, scientists, painters and other brain workers'.[14] This should mean that the social status of actors has risen enormously in China, and that the contempt in which they were once held has vanished.

This is the ideal, but is it the reality? To determine the standing in society of any one group is never easy, and becomes all the more difficult in the case of a Communist country, where the values of the people are radically different from those of a Western democracy. In the last resort, social status means the respect or disrespect of other people, and to determine how the mass of Chinese regard their actors would require a gigantic social survey, which cannot be undertaken at present. It is impossible to do more than offer a few tentative suggestions.

Probably the most important test of social status in China today is political. The fact that the government has deliberately chosen the drama as a significant medium of direct propaganda has inevitably raised the importance of actors as a class and has given them a definite political function. Since the authorities have needed to woo their support, the people's respect for them has risen. On the other hand, the actors do not appear to have fulfilled their political role particularly well, and there is no evidence that, ideologically, they are especially progressive. On this score, the government and many of the people must still have reservations about them.

When the Communists first came to power, Mei Lan-fang, Chou Hsin-fang and a few other leading actors became members of the People's Political Consultative Conference, an organ which enjoyed considerable prestige just after the Communist victory. Moreover, both these artists, together with many others, became members of the Communist Party. These moves were certainly a boost to the acting profession. Yet it is uncertain whether the overall proportion of Party members among actors is as high as among scientists, factory workers or other urban groups. When a man as famous as Mei Lan-fang joins the Party, the news is given prominence in the press, but its importance for the social status of his profession as a whole is little more than marginal.

Another factor likely to encourage respect for actors and actresses among the people of China is the practice whereby many of them work together with peasants and other workers as a means of improving their art and integrating it more closely with popular feeling. The following anecdote, which concerns a famous Szechwanese actress, offers a typical instance:

> Chen Shu-fang once stayed in the home of a peasant woman about her own age [fifty]. They did farm work together. . . . Another time Chen Shu-fang went to work in a brick-kiln. A woman worker noticed that she had no gloves and immediately gave her her own, saying with a smile: 'We're glad you're here. Labour changes people.' Daily contacts with labour and the labouring people gradually made it possible for Chen Shu-fang to portray worker-peasant-soldier heroines on the stage. A new identification of the artist with audiences was built up.[15]

Social status judged from a political point of view can be a changeable phenomenon in contemporary China, because ideological attitudes have not been consistent in every particular. During some periods, such as the early and middle 1950s and the years 1963–66, the specialist or professional has been held in higher regard than at others. The Great Leap Forward (1958–60) and the Cultural Revolution both saw a distinct decline in the status of the specialist, and this no doubt influenced the degree to which the people respected professional actors and actresses.

Despite their overwhelming significance, ideology and politics form a somewhat theoretical gauge of social standing. A more concrete test is the standard of living, which, though it does not carry anything like the importance attached to it in the West, still constitutes to some extent a measure of social status in Communist China.

Actors' salaries vary greatly, ranging from the level of those of the poorest workers to those of the most highly qualified technicians. Before the Cultural Revolution some actors drew incomes as high as that of anyone in the land, and Ma Lien-liang received a salary about five times that earned by Chairman Mao. It is said that, much against his will, he was persuaded to have it drastically reduced.

Medical facilities and housing were greatly improved for actors and their families, as for other sections of the community. Progress was not very rapid, however, and at first many of those who needed these benefits failed to receive them. Articles published by Huang Chen-yüan and others in 1956 revealed the appalling living standards endured by many actors. The lack of medicines, overwork and inadequate diet had led to great hardship. Some artists were reported to be homeless and to be forced to sleep in the theatres; there were even cases of actresses suffering miscarriages caused by bad working conditions.[16]

The government's response to the spate of articles in the press revealing these conditions was to try to improve social security benefits for actors, partly through large grants of state money. Though the government's measures naturally did not solve all the problems immediately, they appear to have resulted in the gradual elimination of the direst cases of poverty. Today the great majority of actors enjoy a standard of living similar to that of urban workers. They are therefore very much better off than the rural peasantry and among the wealthier members of Chinese society.

The granting of social security benefits has solved one aspect of a substantial injustice: the bad treatment traditionally accorded to the theatrical profession as a whole in China. One of the worst features of an actor's life in the past was that in most parts of China he entered upon his career by being forced into an indenture which made him a virtual slave. The Communists claim to have improved greatly the conditions under which young actors are trained:

> The relationship between the master and his apprentice has been entirely reformed and the old contracts have been nullified. The [old training] system will be completely ended in the near future as more of the modern dramatic schools are opened. The first of these – the Experimental Academy of the Drama founded in Peking in

August, 1949, already has 154 students of both sexes from 8 to 19 years of age. They are receiving a complete education not only in dramatic art, but in ordinary school subjects as well, free of charge and with full board and lodging.[17]

The Experimental Academy was later renamed the Chinese Drama School, and in 1952 the age of entry was officially set at ten. The school was held up as a model whose practices should be followed elsewhere, though progress in inducing people to adopt them was slow. In 1955 a special study of China's drama schools was made by a certain Lin Yin, who found conditions in them to be poor. Lin discovered that the teachers at the schools were behaving too arbitrarily towards the students and wrote that 'although the system of beating and cursing [the students] has been essentially abolished in most companies, there are still a few teachers who behave like this towards their disciples'.[18] He also noted that too little care was taken of the children's education and moral upbringing and found cases of tobacco-smoking and drinking among the students. His most serious criticism was that far too little time was devoted to general education; he was afraid that many actors would grow up almost illiterate, just as their predecessors had done in the past. However, he did not mention the use of contracts and indentures, which had presumably disappeared by this time.

Despite the shortcomings mentioned by Lin, this state of affairs represents a tremendous advance on the past. It is true that some attempts had been made before 1949 to improve the conditions under which actors were trained, but they were on a fairly small scale, and few people worried about what went on in the minor drama schools. The Communists have extended the scope of the reforms enormously; this is clear from the fact that Lin Yin felt obliged to complain that some teachers beat their students, for thrashings were taken for granted in the past, except in a few schools. Life for a trainee may have been hard in 1955, but was certainly much better than it had been during the Republican period. Moreover, the efforts of the Communists to spread education (of their own kind, of course) and to stamp out corrupt practices have continued since the 1950s, and conditions in the training-schools have probably improved still further with the intensification of organization since then.

When considering the question of how older professional actors are treated and regarded one is faced, as usual, with conflicting reports. On the one hand, the Chinese press is constantly publishing the personal accounts of actors who are delighted with the improvements in their condition which have occurred under the Communists. For instance, Ch'en Shu-fang has described how the desperate life which she led under the Nationalists caused her to become an opium addict, and how she became completely cured under the care of the new government.[19] On the other hand, the indications are that Ch'en Shu-fang's case can be at least partly balanced by the experiences of others less fortunate than her. In 1952 Chou Yang condemned administrators who were dictatorial towards actors and actresses and admitted that 'there are even some cadres who treat the artistes in the same way as the feudal lords in the past treated them'.[20]

It takes time to change the attitudes of a nation, and it would be surprising if there were no remnants of former customs after only a few years of Communist government. A few cadres like the ones to which Chou Yang referred may still exist even now. But the overall thrust of social pressure and education today is in the direction of a greater respect for 'theatrical workers'. In the course of modernization Western societies have largely forgotten the contempt in which actors were once held in their midst. It is perfectly natural that a similar process of reform should now be taking place in China.

During the Cultural Revolution certain people continued to be criticized for wrong attitudes towards the acting profession. But this time their fault lay not in despising the ordinary artist but in fawning on the 'big stars'. Many of these the Red Guards condemned as 'monsters and demons' for their alleged attempts to carve out comfortable and famous careers for themselves and for their selfish lack of interest in the fortunes of others. Worse still, some Maoist factions accused the 'stars' of trying to revive China's ancient culture, an activity which the revolutionaries regarded as intolerable.[21] Considering the praise formerly lavished by the government on men like Mei Lan-fang, it is ironic to find famous actors considered arrogant and powerful enough to require cutting down to size.

It remains, then, a serious objective of the Maoists to raise actors to the same social level as people in other occupations, and also to even out the differences in status among the actors themselves. The present government gives the people greater direct encouragement to go to the theatre, and to establish their own amateur groups, than any previous one ever did. The reasons for these changes lie in the Communists' ideology generally, not simply in their desire to eliminate social stratification and privilege. The ideological and ethical content of the drama is more all-pervasive and intense than it was at any time during the imperial or Republican periods. The theatre and the actor are certainly useful to the revolution because of their power to transmit propaganda. And, for a contemporary Maoist, to serve the revolution is the ultimate virtue.

12 The Development of the Theatre from 1949*

The policies of the present Chinese government in theatrical matters have aroused much controversy both inside China and elsewhere. In the previous two chapters I have tried to set them in a political and social framework. It now remains to comment on some of the government's methods of popularizing drama, and to attempt an assessment of the Chinese theatre's progress since the Communist victory in 1949. In particular, it may be useful to describe the artistic and technical features of the modern drama, since these have been much debated.

THE TRADITIONAL DRAMA

It did not take China's new leaders long to embark on their programme of revitalizing the theatre. In 1959 the great actor Mei Lan-fang wrote: 'From 1951 on, provincial and other local government bodies sent a number of workers out, with generous financial aid, to explore the local opera in their areas. Old actors were located. Existing companies were aided. New ones were set up. Ancient plays and musical scores, sometimes existing only in the memories of singers and musicians, were rescued from oblivion. Something like 50,000 old plays have been brought to light.'[1]

In October and November 1952 the First National Festival of Classical and Folk Drama was held in Peking. Some thousand actors attended and performed nearly a hundred individual pieces, representing twenty-three different styles of local drama from all parts of the country. The festival was intended partly to demonstrate how far the nation's traditional drama had already been revived, and in his

* See Ills. 32–35, pp. 142–44.

concluding speech, made on 14 November, Chou Yang remarked that 'a national drama festival on such a large scale is the first of its kind in Chinese history'. The authorities also made it clear, however, that they hoped to stimulate theatrical reform through the festival, which was planned as a kind of contest. Chou remarked that 'prizes have been awarded to good operas and performances in order to encourage the reform of our dramatic art. These awards show what we approve and what we oppose.'[2] The holding-up of model examples had been a standard means of encouraging hard work since 1949, and, by his observation that 'contests are undoubtedly a good way of fostering the development of the drama', Chou Yang showed what he expected to result from the event.

The revival of the classical theatre continued, and many festivals were held in other parts of the country. In the autumn of 1954 exponents of many regional styles from east China were given their chance to compete in an important festival held in Shanghai, and provincial capitals followed suit. Theatrical performances also became unusually frequent and varied during the National Day holidays early in October each year. The largest such festival was held in Peking from 21 September to 10 October 1959 to celebrate the tenth anniversary of the founding of the People's Republic. There was a much stronger emphasis on Peking Opera than during the festival of 1952, and spoken plays, including a few by foreign dramatists (Shakespeare among them) were performed. The audiences also had the opportunity of seeing dramas in such major regional styles as Shaohing, Kwangtung and Hupeh Opera.

Despite the large number of old plays which, according to Mei Lanfang's claim, have been brought to light, the dramas shown in Peking and elsewhere have tended to be stereotyped in their themes, and only during festivals has a wide variety been performed. The fairy-tale play *The White Snake*,[3] and dramas on the love of Liang Shan-po and Chu Ying-t'ai, were performed so frequently that the people became tired of them. Indeed, lack of variety has been an endemic problem which largely accounts for the decline of popular interest in the traditional theatre just before mid-1964.

Another method used to spread the popularity of the drama was to give wide publicity to famous actors, especially old ones. Almost all the leading actors of Peking Opera and of the regional styles either remained in China after the Communists came to power or returned there after a few years' unsuccessful effort at making a living in Hong

197

Figs. 3 and 4 Two scenes from *Pai-she chuan* (*The White Snake*), adapted by T'ien Han from an ancient story. *Above*, the scholar-lover (*hsiao-sheng*, right) lends his umbrella to the beautiful woman (*ch'ing-i*, second from left), formerly a white snake. On her left is her maid-servant (*hua-tan*). He goes to her house the next day to take back his umbrella; the two fall in love, and they marry. *Below*, the beautiful woman (left) and the scholar-lover (centre) drink wine just after their marriage. On the right is a maid-servant. Seal engravings, Ch'ing period.

Kong or elsewhere. The list of actors who took part in the festival of 1959 is an impressive one. Among exponents of the Peking Opera were three of the 'four great *tan*', Mei Lan-fang, Shang Hsiao-yün and Hsün Hui-sheng (the fourth, Ch'eng Yen-chiu, had died in 1958), in addition to such well-known figures as Li Shao-ch'un, Ma Lien-liang, T'an Fu-ying, Yeh Sheng-lan and Yüan Shih-hai. The provinces also sent their best actors and actresses. Hung-hsien-nü and Ma Shih-tseng came from Canton; and from Shanghai Yü Chen-fei, perhaps the most famous *K'un-ch'ü* actor of recent times, and Hsü Yü-lan, a Shaohing Opera actress with a voice as beautiful as any I have heard in China.

Among the older actors none has been more lauded in the press than Mei Lan-fang, Chou Hsin-fang and Kai Chiao-t'ien. In 1955 there was a great fanfare to commemorate Mei's and Chou's fiftieth anniversaries on the stage, and the following year celebrations were held in Shanghai to honour the sixty years as an actor of Kai Chiao-t'ien, who was then aged seventy. The government has also encouraged these and other actors to record their lives and art in print. Mei and Kai have narrated their autobiographies in detail to amanuenses specially designated to write them down.[4] The attitudes of the older actors were also held up for praise. In one monthly journal we read of Mei Lan-fang and Chou Hsin-fang: 'It is correct to learn from them . . . their enthusiasm for artistic reform and penchant for revolution. The prominence of Mr Mei and Mr Chou in the performing arts cannot be separated from their progressive thought.'[5]

During the Cultural Revolution, however, virtually all the leading actors of the traditional theatre came under heavy attack. Horrific reports on the fate of some of them percolated to Hong Kong and were taken up eagerly in Taiwan. The press there claimed, for example, that Chou Hsin-fang had been beaten savagely by Red Guards and had died later in hospital as a result.[6] After the Cultural Revolution this situation was reversed, and the practice of encouraging drama by publicizing the activities of famous actors and actresses re-emerged.

Before the eclipse of the traditional theatre, the Communist effort to promote it had extended also to the gramophone. Records of traditional drama were available in large numbers in China's big cities. Such major styles as the Peking Opera were represented best, but it was possible to buy excerpts from plays even in quite obscure local styles. Many of the most famous plays, such as the Peking Opera *The White Snake*, the Shaohing Opera *Liang Shan-po and Chu Ying-t'ai* and the *Li-yüan hsi Ch'en San and Wu-niang*, were recorded complete on long-playing records, and many others were available in part, either on long-playing records or on the old-fashioned 78 r.p.m. records. The Chinese also followed a custom now well established in the West, that of re-recording popular excerpts sung by famous artists of the past. For instance, three long-playing records were made of Yü Shu-yen's old 78 r.p.m. records and six of Mei Lan-fang's. It is worth remarking, too, that records of traditional dramas were available in virtually all China's largest cities even after (in 1964) the works had ceased to be performed on the stage. As a resident in China, I was able to buy records of a wide range of regional drama in the music shops until as late as August 1966. It was not until the Red Guards came into the streets of Peking in that month that the record shops began to sell records of modern drama only.

On the other hand, cinemas had discontinued showing films of traditional plays at about the same time that stage performances of them ceased to be given. Previously, a number of dramas in local styles had been filmed and shown frequently. One example was *Liang Shan-po and Chu Ying-t'ai*, which became extremely popular both inside China and outside it. The technical standards of these films are extremely high, and during the 1950s and early 1960s they were instrumental in spreading goodwill for the present government, especially among Chinese in Hong Kong.

It is not only films that have brought the theatrical arts of mainland China to the outside world. The best troupes have visited countries as widely separated geographically and politically as Japan, Australia, the United Arab Republic, Hong Kong and France. Actors of the traditional Peking Opera have visited Europe (including London, on one occasion) three times since the Communists came to power in China: in 1955, 1958 and 1964. Their productions were received enthusiastically both by audiences and critics, and even 'led to several artistic creations by major figures of the contemporary French theatre world'.[7]

THE MODERN DRAMA

Although the Chinese theatre has exerted some influence in the West, the impact of the Western theatre on China has been much greater, and the modern Chinese drama owes a great deal to European models. The spoken play and ballet are of entirely Western origin, and even the revolutionary plays show Western influence to a marked degree.

As I have explained in earlier chapters, the spoken play fulfilled an important role before 1949 in popularizing drama on contemporary themes. It was natural, therefore, that the Communist government should strongly foster the spoken play; as T'ien Han remarked, it was the form 'most able to express the realistic struggle of life'.[8] It is especially suitable for amateurs, being easier to compose and perform than the traditional Chinese play. The authorities showed their support for the spoken, as they had done for the traditional, play by organizing festivals. The most important of these was held in Peking from 1 March to 4 April 1956, during which time some fifty plays were performed. Some of the best playwrights of the period before 1949 continued to write after the Communist victory, although they were much less prolific and, in the view of most Western critics, produced work of a lower standard. Virtually all the veteran dramatists of the spoken play, such as Ts'ao Yü and T'ien Han, were savagely criticized during the Cultural Revolution, and even before that campaign had begun the spoken play had been adopted by younger, politically more progressive writers. In my view the examples written and performed in China today are of poor quality. Chinese actors still do not appear to be at ease when performing this non-Chinese type of drama, and the manner in which the themes are presented remains too brash to carry conviction.

Another foreign form which the Chinese have grafted on to their own culture is opera of the Western type. This form (*ko-chü*) has been to some extent adapted by the Chinese to their own theatrical traditions. *Ko-chü*, however, differs from the pre-1949 classical theatre in several respects: scenery is employed, stage conventions are much closer to those of Western opera, costumes are less traditional in style, there are little or no acrobatics, and characters are not classified according to the old categories (*sheng, tan* and so on). The texture of the singers' voices is more similar to that of singers in Western opera than to that of actors in the traditional Chinese theatre, though it does possess a certain Chinese quality. Western instruments predominate in the orchestra. Melody is based on the Western scales (though some Chinese characteristics are present), and the harmony is of the Western type.

The Communists first adapted the Western opera to their own needs during the period (from December 1936 until March 1947) when Yenan was their capital, and they have fostered it ever since. However, progress in developing a good national repertoire of *ko-chü* has been slow, and there have been many complaints that authors and composers have paid too little attention to this form. A case in point is furnished by a letter written early in 1963 to the editor of *Theatre News* by a professional *ko-chü* actor in Hupeh.[9] He noted that there were nine *ko-chü* companies in his province, but that 'the problem of items for these troupes could not be solved'. 'Dear author and composer comrades,' he concluded, 'we stretch out our two hands to you for help, in the hope that you will give enthusiastic support.' Whether this particular actor received the help which he sought has not been recorded, as far as I know, but it is worth pointing out that none of the 'model' dramas written after the Cultural Revolution is a *ko-chü*, even though they include ballets and a symphony.

Possibly the most famous example of this Sinicized Western opera is *The White-haired Girl*, by Ho Ching-chih and Ting Yi, which was first performed in Yenan in April 1945. The story is believed by many Chinese to be true, and, though documentary proof is still lacking, the claim is not beyond the realms of possibility. The plot concerns a young peasant girl called Hsi-erh. Her father is desperately poor and, unable to pay his rent, is forced to sell her into slavery to the landlord. Then, overcome by remorse and despair, he commits suicide. Meanwhile, Hsi-erh, raped by her master, flees to the mountains, where she bears a child and undergoes privations so harsh that her hair turns white. Because of her unusual appearance, the local folk believe that she is a goddess and are consequently terrified of her. She is finally brought back to society by the Communist cadres of the Eighth Route Army. The moral of the opera is stated in the last scene but one: 'The old life forced men to turn into ghosts. . . . The new life changes ghosts into men.'[10] The final scene shows Hsi-erh taking the lead in accusing the landlord of his crimes.

The tunes of the opera are based largely on folk melodies. Since the stage movements, decor and style of singing owe far more to European (especially Russian) models than to Chinese, there is a curious mixture of cultures in this work. As a stage piece, it seems to me too long to be fully effective. Yet the moral message is blended with a very human story, and I found parts of *The White-haired Girl* extremely moving. I could certainly see that it was tremendously popular with the Chinese.

The plot of *The White-haired Girl* has been treated as a spoken play and has been adapted to several styles of regional Chinese theatre. In 1958 it was performed in a Peking Opera version, with an excellent cast, including Tu Chin-fang, 'Mei Lan-fang's successor', as Hsi-erh and Yüan Shih-hai as the landlord. It has also been filmed and, most important of all, has been adapted as a ballet which has come to be regarded as a 'model' drama. Curiously enough, this adaptation was made not in China but in Japan, where, early in 1955, the members of a certain ballet company 'were moved by the image of the "white-haired girl" ' in the Chinese film which they had seen and 'planned by this work to hasten cultural exchanges between China and Japan'.[11] In China itself *The White-haired Girl* was first adapted as a ballet in 1965 in Shanghai, where Chiang Ch'ing, who had for some time been trying, against opposition, to have such an idea accepted, enjoyed particularly strong influence. Since the Cultural Revolution, this ballet version also has ranked among the model dramas, and it was filmed in 1971.

Certain changes have been made in the story for this ballet, designed to intensify the portrayal of class struggle and the heroism of the people. In the new version Hsi-erh's father does not commit suicide, an act which would run counter to the theme of struggle against oppression, but is murdered by the landlord's henchmen. Hsi-erh is not raped, for the revolutionary masses cannot submit to such treatment, and consequently bears no child. It is other forms of suffering in the mountains that cause her hair to go white.

To my mind, the story was more dramatic in the original operatic version. Nevertheless, it seems to me that the arrangers have made the new version extremely convincing. In the scene in which Hsi-erh's hair goes white, there are successive vignettes showing the heroine fleeing from wild animals and undergoing other hardships. These vignettes are performed alternately by two ballerinas, so that the progressive transformation in the colour of the hair is shown very clearly and with great dramatic intensity. The music of the original *ko-chü* version is largely retained, and there are even singers in the pit who sing the principal songs from the *ko-chü*. One definite improvement is that the ballet is somewhat shorter than the *ko-chü* and thus both sharper and, to me at least, more moving.

There is a brief love scene in the ballet between Hsi-erh and an old village friend who has joined the Eighth Route Army. Although love interest has not been a significant feature of modern Chinese drama, especially since 1966, it is certainly not excluded altogether. When I questioned him on this point, Li Hsi-fan, the head of the literature and arts section of the *People's Daily*, assured me that love scenes were perfectly acceptable, provided they were 'proletarian'. He even suggested that they might play a more important part in Chinese drama in the future.

Besides the spoken play, *ko-chü* and ballet, the Chinese have also experimented in a form which they have described as a 'large-scale historical poem with music and dancing'.[12] The piece which has been referred to thus is *Tung-fang hung* (*The East is Red*), which was first performed during the National Day holidays of 1964 to mark the fifteenth anniversary of the founding of the People's Republic. It combined singing, dancing and recitation and contained a great deal of large-scale choral music. The orchestra used was Western in composition, the harmony was of Western character, and much care and effort had obviously been lavished on the spectacular sets. The piece, which was extravagantly praised in the press, was a realistic dramatization of the development of the Chinese revolution from the 1920s until the Communist victory.

In technical respects, the performance of *The East is Red* which I saw was impressive. Artistically, the work was considered too naïve by most Western spectators, though the Chinese audiences appeared to be extremely enthusiastic. One Western journalist wrote: 'It seems fairly certain that whatever the more sophisticated Chinese think about the dreariness of the endless propaganda themes, some of the message still gets across to the majority. After all in the West people grumble at advertising and sometimes laugh at its obviousness, but they continue to buy the products.'[13] Though political propaganda and commercial advertising differ widely in many ways, the comparison drawn here concerning their techniques and effect is surely apt. Yet it is only fair to add that *The East is Red* did not survive the Cultural Revolution and has not been revived since.

Despite the importance to them of Western theatrical forms, the Chinese have devoted even more attention to the modernization and revolutionizing of the Peking Opera and other styles which are the legacy of their own history. Though these styles were never completely static, and have developed continually, the Communists have not found it easy to introduce sudden changes into the traditional Chinese theatre while retaining its vital dramatic qualities.

The reform of the classical drama in the 1950s (see pp. 166–67) simply involved the preparation of new arrangements of old plays. The launching of the revolutionary drama called for much more radical changes. Completely new texts had to be written, and costumes and stage movements had to be made more realistic. The old categories of the Peking Opera actors (the scholar-lover with his falsetto voice, the bearded old man, the warrior and the female impersonator) were abandoned. Men no longer play female parts on the Peking stage and strong pressures are at work to discontinue the all-female casts of the Shaohing Opera.

But the question remains: how much should be retained from the past? Different producers have given different answers, and the diversity of opinion on this point, judging from the performances of modern plays which I have seen, is surprising. In some productions, the influence of the classical theatre is very strong, and it is still common to see battle scenes shown by means of the acrobatics which were so popular in the past. In one performance which I saw in a small theatre in Nanking before the Cultural Revolution, the actors' movements were so close to those of the traditional style that one could almost have imagined that the troupe was presenting a classical piece. In Peking I saw a delightfully amusing one-act play performed by actors from a remote region of Shantung province. Only two characters, a man and a woman, were involved in the action, which was set in a commune and took place on a small boat crossing a river. The players mimed the movement of the boat in the traditional manner: they remained always the same distance apart, the woman performed a graceful sinking motion, while the man rose gently, and *vice versa*. In its mime the piece is strongly reminiscent of the classical *Autumn River*, which describes the escape of a nun from her convent in pursuit of her lover. This piece, too, takes place in a boat and is cast for only two characters: the nun and a boatman. The actors mime the movement of the boat in the way described above.

There are many modern dramas, however, which reveal a drastic departure from classical models. The traditional costumes and stylized gestures and acting have disappeared, and realism is so dominant, both in the texts and in the production, that only the language, the melodies and a few of the orchestral instruments indicate that the dramas are of Chinese origin. I have also seen Peking operas in which even the music differed so greatly from traditional patterns that it was virtually impossible to identify it as Peking Opera music.

Such cases are exceptional, since one of the chief bonds between the modern and the classical Chinese drama rests in the music. Before the Cultural Revolution, most people appeared to agree that there was no need to interfere much with the music of the classical dramas. This is borne out by an authoritative article on the relationship between the traditional music and the modern drama, published, with the explicit approval of the editor, in an influential Shanghai newspaper in 1965.[14] The author definitely favoured the retention of most features of the old style of music, and did not want the music of the Peking Opera to be Westernized. He quoted the view of those who held that the music of the Peking Opera 'was a product of the feudal period and expressive of emperors, kings, generals and ministers or scholars and beauties, all of whom belonged to the exploiting classes'. He considered this a one-sided opinion, and an insufficiently strong argument for rejecting the traditional music. Sung by proletarian actors, he argued, this music was perfectly appropriate for the expression of proletarian emotions.

During the Cultural Revolution, Western instruments were introduced into the Peking Opera on a large scale, and this innovation still survives in all performances of the model dramas. In some of these, Western instruments are never silent for long, although in others there are long passages in which only traditional Chinese instruments accompany the singers. Li Hsi-fan told me that he considered that Western instruments could express heroism more forcefully than Chinese, and that the new music of the Peking Opera was more appropriate for the model dramas, with their renewed emphasis on the class struggle and on the idealism and courage of the Communist heroes. While I agree with this view, I do not find the mixture of Chinese and Western instruments aesthetically satisfying. It seems to me that the Chinese use European instrumentation too brashly, and that they have much to learn before they can adapt it properly to their own drama. Eventually they may well be successful in this. In any case, as Li Hsi-fan pointed out, many instruments now regarded as Chinese (for example the *hu-ch'in* and the *p'i-p'a*), came originally from other countries. The violin or trumpet may, likewise, become so fully assimilated in Chinese music that it will no longer be possible to consider them exclusively 'Western'. The fact remains, however, that the post-1966 model dramas do not sound much like the old Peking Opera.

At present it seems that the mixed orchestra will be a permanent feature of the modern Peking Opera. In amateur productions of model dramas, however, it is still common for only Chinese instruments to be played. This was the case at a children's performance of scenes from Peking Operas which I saw in Shenyang in June 1973. The music sounded almost the same as that of a classical drama performed during the pre-Communist era. For those who find it difficult to play, or to obtain, Western instruments, this use of traditional Chinese instruments seems perfectly reasonable, even in the eyes of those who regard the blending of Chinese and Western instruments as desirable.

The development of the modern Chinese theatre, then, has been changeable and uneven. This is also shown by the extent to which these plays have been performed in recent years.

The First Festival of Peking Operas on Contemporary Themes, held in Peking in 1964, seems to have been successful and was followed by a similar festival in Shanghai the following year. From the autumn of 1964 until mid-1966 a constant stream of companies from different provinces visited the capital to demonstrate how the exponents of the regional styles were following the example of the Peking Opera by concentrating on revolutionary themes. Moreover, the greatest actors of the day had taken the cue from the Festival of 1964 and, whatever their private thoughts, were energetically trying to establish reputations as revolutionary actors. Ma Lien-liang sometimes appeared in contemporary heroic roles. Hung-hsien-nü performed magnificently in the modern drama, both in Canton and in Peking. In Shanghai I saw Hsü Yü-lan play the part of the progressive Party Secretary of a nightsoil-collecting unit; her voice was as splendid as ever, even though her acting was somewhat stiff.

This copious activity was practically halted by the outbreak of the Red Guard movement in August 1966. Almost all the theatres closed down, while their members set about the formidable task of deciding on the future direction which their work should take; which actor was revisionist and which a genuine revolutionary, which plays were 'poisonous weeds' and which 'held high the red banner of Mao Tse-tung's thought'. The dramatic diet of the Chinese was reduced to a very few 'model theatrical works'. Even these model plays became suspect, and revised versions have been used for recent performances.

Probably the most famous of these works is *The Story of the Red Lantern*. At first, this was a Shanghai Opera; later it was adapted as a Peking Opera for the festival of 1964. It tells the story of three revolutionaries, each of a different generation, who live together as a family, although they are not in fact related. Li Yü-ho is a middle-aged railway worker who took part in the great railway strike on the Peking-Hankow line in 1923. At that time, Li Yü-ho had found a little girl, T'ieh-mei, whose parents had been killed in the strike, and adopted her as his daughter. He also adopted as his mother an old woman whose husband, a friend of his, had been killed during the strike. Li Yü-ho becomes an underground Communist agent during the War against Japan. The plot of the play concerns his attempt to carry an important secret code to the Chinese guerillas. He is betrayed to the Japanese general, Hatoyama, by a former friend, and the Japanese capture him, together with T'ieh-mei and his adopted mother. They search the house of the three revolutionaries for the secret code, but without success. They thereupon torture Li Yü-ho and the old woman in an effort to force them to reveal the whereabouts of the code. When this scheme fails, they execute both the railway worker and his adopted mother in front of Li T'ieh-mei, hoping to frighten her into giving them the information. She resists these pressures courageously, however, is released, and eventually reaches the guerillas, and delivers the code.

Despite its heavy propaganda content, *The Story of the Red Lantern* is exciting on the stage and in parts highly dramatic. At its first performances in Peking in 1964 the role of Li Yü-ho was played by Ch'ien Hao-liang, one of the best of the younger Peking Opera actors, and that of Hatoyama by Yüan Shih-hai. Yüan portrayed the Japanese general as cruel, but also as highly intelligent and not without a certain dignity. This is significant, for in Chinese plays at that time American villains, at any rate, were allowed no redeeming features.

The onset of the Cultural Revolution brought about changes in the portrayal of Hatoyama, as in other aspects of the modern drama in general. The following declaration is typical of what the Red Guards were saying at that time about the theatre:

> The handful of counter-revolutionary revisionists in the theatre, in collusion with the counter-revolutionary revisionists in the old Propaganda Department of the Party's Central Committee and in the old Ministry of Culture . . . paid no attention to Li Yu-ho and went to great pains to give more perfect expression to the inner world of Hatoyama. They not only brought on to the stage again and again the man who betrays Li Yu-ho, but smuggled in the 'traitor's philosophy' of China's Khrushchov [*sic*; Liu Shao-ch'i], saying that 'there must be some reason for him to turn traitor.' They wanted to make him into someone who arouses 'sympathy'. It was only after Chiang Ching's severe criticism that this scheme was smashed.[15]

The latest version of *The Story of the Red Lantern*, which was adopted in May 1970 and later filmed, incorporates these ideas of Chiang Ch'ing and the Red Guards. The main emphasis is now on class struggle and on the heroism of Li Yü-ho, and Hatoyama is shown as brutal and stupid. These and other changes are clearly apparent from a comparison of the 1964 version with the film (and gramophone recording) of the 1970 version, in which the actors who took part in the earlier production have been retained. While the 1970 version of *The Story of the Red Lantern* is more exciting, and sharper in dramatic tension, than the 1964 version, the characters have become somewhat stilted. There is a certain logic in the arguments put forward by Chiang Ch'ing and her followers. If one sees this drama as a depiction of class struggle, then it is arguable that one should delineate the class attributes of each character as clearly as possible. But there is surely the danger that, if every detail of a drama is worked out explicitly to fit an ideology, the result will seem contrived and unconvincing.

The strict ideological approach is maintained also in *Azalea Mountain* (*Tu-chüan shan*), the final text of which was published in September 1973. The action takes place in Azalea Mountain, in the Hunan-Kiangsi border region, in the spring of 1928. The main author of the drama, Wang Shu-yüan, tells us that the azalea, with its bright red colour, symbolizes the revolution, and that this is why he chose the name.[16] The drama concerns the struggle of a peasant partisan group against reactionary 'civil guards'. The peasant leader, Lei Kang, is enthusiastic but impetuous, and his forces lack the guidance of a political party or an ideology. They are provided with both at the vital moment when the partisans rescue from the civil guards a Communist Party member called K'o Hsiang, who turns out to be a woman. Clear-headed and invariably sound in judgment, she leads the partisans to victory against the civil guards. In particular, she manages to expose a hidden traitor in the partisan forces, the deputy leader Wen Ch'i-chiu, who has all the time been working for the enemy. The story is set in the period when Mao Tse-tung was setting up the first Communist guerilla base areas, and in the same region. It ends with the partisans setting off to join the Communist leader.

According to the commentaries published in the Chinese press, the central point of *Azalea Mountain* lies in the distinction between the traditional peasant rebellion of dynastic times and the revolution led by the Communist Party and inspired by Marxist-Leninist ideology. The following statement expresses this idea clearly:

> This opera is a mirror of history. It is a microcosm of the hundreds of peasant uprisings and peasant wars, great and small, that erupted

throughout 2,000 years of Chinese history. Although these peasant uprisings and peasant wars dealt a blow to the feudal regime . . . they were invariably used by the landlords and the nobility as a lever for bringing about dynastic change and, therefore, ended in defeat. The basic reason for their failure was that in those days . . . no proletariat arose, so there was neither correct leadership from a proletarian political party nor a correct line. And the fundamental reason why the armed peasants led by Lei Kang on Azalea Mountain did not repeat history's tragedies was that they had Party leadership in the person of Ko Hsiang and her firm implementation of Chairman Mao's line in army building.[17]

Another political issue to emerge from this drama is that of women's status. It is quite common in Chinese dramas of the Communist period for the leading positive character to be female. Nevertheless, K'o Hsiang is a new type of heroine. In earlier model dramas there have been runaway slave-girls who joined the revolution, or female Party secretaries in a commune or city organization; but until September 1973 the heroic guerillas, or military Party leaders, were all men. The significance of the fact that K'o Hsiang is a woman is accentuated by the scenes in which Wen Ch'i-chiu suggests to Lei Kang that he has lost his power of judgment through being too much under the thumb of a woman. This no doubt reflects the problem of equality between the sexes, which still exists in China today, even after twenty-five years of Communist government.

During my tour of China in mid-1973 I was struck by the narrowness of the people's theatrical life. It was narrow not in the sense that few people have the opportunity to enjoy the theatre (in fact, greater numbers patronize it than ever before), but in the range of plays performed and in their themes. Not many dramas are available for widespread professional performance, and even amateurs tend to adhere to stereotyped themes.

However, the number of officially accepted plays is increasing and seems likely to increase even more rapidly during the next few years. I have already noted that the traditional theatre seems likely to return to popular favour in due course. On a more general plane the process which the Chinese call *ting-hsing* ('establishing the form') should be mentioned. A drama is first written and performed in a certain region. The people and the actors then discuss it and put forward suggestions for improvement. Changes are made, the revised version is performed, and criticism is again invited. This process may continue for several years. Only after a final approved version emerges is the drama performed outside its region of origin, since its 'form' is now considered 'established'. While in China, I learned that there are a vast number of dramas currently undergoing experimentation of this kind, as a prelude to eventual official acceptance. One should not assume, therefore, from the small number of model plays currently being performed that the theatre is all but dead in China.

More disturbing than the paucity of themes, at present, is the narrowness of Chinese attitudes to the theatre. In general, the people do not know of theatrical developments outside China, nor are they interested in them. This trend has become more pronounced since the onset of the Campaign to Criticize Lin Piao and Confucius, which has resulted in numerous vigorous attacks in the Chinese press on the bourgeois quality of music and the theatre in the West. It remains to be seen if this attitude is permanent or not, but it is surely no more helpful for a Chinese to damn all Western art than it is for somebody brought up in the European tradition to denigrate all the model dramas of the Chinese. I am certainly not implying here that the Chinese should adopt foreign culture uncritically: in my opinion it would be disastrous if they did so. I am only suggesting that the exchange of views and attitudes which could follow China's closer contact with other countries would be very beneficial to its theatre, and, indeed, to that of the other countries concerned.

Whatever attitude the Chinese adopt towards non-Chinese art in the future, the basic framework of their own theatrical art will probably remain modern and revolutionary. Yet this need not preclude the composition of masterpieces. Even though many of the modern plays are poor, some stand out, either for their highly dramatic qualities, or for their wit. Art which carries a sharply defined message is not necessarily bad; many would argue, indeed, that there is no point in art of any other kind. When first-rate works are produced they are not generally regarded as mere vehicles of propaganda, even when their content is essentially doctrinal. Christian artists, for instance, are universally acknowledged to have built up a magnificent tradition, although their works undoubtedly contain religious propaganda. The countries of Eastern Europe have already produced theatrical masterpieces based on socialist doctrines. The beginnings of such a development can be discerned in China also, and could easily lead to creation of a magnificent body of drama.

Notes to the Text

Full details, including translations of titles, are only given for publications not cited in the Bibliographical Notes, to which readers are referred. Details of publications cited in the Bibliographical Notes are given in the Part which corresponds to the relevant Part of the text, unless it is otherwise indicated.

INTRODUCTION

1 *Ch'ü-tsao* ('Language of Dramas'; first published 1580). Reprinted in the collection *Chung-kuo-tien hsi-ch'ü lun-chu chi-ch'eng* ('Collections of Writings on the Chinese Classical Drama', 10 vols, Peking, 1959 and 1960), vol. 4, p. 27.
2 *Yü-ming t'ang ch'üan-chi* ('Complete Works of T'ang Hsien-tsu'), chap. 4. I have quoted the translation by Josephine Huang Hung in *Ming Drama* (Taipei, 1966), p. 136.
3 There is a complete English translation of this drama by Gladys Yang and Yang Hsien-yi: *The Palace of Eternal Youth* (Peking, 1955).
4 The quoted phrases are from A. C. Scott, *The Classical Theatre of China* (London, 1957; Taipei, 1967), p. 51.
5 Colin Mackerras, 'The Growth of the Chinese Regional Drama in the Ming and Ch'ing', *Journal of Oriental Studies*, IX, 1 (January 1971), pp. 84–90.
6 Ou-yang Yü-ch'ien, 'T'an Erh-huang hsi' ('Talking of Erh-huang Drama'), in Cheng Chen-to, ed., *Chung-kuo wen-hsüeh yen-chiu* ('Research on Chinese Literature', Shanghai, 1927; Hong Kong, 1963), p. 491.
7 *Ch'in-yün hsieh-ying hsiao-p'u* (written *c*. 1780). Reprinted in *Shuang-mei ching-an ts'ung-shu* (a collection compiled by Yeh Te-hui, 1903–11), pp. 9bff.
8 A. C. Scott, op. cit., p. 74.

CHAPTER ONE

THE DEVELOPMENT OF THE PEKING OPERA UNTIL 1860

1 *Meng-chung yüan*, preface. *Meng-chung yüan* ('Love in a Dream') is a drama by Chang Chien, completed in 1699. It was first published in 1750, and the preface refers to that year.
2 Yang Mou-chien, *Hsin-jen kuei-chia lu*, p. 578.
3 Hsiao T'ieh-ti tao-jen, *Jih-hsia k'an-hua chi*, p. 266.
4 Wu Ch'ang-yüan, *Yen-lan hsiao-p'u*, p. 125.
5 Chang Tz'u-hsi, ed., *Pei-ching li-yüan chang-ku ch'ang-pien*, p. 1,637.

6 Chao I, *Yen-p'u tsa-chi*. Reprinted in *Ou-pei ch'üan-chi* ('Complete Works of Chao I', 1877), chap. 1, p. 10a.

7 Some writers claim that the main purpose of Wei Ch'ang-sheng's arrival in Peking in 1779 was to celebrate Ch'ien-lung's seventieth birthday. This is certainly possible, but there is no direct evidence for it in the primary sources.

8 Su-hai an chü-shih, *Yen-t'ai hung-chao chi*, pp. 563–4.

9 For a more detailed account of the growth of the Peking Opera, see Colin Mackerras, *The Rise of the Peking Opera 1770–1870: Social Aspects of the Theatre in Manchu China.*

CHAPTER TWO

ACTORS OF THE LATE CH'ING PERIOD

1 Chou Chih-fu, *Tu-men chi-lüeh chung chih hsi-ch'ü shih-liao*, pp. 82ff.

2 *Kuo-chü man-t'an*, vol. 1, p. 54.

3 *Ch'ing-tai P'i-huang ming-chüeh chien-shu*, p. 4.

4 Ch'en Yen-heng, *Chiu-chü ts'ung-t'an*, p. 1,601.

5 Ch'en Tan-jan, *I-ling chuan*, p. 1,340.

6 For a more detailed account of Ch'eng Chang-keng's career, see Colin Mackerras, *The Rise of the Peking Opera 1770–1880: Social Aspects of the Theatre in Manchu China*, pp. 176–84.

7 Chang Tz'u-hsi, *Yen-tu ming-ling chuan*, p. 2,154.

8 Hatano Kenichi, *Ching-chü erh-pai nien chih li-shih*, p. 32.

9 Ibid., pp. 31–32.

10 Ibid., pp. 55–56.

11 Ibid., pp. 42–43.

12 Wang Meng-sheng, *Li-yüan*

chia-hua ('Stories on the Theatre', Shanghai, 1915), p. 73.

13 Hatano Kenichi, op. cit., p. 56.

CHAPTER THREE

THE PEKING THEATRE OF THE REPUBLIC

1 Until 1914 Peking's dramatic troupes were referred to as *pan*; from 1914, as *she*.

2 *Ching-chü erh-pai nien chih li-shih*, p. 88.

3 *T'an ssu-chüeh*, p. 125.

4 Loc. cit.

5 *T'an Yü Shu-yen* ('Talking about Yü Shu-yen', Hong Kong, 1953), p. 156.

6 Op. cit., p. 106.

7 Ibid., p. 120.

8 Hatano Kenichi, loc. cit.

9 Ch'i Ju-shan, op. cit., p. 67. Ch'i is quoting two actors who had acted with Yang in the imperial palaces.

10 Chou Chih-fu, *Chen-liu ta-wen*, p. 87.

11 Op. cit., p. 93. Mei Lan-fang does not mention this story in his autobiography. However, he does record Yang's kindness to him as a child. 'He would often take me to school. I sometimes rode on his shoulders, and he would tell me folk stories, buy me sweet gourds and make me feel happy and cheerful.' (*Wu-t'ai sheng-huo ssu-shih nien*, vol. 1, pp. 21–22).

12 Hatano Kenichi, op. cit., p. 168.

13 See John Willett, trans. and ed., *Brecht on Theater* (New York, 1964), p. 94.

14 *Hsi-chü pao*, 16 (April 1955), p. 5.

15 Loc. cit.

16 Quoted in A. C. Scott, *Mei Lan-fang, Leader of the Pear Garden*, p. 93.

17 Quoted in Hui-chai, *Hsi-ch'ü ts'ung-hua* ('Collected Words on Theatre', Hong Kong, 1957), vol. 1, pp. 43–44.
18 Chang Tz'u-hsi, *Yen-tu ming-ling chuan*, pp. 2,170–71.
19 The name of this city was changed to Peiping when Chiang Kai-shek adopted Nanking as his capital in 1928. For the sake of convenience, however, I have decided to refer to the city as Peking throughout this book.
20 Hui-chai, op. cit., vol. 1, p. 40.
21 The friend was a scholar and journalist named Pu Lin-wu. He is quoted in Hatano Kenichi, op. cit., pp. 230–31.
22 Quoted in Li Yen-hui, *Hsientai Chung-kuo hsi-chü chien-shih* ('Simple History of Modern Chinese Drama', Singapore, 1959), p. 22.
23 *Hsi-chü* ('Drama'), quoted and translated in A. R. Davis, 'Out of "Uncle Tom's Cabin"', Tokyo 1907: A Preliminary Look at the Beginnings of the Spoken Drama in China', *The Journal of the Oriental Society of Australia*, VI, 1 and 2 (1968–69), p. 46.
24 Chao Ming-i, 'Hua-chü yüntung san-shih nien kai-kuan (1907–1937)' ('General View of the Spoken Play Movement over the Thirty Years 1907–1937'), *Hsi-chü lunts'ung* 3 (August 1957), p. 35.

CHAPTER FOUR

ACTORS IN PEKING SOCIETY

1 Quoted in A. M. Nagler, *A Source Book in Theatrical History* (New York, 2nd ed., 1959), pp. 433–4.
2 *Ching-chü chih pien-ch'ien*, p. 48b.
3 *Hsi-chieh hsiao chang-ku*, p. 42.

4 *Studies on the Population of China, 1368–1953* (Cambridge, Massachusetts, 1959), pp. 270ff.
5 *Wu-t'ai sheng-huo ssu-shih nien*, vol. 1, p. 61.
6 Yang Mou-chien, *Meng-hua so-pu*, p. 754. It may be added that the Standard Histories of the Five Dynasties period (907–60) confirm that Chuang-tsung loved to act. However, there is no evidence that he performed *ch'ou* roles. These are not mentioned at all in works dating from earlier than the Yüan period.
7 *Hsi-pan*, p. 31a.
8 The texts of the inscriptions are in Chang Tz'u-hsi, ed., *Pei-ching li-yüan chin-shih wen-tzu lu*.
9 *Hsi-chieh hsiao chang-ku*, p. 155.
10 See J. S. Burgess, *The Guilds of Peking* (New York, 1928), p. 140. Burgess is here quoting a representative of the actors' guild.
11 Quoted in A. M. Nagler, op. cit., p. 177.
12 *Chung-kuo ling-jen hsüeh-yüan chih yen-chiu*, p. 237.
13 This statement is based on a survey of the class background of actors carried out by P'an Kuang-tan in the 1930s (see ibid., pp. 224–7).

CHAPTER FIVE

THE THEATRE IN PEKING SOCIETY

1 *Meng-hua so-pu*, p. 704.
2 Ibid., p. 705.
3 Shih-i, *Tu Yüeh-sheng wai-chuan* ('Unofficial Biography of Tu Yüeh-sheng', Hong Kong, 1962), p. 154.
4 See Chou Chih-fu, *Tu-men chi-lüeh chung chih hsi-ch'ü shih-liao*, pp. 141ff.
5 Op. cit., p. 704.
6 Quoted in A. M. Nagler, *A*

Source Book in Theatrical History (New York, 2nd ed., 1959), p. 476.

7 *Chin-t'ai ts'an-lei chi*, pp. 527–8.

8 *Hsi-chieh hsiao chang-ku*, p. 182.

9 Quoted in A. M. Nagler, op. cit., pp. 117–18.

10 *Kuo chü man-t'an*, vol. 1, p. 167.

11 See Wang Hsiao-ch'uan, *Yüan Ming Ch'ing san-tai chin-hui hsiao-shuo hsi-ch'ü shih-liao*, p. 68.

12 I have quoted this edict at greater length in *The Rise of the Peking Opera 1770–1870: Social Aspects of the Theatre in Manchu China*, p. 217.

13 See Wang Hsiao-ch'uan, op. cit., pp. 74–75.

14 Quoted in A. M. Nagler, op. cit., p. 115. I have modernized the spelling.

CHAPTER SIX

THE THEATRE IN CHINESE SOCIETY

1 Sidney Gamble writes in his *Ting Hsien, A North China Rural Community* (New York, 1954), p. 410, that in Tinghsien in the late 1920s 'The city, two of its three suburbs, and 35 out of 453 towns and villages held fairs'.

2 Quoted in Tanaka Issei, ed., *Shindai chihō geki shiryō shū*, vol. 2, p. 86.

3 Quoted in ibid., p. 9.

4 Quoted in ibid., p. 29. This excerpt is from an Anhwei document of *c.* 1905.

5 See Tanaka's article 'Min-Shin Kahoku chihō geki no kenkyū', *Hokkaidō daigaku bungakubu kiyō*, XVI, 1 (1968), pp. 219–52. Tanaka is referring specifically to north China in this article, but his conclusion can also be applied to the south.

6 Tu Li-fang, 'Lun Lung-yen tsa-hsi' ('On the Tsa-hsi Drama of Lung-yen'), *Hsi-ch'ü yen-chiu* ('Drama Research'), 6 (1958), p. 111.

7 'Village Opera', *Selected Stories of Lu Hsun*, trans. Gladys Yang and Yang Hsien-yi (Peking, 1954), p. 89. The story quoted is dated October 1922 and is contained in the collection *Na-han* ('Call to Arms').

8 Quoted in Tanaka Issei, *Shindai chihō geki shiryō shū*, vol. 1, p. 37.

9 Gladys Yang and Yang Hsien-yi, trans., op. cit., p. 84.

10 Quoted in Tanaka Issei, 'Shindai shoki no chihō geki ni tsuite', p. 150.

11 During the Sung dynasty (960–1279) there were many public theatres in the amusement centres of China's largest cities, especially Kaifeng and Hangchow. Most of the playhouses were covered, but some were in the open air. However, they went out of fashion in the Yüan (1280–1368) and Ming (1368–1644) periods.

12 *Chung-kuo ch'ang-chi shih* ('History of Chinese Prostitution', Shanghai, 1934), p. 332.

13 Quoted in A. M. Nagler, *A Source Book in Theatrical History* (New York, 2nd ed., 1959), pp. 178–9.

14 Quoted in Chou Chih-fu, *Ching-hsi chin pai-nien so-chi*, p. 83 (Bibliog. Notes, Part One).

15 See Samuel C. Chu, *Reformer in Modern China, Chang Chien, 1853–1926* (New York and London, 1965), p. 170.

16 This was printed in 1921 and is quoted by Tanaka Issei in 'Shindai shoki no sōzoku engeki ni tsuite', p. 108.

17 From the clan records (printed *c.* 1865) of a Mao family of Yuyao in Chekiang province. Quoted by Tanaka Issei, op. cit., p. 113.

CHAPTER SEVEN

SHANGHAI AND THE LOWER YANGTZE VALLEY

1 'The Salt Merchants of Yangchou: A Study of Commercial Capitalism in Eighteenth-century China', *Harvard Journal of Asiatic Studies*, XVII (1954), p. 130.
2 Quoted in Chou I-pai, *Chung-kuo hsi-ch'ü lun-chi*, p. 216.
3 Chao Ching-shen, *Hsi-ch'ü pi-t'an*, p. 209.
4 *Su-chü ch'ü-tiao chieh-shao* ('Introduction to the tunes of Soochow Opera', Nanking, 1955, 1959), p. 2.
5 Li Tou, *Yang-chou hua-fang lu* ('Records of Yangchow's Decorated Pleasure Boats', Peking, ed. of 1960), p. 130. This work was completed in 1794.
6 Quoted in Meng Yao, *Chung-kuo hsi-ch'ü shih* ('History of Chinese Drama'), pp. 666–7.
7 A revised version of this Shaohing opera has been recorded complete under the auspices of the present Chinese government. The title roles are acted by Fan Juichüan (Liang) and Fu Ch'üanhsiang; the record numbers are DM-6063-6066. The text may be found, together with musical scores of certain sections and an explanatory article, in *Hsi-ch'ü hsüan*, vol. 1, pp. 315ff.
8 *Wu-t'ai sheng-huo ssu-shih nien*, vol. 1, pp. 46–47 (Bibliog. Notes, Part One).
9 *Ching-chü erh-pai nien chih li-shih*, p. 118 (Bibliog. Notes, Part One).
10 See Kai Chiao-t'ien, ed. Ho Man and Kung I-chiang, *Fen-mo ch'un-ch'iu*, p. 11.
11 See *Hua-tung hsi-ch'ü chü-chung chieh-shao*, vol. 1, p. 77.
12 Chao Ching-shen, op. cit., p. 220.
13 T'ien Han, Ou-yang Yü-ch'ien and others, ed., *Chung-kuo hua-chü yün-tung wu-shih nien shih-liao chi* ('A Collection of Fifty Years of Material on the Chinese Spoken Play Movement', Peking, 1958), p. 52.
14 See Ibid., p. 144.
15 See Ibid., p. 159.
16 This play has been translated into English by Wang Tso-liang and A. C. Barnes. The first edition was published in Peking in 1958 and the second in 1964. For critical comment on Ts'ao Yü's works see Joseph S. M. Lau, *Ts'ao Yü, The Reluctant Disciple of Chekhov and O'Neill, A Study in Literary Influence* (Hong Kong, 1970).
17 K'an-wai jen and others, *Ching-chü chien-wen lu* ('Records of Things Seen and Heard about Peking Opera', Hong Kong, 1973), p. 107.
18 'Hsi-chü chieh ts'an-chia hsinhai ko-ming ti chi-chien shih' ('A Few Matters on the Participation of the Theatre World in the 1911 Revolution'), *Hsin-hai ko-ming hui-i lu* ('Recollections on the 1911 Revolution', Peking, 1961), vol. 1, p. 351. Also in *Mei Lan-fang wen-chi* ('A Collection of Essays by Mei Lanfang', Peking, 1962), p. 196.

CHAPTER EIGHT

THE SOUTH-EASTERN PROVINCES: FUKIEN AND KWANGTUNG

1 See *Hua-tung hsi-ch'ü chü-chung chieh-shao*, vol. 1, p. 99.
2 The text of this piece, together with two articles about it and musical scores of some sections, may be found in *Hsi-ch'ü hsüan*, vol. 4, pp. 99–193. The modern version

is based on the sixteenth-century drama, a folk-song and novel on the same theme and 'the oral records of the old artist Ts'ai Yu-pen' (see p. 192). The drama has been recorded on long-playing records nos. M-663-665, with Ts'ai Ya-chih (Ch'en) and Su Wu-shui in the title roles. In his book *Li-ching chi hsi-wen yen-chiu* (Taipei, 1970), pp. 23–127, Wu Shou-li has reproduced the sixteenth-century version photographically, rewritten the text of the drama in clearer characters, with punctuation, and added a commentary. On pp. 2–5, Wu puts forward good evidence for his view that, despite the date of the surviving text, the drama itself was actually written somewhat earlier, probably in the fifteenth century, though possibly in the late fourteenth.

3 Chou I-pai, *Chung-kuo hsi-ch'ü lun-chi*, p. 363, or Ou-yang Yü-ch'ien, ed., *Chung-kuo hsi-ch'ü yen-chiu tzu-liao ch'u-chi*, p. 175.

4 This *Yüeh-chü* is quite different from the *Yüeh-chü* (Shaohing Opera) discussed in Chapter Seven. The sound of the syllable *yüeh* is identical in both names, but the Chinese characters are different.

5 W. C. Milne, *Life in China* (London, 1857), p. 307.

6 *Meng-hua so-pu*, p. 754 (Bibliog. Notes, Part One).

7 Ou-yang Yü-ch'ien, ed., *Chung-kuo hsi-ch'ü yen-chiu tzu-liao ch'u-chi*, p. 110.

8 See Liang Ting-fen, and others, *P'an-yü hsien hsü-chih* ('Supplementary Gazetteer of P'anyü County', Taipei, 1967), p. 625. This work was completed in 1931.

9 Loc. cit.

10 Loc. cit.

11 Ou-yang Yü-ch'ien, ed., op. cit., p. 117.

12 See Tanaka Issei, ed., *Shindai chihō geki shiryō shū*, vol. 2, p. 84.

13 See Mai Hsiao-hsia, 'Kuang-tung hsi-chü shih-lüeh', *Kuang-tung wen-wu* ('Cultural things of Kuang-tung', Hong Kong, 1941), vol. 3, pp. 154–5.

14 Shen Chi, *Ma Shih-tseng ti hsi-chü sheng-ya* ('Ma Shih-tseng's Theatrical Career', Canton, 1957), p. 6.

15 This actor's surname is pronounced Ching in Peking and Ling in Kwangtung.

16 Shen Chi, op. cit., p. 91.

17 Ou-yang Yü-ch'ien, ed., op. cit., p. 140.

CHAPTER NINE

THE MIDDLE YANGTZE REGION: HUPEH AND SZECHWAN

1 See Ou-yang Yü-ch'ien, ed., *Chung-kuo hsi-ch'ü yen-chiu tzu-liao ch'u-chi*, p. 34.

2 Ibid., p. 46.

3 *Chü-hua*, p. 46.

4 See A. W. Hummel, ed., *Eminent Chinese of the Ch'ing Period (1644–1912)* (Washington D.C., 1943–44), p. 38.

5 *Ch'uan-chü ch'ien-t'an* ('Simple Talks on Szechwanese Opera', Chungking, 1955), p. 25.

6 Op. cit., p. 47.

7 See D. Kalvodová, 'The Origin and Character of the Szechwan Theatre', *Archiv Orientální*, 34 (1966), p. 519.

8 Tung-ni, 'Ch'uan-chü tso-chia Chao Hsi chi ch'i "Ch'ing-t'an"' ('The Szechwanese Opera Author Chao Hsi and his *Ch'ing-t'an*'), *Hsi-chü lun-ts'ung* ('Collection of Discussions on Drama'), 4 (Nov. 1957), p. 158.

9 'San-ch'ing hui ho K'ang Tzu-lin' ('The San-ch'ing Company and K'ang Tzu-lin'), *Ssu-ch'uan hsi-ch'ü* ('Szechwanese Drama'), 1 (Oct. 1958), p. 32. This article was reprinted under the title ' "San-ch'ing hui" ho K'ang Chih-lin' ('The San-ch'ing Company and K'ang Chih-lin') in *Ch'uan-chü i-shu yen-chiu* ('Research on Szechwanese Opera Art', Chungking, 1961), vol. 2; the passage quoted is on p. 83.

10 *Ssu-ch'uan hsi-ch'ü*, 2 (Nov. 1958), p. 19; *Ch'uan-chü i-shu yen-chiu*, vol. 2, p. 84.

11 *Ssu-ch'uan hsi-ch'ü*, 2 (Nov. 1958), p. 20; *Ch'uan-chü i-shu yen-chiu*, vol. 2, p. 87.

12 *Ssu-ch'uan hsi-ch'ü*, 3 (Dec. 1958), p. 36; *Ch'uan-chü i-shu yen-chiu*, vol. 2, p. 92.

CHAPTER TEN

GOVERNMENT POLICY TOWARDS THE THEATRE

1 'Talks at the Yenan Forum on Literature and Art', *Selected Works of Mao Tse-tung* (Peking, 1965), vol. 3, p. 86.

2 Ibid., p. 90.

3 'On New Democracy', *Selected Works of Mao Tse-tung*, vol. 2, p. 381.

4 *Hsi-chü pao*, 12 (Dec. 1954), p. 27.

5 Ibid., 50 (July 1957), p. 18.

6 *Hsi-ch'ü yen-chiu*, 4 (1958), p. 5.

7 See *Far Eastern Economic Review*, XLIV, 13 (25 June 1964), p. 634.

8 *Kuang-ming jih-pao*, 14 Sept. 1963.

9 *Hung-ch'i*, 96 (1964), p. 58.

10 *Yang-ch'eng wan-pao* ('Canton Evening News'), 3 July 1965, quoted in Eng. trans. in *Current Scene*, III, 29 (15 Oct. 1965), p. 7.

11 *Chieh-fang chün wen-i*, 10 Sept. 1967, quoted in Eng. trans. in *Selections from China Mainland Magazines*, 605 (11 Dec. 1967), p. 7.

12 Loc. cit.

13 New China News Agency, English Version, 6 Feb. 1968.

14 *Yang-ch'eng wan-pao*, 20 June 1963, quoted in Eng. trans. in *Current Scene*, III, 9 (15 Dec. 1964), p. 3.

15 Fredric Kaplan in *Far Eastern Economic Review*, loc. cit., p. 635.

16 *Wen-hui pao*, 19 June 1965.

17 *Hsin-min wen-pao* ('New People's Literary Newspaper'), Shanghai, 11 Jan. 1964.

18 Fredric Kaplan in *Far Eastern Economic Review*, loc. cit., p. 636.

19 See *China Notes*, 334 (23 Oct. 1969); *Hung-ch'i*, 217 (Sept. 1969), p. 39.

20 Cited in Note 16, above.

21 *Chung-kuo hsin-wen (t'ung-hsün kao)* ('Chinese News (Information Draft)'), 22 May 1972, p. 22.

CHAPTER ELEVEN

THE THEATRE AND THE ACTOR

1 *Hsi-chü pao*, 17 (May 1955), p. 53. The letter is dated 10 March.

2 Ibid., 25 (Jan. 1956), p. 41.

3 New China News Agency, English Version, 16 Nov. 1969.

4 *Peking Review*, VIII, 48 (26 Nov. 1965), p. 31.

5 *Kuang-ming jih-pao*, 29 Mar. 1964.

6 *China Reconstructs*, X, 2 (Feb. 1961), p. 17.

7 *Hsi-chü pao*, 33 (Sept. 1956), p. 4.

8 Loc. cit.

9 *Hsin Chung-hua pan-yüeh k'an* ('New China Semi-monthly'), XIV, 19 (1 Oct. 1951), p. 33.

10 *China Reconstructs*, II, 2 (Mar.–Apr. 1953), p. 49.
11 *Ssu-ch'uan hsi-ch'ü*, 1 (Jan. 1959), p. 18.
12 *Wen-hui pao*, 19 June 1965.
13 *Amateur Theatre in China 1949–1966*, p. 10.
14 *People's China*, III, 1 (1 Jan. 1951), p. 13.
15 *Peking Review*, XVI, 22 (1 June 1973), p. 23.
16 *Hsi-chü pao*, 33 (Sept. 1956), pp. 4–7. Similar articles appeared in many Chinese newspapers at about the same time.
17 *People's China*, loc. cit., p. 29.
18 *Hsi-chü pao*, 22 (Oct. 1955), p. 49.
19 *China Reconstructs*, VIII, 7 (July 1959), pp. 14–16.
20 Chou Yang, *China's New Literature and Art, Essays and Addresses* (Peking, 1954), p. 109.
21 See, for example, *Wen-hui pao*, 20 May 1968.

CHAPTER TWELVE

THE DEVELOPMENT OF THE THEATRE FROM 1949

1 *China Reconstructs*, VIII, 10 (Oct. 1959), p. 20.
2 Chou Yang, *China's New Literature and Art, Essays and Addresses* (Peking, 1954), pp. 103–5.
3 *The White Snake* (*Pai-she chuan*) has been adapted by T'ien Han from an ancient story. It concerns a beautiful woman (in fact, a transformed snake) who marries a young scholar. A Buddhist monk tries to break up the marriage and succeeds in imprisoning the girl in a pagoda. In the end the pagoda collapses, and she escapes. The work has been translated into English by Gladys Yang and Yang Hsien-yi: *The White Snake, A Peking Opera* (Peking, 1957).
4 See Bibliog. Notes, Parts One and Two respectively.
5 *Hsi-chü pao*, 16 (Apr. 1955), p. 9.
6 See, for example, *Chung-yang jih-pao* ('Central Daily'), 22 Sept. 1966.
7 L. C. Pronko, *Theater East and West, Perspectives towards a Total Theater* (Berkeley and Los Angeles, 1967), p. 43.
8 *Hsi-chü pao*, 27 (Mar. 1956), p. 4.
9 Ibid., 170 (Feb. 1963), p. 18.
10 Ho Ching-chih and Ting Yi, trans. Gladys Yang and Yang Hsien-yi, *The White-haired Girl* (Peking, 1954), p. 89.
11 *Hsi-chü pao*, 17 (May 1955), p. 55.
12 See ibid., 190 (Oct. 1964), p. 2.
13 Colina MacDougall in *Far Eastern Economic Review*, XLIX, 12 (16 Sept. 1965), p. 521.
14 *Wen-hui pao*, 4 Oct. 1965.
15 *Peking Review*, X, 48 (24 Nov. 1967), p. 37.
16 *Chinese Literature*, 1 (Jan. 1974), p. 119.
17 *Peking Review*, XVII, 4 (25 Jan. 1974), p. 12.

Bibliographical Notes

PART ONE

THE THEATRE IN PEKING BEFORE 1949

Already there exists a good literature in the Western languages on the Peking Opera, including books on the stage conventions, costumes and dramas. The best of them is probably A. C. Scott, *The Classical Theatre of China* (London, 1957; Taipei, 1967). This work gives brief biographical notes on several famous actors of the past and present, but, like the other books, does not give detailed treatments either of the history of the Peking Opera or of its function in society. The only Chinese actor accorded a full-length biography in a European language is Mei Lan-fang; see A. C. Scott, *Mei Lan-fang, Leader of the Pear Garden* (Hong Kong, 1959). The early history of the Peking Opera is treated in Colin Mackerras, *The Rise of the Peking Opera 1770–1870: Social Aspects of the Theatre in Manchu China* (Oxford, 1972). A. C. Scott has made a significant study of the place of the theatre in Chinese society in the chapter on China in his book *The Theatre in Asia* (London, 1972; New York, 1973). By far the most comprehensive study of the

music is Gerd Schönfelder, *Die Musik der Peking-Oper* (Leipzig, 1972).

The Chinese sources naturally remain the basis of research into the Peking Opera and its history. By far the most valuable collection of primary sources written before 1911 is Chang Tz'u-hsi, ed., *Ch'ing-tai Yen-tu li-yüan shih-liao* ('Historical Material on the Peking Theatre of the Ch'ing Dynasty', 4 vols, Peiping, 1934–37; reissued, Taipei, 1965). The latter edition is the one to which references are made in the Notes to the Text. It has also been reissued as part of the larger collection *P'ing-chü shih-liao ts'ung-k'an* ('Collection of Materials on Peiping Opera', Taipei, 1974). Chang Tz'u-hsi spent several years looking for reliable editions of old books on the Peking theatre. I list below, in order of their appearance, some of the most valuable books in this collection:

VOL. 1

Wu Ch'ang-yüan, *Yen-lan hsiao-p'u* ('A Short Treatise on the Epidendrums of Peking', completed in 1785). The title was chosen in honour of one particular actor who was famous for his drawings of epidendrums.

Hsiao T'ieh-ti tao-jen, *Jih-hsia k'an-*

hua chi ('Records of Watching Flowers in Peking', written in 1803). The 'flowers' of the title refer to the boy actors who were frequently homosexual favourites. It may be because of his relationship with them that the author has written under a pen-name.

Chang Chi-liang, *Chin-t'ai ts'an-lei chi* ('The Cruel Tears of the Stage', completed in 1829)

Su-hai an chü-shih, *Yen-t'ai hung-chao chi* ('Traces of Past Events on the Peking Stage', completed in 1832)

Yang Mou-chien, *Hsin-jen kuei-chia lu* ('Records of the Years 1831–34', completed in 1842)
VOL. 2

Yang Mou-chien, *Ch'ang-an k'an-hua chi* ('Records of Watching Flowers in Peking', completed in 1837)

Yang Mou-chien, *Meng-hua so-pu* ('Fragmentary Notes on Dreams and Flowers', completed in 1842)
VOL. 3

Ch'en Tan-jan, *I-ling chuan* ('Biographies of Different Actors', written c. 1910)

Wu Tao, *Li-yüan chiu-hua* ('Stories of the Theatre', written in the late nineteenth century)

Ch'en Yen-heng, *Chiu-chü ts'ung-t'an* ('Collected Chats on Old Dramas', first published 1934)

Chang Tz'u-hsi, ed., *Pei-ching li-yüan chang-ku ch'ang-pien* 'Historical Records of the Peking Theatre', first published 1934)

Chang Tz'u-hsi, ed., *Pei-ching li-yüan chin-shih wen-tzu lu* ('Corpus of Inscriptions on the Peking Theatre', first published 1934)
VOL. 4

Chang Tz'u-hsi, *Yen-tu ming-ling chuan* ('Biographies of Peking's Famous Actors', first published 1937)

The greatest recent writer on the Peking theatre is Ch'i Ju-shan, who died in Taipei in 1962. His many works were collected in *Ch'i Ju-shan ch'üan-chi* ('The Complete Works of Ch'i Ju-shan', Taipei, 1964). I list below those which I have found most valuable while writing the present book:

VOL. 1
Hsi-pan ('Troupes', Peiping, 1935)
VOL. 2
Ching-chü chih pien-ch'ien ('Changes in Peking Theatre', Peiping, 1935)
VOL. 3
Kuo-chü man-t'an ('Miscellaneous Talks on Peking Drama')
VOL. 4
Ch'ing-tai P'i-huang ming-chüeh chien-shu ('Short Accounts of Famous Peking Opera Actors in the Ch'ing Dynasty')
T'an ssu-chüeh ('On Four Actors')
Hsi-chieh hsiao chang-ku ('Anecdotes of the Theatrical World')

The greatest living authority on the Peking Opera is Chou Chih-fu. Five of his many works were written as a series called *Chi-li chü hsi-ch'ü ts'ung-shu* ('Chi-li chü's Series on the Theatre'). Of the five, the two most relevant to the present study are:
No. 1, *Tu-men chi-lüeh chung chih hsi-ch'ü shih-liao* ('Historical Material on the Theatre in the Peking Guide-books Tu-men chi-lüeh', Shanghai, 1932)
and No. 5, *Chin pai-nien ti Ching-chü* ('One Hundred Years of Peking Opera', Hong Kong, 1962).
Chou Chih-fu's other works include *Ching-hsi chin pai-nien so-chi* ('Miscellaneous Accounts of the Peking Opera during the Last Hun-

dred Years', Hong Kong, 1951; first published in Shanghai, 1932, as No. 3 of the series *Chi-li chü hsi-ch'ü ts'ung-shu*, and reissued, photographed from the edition of 1932, as part of the collection *P'ing-chü shih-liao ts'ung-k'an*, cited above) and *Chen-liu ta-wen* ('Chen-liu Answers Questions', Hong Kong, 1955).

In addition to the specialized works noted above, the best general histories of the Chinese drama contain much information about the Peking Opera. The following four are good examples:

Aoki Masaru, trans. from the Japanese into Chinese by Wang Ku-lu, *Chung-kuo chin-shih hsi-ch'ü shih* ('A History of Recent Chinese Theatre', Shanghai, 1936, 1958)

Chou I-pai, *Chung-kuo hsi-chü shih* ('A History of the Chinese Drama', 3 vols, Shanghai, 1953)

Hsü Mu-yün, *Chung-kuo hsi-chü shih* ('A History of the Chinese Drama', Shanghai, 1938). This book is more concentrated on the Peking Opera than the other three listed here.

Meng Yao, *Chung-kuo hsi-ch'ü shih* ('A History of the Chinese Stage', 4 vols, Taipei, 1969)

Finally, several works on particular aspects of the Chinese theatre before 1949 should be mentioned:

Chou I-pai, *Chung-kuo chü-ch'ang shih* ('A History of Chinese Theatres', Shanghai, 1936). The author deals with the structure of stages and with theatre architecture.

Hatano Kenichi, trans. from the Japanese into Chinese by Lu-yüan hsüeh-jen, *Ching-chü erh-pai nien chih li-shih* ('The History of Peking Opera over the Last Two Hundred Years', Shanghai, 1926; reprinted as part of the collection *P'ing-chü shih-liao ts'ung-k'an*, cited above). This book is devoted to the biographies of famous actors. Despite its title, it contains almost no information about actors who flourished before 1840.

Mei Lan-fang, *Wu-t'ai sheng-huo ssu-shih nien* ('Forty Years on the Stage', 2 vols, Shanghai, 1952–54; Peking, 1961). Mei Lan-fang's autobiography down to 1949, narrated to an amanuensis, Hsü Chi-ch'uan, who wrote down and edited the story.

P'an Kuang-tan, *Chung-kuo ling-jen hsüeh-yüan chih yen-chiu* ('Research into the Family Relations of Chinese Actors', Changsha, 1941). P'an deals extensively with the social status of actors in China.

Su Hsüeh-an, *Ching-chü ch'ien-pei i-jen hui-i lu* ('Reminiscences of Peking Opera Artists of the Previous Generation', Shanghai, 1958). This book contains numerous anecdotes and details from the lives of actors of the late Ch'ing and Republican periods, and comments on the plays which each performed.

Wang Hsiao-ch'uan, *Yüan Ming Ch'ing san-tai chin-hui hsiao-shuo hsi-ch'ü shih-liao* ('Historical Material on the Prohibited and Burnt Novels and Dramas of the Yüan, Ming and Ch'ing', Peking, 1958).

PART TWO

THE THEATRE OUTSIDE PEKING BEFORE 1949

The Chinese regional drama has received very little attention from Western writers. A preliminary study of its early development in English is Colin Mackerras, 'The Growth of the Chinese Regional Drama in the Ming and Ch'ing', *Journal of Oriental Studies*, IX, 1 (January 1971), pp. 58–91. By far the most important sources, however, are in Chinese and Japanese. A great deal of primary material has been collected in *Chung-kuo ku-tien hsi-ch'ü lun-chu chi-ch'eng* ('Collections of Writings on the Chinese Classical Drama', 10 vols, Peking, 1959 and 1960). For the purposes of the present book, two works in this collection, both in vol. 8, are particularly relevant. They are Chiao Hsün, *Hua-pu nung-t'an* ('Peasant Talks on the Regional Drama', written in 1819), and Li T'iao-yüan, *Chü-hua* ('On the Drama', completed *c.* 1775). A much more recent but significant primary source is Kai Chiao-t'ien, *Fen-mo ch'un-ch'iu* ('My Life on the Stage', Peking, 1959). This book is a collection of articles dictated by Kai Chiao-t'ien and copied down by Ho Man and Kung I-chiang. They were originally published separately in *Hsi-chü pao* ('Theatre News').

The foremost contemporary authority on the function of the theatre in Chinese society is the Japanese Tanaka Issei. He has written several outstandingly brilliant articles on the subject, including the following: 'Shindai shoki no chihō geki ni tsuite' ('On the Regional Drama of the Early Ch'ing'), *Nippon-Chūgoku-gakkai-hō* ('Bulletin of the Sinological Society of Japan'), 17 (1965), pp. 143–54 'Shindai shoki no sōzoku engeki ni tsuite' ('On the Clan Drama of the Early Ch'ing'), *Tōhōgaku* ('Eas-

tern Studies'), 32 (1966), pp. 102–116 'Min-Shin Kahoku chihō geki no kenkyū ('Research on the Local Drama of North China in the Ming and Ch'ing Dynasties'), *Hokkaidō daigaku bungakubu kiyō* ('Records of the Department of Literature of Hokkaidō University'), XVI, 1 (1968), pp. 97–269 'Nan-Sō jidai no Fukuhen chihō geki ni tsuite' ('On Local Drama in Fukien in the Southern Sung Period'), *Nippon-Chūgoku-gakkai-hō* ('Bulletin of the Sinological Society of Japan'), 22 (1970), pp. 102–118 'Development of Chinese Local Plays in the 17th and 18th Centuries' (in English), *Acta Asiatica, Bulletin of the Institute of Eastern Culture*, 23 (1972), pp. 42–62 He has also collected together a large number of primary administrative documents relating to the drama of the Ch'ing period. However, he has added no comment on the extracts included. The title of this collection is *Shindai chihō geki shiryō shū* ('Collections of Material on the Regional Drama of the Ch'ing', 2 vols, Tokyo, 1968).

The histories of the styles of regional drama have been treated in a number of works published recently on the Chinese mainland. The following four are among the most notable:
Chao Ching-shen, *Hsi-ch'ü pi-t'an* ('Sketches on Drama', Peking, 1962)
Chou I-pai, *Chung-kuo hsi-ch'ü lun-chi* ('Anthology of Essays on Chinese Drama', Peking, 1960)
Hua-tung hsi-ch'ü chü-chung chieh-shao ('An Introduction to the Kinds of Drama in the Theatre of

East China', 6 vols, Shanghai, 1955). This work contains articles by various contributors working under the general supervision of the East China Drama Research Institute. The history, tunes and structure of each form of local drama are described in considerable detail, and musical scores are included. The information presented has been based largely on field work.

Ou-yang Yü-ch'ien, ed., *Chung-kuo hsi-ch'ü yen-chiu tzu-liao ch'u-chi* ('First Collection of Research Material on Chinese Drama', Peking, 1957). The editor has collected seven articles by four distinguished writers, including Chou I-pai and himself.

The general histories already mentioned under Part One provide a certain amount of material on the regional theatre, and some of the provincial cultural bureaux and drama units have issued booklets on those local forms of drama which are most popular in their own districts. But probably the most comprehensive single contribution on a particular form of regional theatre is Mai Hsiao-hsia's study of the Kwangtung Opera, 'Kuang-tung hsi-chü shih-lüeh' ('Outline of the History of the Kwangtung Theatre'), in *Kuang-tung wen-wu* (3 vols, Hong Kong, 1941), vol. 3, pp. 141–85. A recent publication, especially valuable for its material on the theatrical history of Shanghai in the late Ch'ing and Republican periods, is K'an-wai jen and others, *Ching-chü chien-wen lu* ('Records of Things Seen and Heard about Peking Opera', Hong Kong, 1973). One should also mention Wu Ch'ien-ching, 'Ts'ung nan-hsi t'an tao Ch'ing-yang tiao' ('Talking of the

Ch'ing-yang tiao from the Southern Drama'), *An-hui shih-hsüeh t'ung-hsün* ('Anhwei Bulletin on Historiography'), 11 (1959), pp. 15–31.

Of particular relevance to the regional drama is the series *Chung-kuo ti-fang hsi-ch'ü chi-ch'eng* ('Collections of Chinese Regional Drama', Peking, 1958–63). To each province (with a few exceptions) and the two cities of Peking and Shanghai are devoted one or two volumes of group authorship. These explain the regional style of the area in question and give the texts of illustrative pieces.

The four volumes of the *Hsi-ch'ü hsüan* ('Selections of Drama', Peking, 1958–59) contain the texts of twenty-two pieces in local styles from various parts of the country. This work is particularly useful in that it provides musical tablatures of extracts from each drama included, together with explanations and critiques.

PART THREE

THE COMMUNIST PERIOD

A great deal has been written about the drama reform both inside China and in other countries. The most recent and comprehensive book on the subject is Chao Ts'ung, *Chung-kuo ta-lu ti hsi-ch'ü kai-ko (1942–1967)* ('Drama Reform in Mainland China 1942–1967', Hong Kong, 1969). In English the largest book on the recent Chinese theatre is Lois Wheeler Snow, *China on Stage: An American Actress in the People's Republic* (New York, 1972), which includes official texts of four of the model dramas. A more specialized but much shorter book is Hua-Yuan Li Mowry, *Yang-pan Hsi,*

New Theater in China (Berkeley, 1973). Some slighter studies are Richard F. S. Yang, 'The Reform of Peking Opera under the Communists', *The China Quarterly*, 11 (July–September 1962), pp. 124–39; Colin Mackerras, *Amateur Theatre in China 1949–1966* (Canberra, 1973); and Colin Mackerras, 'Chinese Opera after the Cultural Revolution (1970–72)', *The China Quarterly*, 55 (July–September 1973), pp. 478–510. For the theatre of contemporary China, however, most of the principal sources, both primary and secondary, are contained in periodicals. Below is a list of some of the relevant newspapers and journals.

China Notes, Hong Kong
The China Quarterly, London
China Reconstructs, Peking
Chinese Literature, Peking
Current Scene, Developments in Mainland China, Hong Kong

Far Eastern Economic Review, Hong Kong
Hsi-chü pao ('Theatre News'), Peking, suspended in 1966
Hsi-ch'ü yen-chiu ('Drama Research'), Peking, suspended in 1959
Hung-ch'i ('Red Flag'), Peking
Jen-min jih-pao ('People's Daily'), Peking
Kuang-ming jih-pao ('Kuang-ming Daily'), Peking
New China News Agency, daily issues from Peking and Hong Kong
Peking Review, Peking
People's China, Peking (the predecessor of *Peking Review*)
Selections from China Mainland Magazines, Hong Kong
Ssu-ch'uan hsi-ch'ü ('Szechwanese Theatre'), Chengtu (publication has now ceased)
Survey of China Mainland Press, Hong Kong
Wen-hui pao, Shanghai

Chronological Table

Reign-title or Period	Political Events in China	Events in the Chinese Theatre
Yung-cheng 1723–36		*c.* 1730 Beginnings of Kwangtung Opera (*Yüeh-chü*)
		1732 First evidence of actors' guild (Li-yüan kuan) in Peking
Ch'ien-lung 1736–96	Period of growth and prosperity ending in crises	*c.* 1740 Court theatre organization set up
	1758–59 The Ch'ing conquer Turkestan	
		1779 Clapper actors, led by Wei Ch'ang-sheng, enter Peking
		1785 Clapper actors banned from Peking
		1790 Anhwei actors enter Peking for Ch'ien-lung's eightieth birthday. Beginnings of Peking Opera
	1793 Lord Macartney leads British delegation to China	
	1795 White Lotus rebellion begins	
Chia-ch'ing 1796–1820	1799 Death of Ho-shen, corrupt minister of Ch'ien-lung. Death of Ch'ien-lung	
		1800 Wei Ch'ang-sheng returns to Peking

Reign-title or Period	Political Events in China	Events in the Chinese Theatre
Chia-ch'ing 1796–1820 (continued)		1802 Wei Ch'ang-sheng dies
	1804 White Lotus rebellion suppressed	
		1812 Ch'eng Chang-keng, Peking Opera actor, born in Anhwei
Tao-kuang 1820–50		c. 1827 Hupeh actors introduce Hupeh Opera to Peking
		1832 Mi Hsi-tzu, first of the great *lao-sheng* Peking Opera actors, dies
	1839 Lin Tse-hsü sent to Canton to prevent import of opium into China. Opium War begins	
		1841 Sun Chü-hsien, Peking Opera actor, born in Tientsin
	1842 Opium War ended by Treaty of Nanking. Many concessions made to Britain	
		1847 T'an Hsin-p'ei, Peking Opera actor, born 23 April in Hupeh
	1850 Taiping revolution begins	c. 1850 Ho-ch'un company of Peking disbands
Hsien-feng 1850–61	1851 Formal proclamation by Taipings	
	1853 Taipings capture Nanking	

227

Reign-title or Period	Political Events in China	Events in the Chinese Theatre
Hsien-feng 1850–61 (continued)	1856 'Arrow' war begins with Britain and France	
	1857 Canton occupied by British and French troops	
	1860 British and French troops occupy Peking. Hsien-feng flees to Jehol	1860 Ch'eng Chang-keng and other actors of Peking city perform at court for a short period
		1861 Li Wen-mao, Kwangtung Opera actor and founder of an independent kingdom in Kwangsi, dies after capture of his capital by the Ch'ing
T'ung-chih 1861–75	T'ung-chih Restoration	
	1864 Nanking taken by Ch'ing army	
		1868 Proscription against Kwangtung Opera troupes rescinded after about fifteen years' enforcement
	1870 Tientsin massacre undermines Sino-Western relations	1870 K'ang Chih-lin, Szechwanese actor, born 13 February
Kuang-hsü 1875–1908	Period of slow modernization	
	1875 Rise of Empress Dowager Tz'u-hsi's power	
		1877 Yang Hsiao-lou, *wu-sheng* Peking Opera actor, born 14 December

Reign-title or Period	Political Events in China	Events in the Chinese Theatre
Kuang-hsü 1875–1908 (continued)		*c.* 1880 Ch'eng Chang-keng dies
	1884–85 Sino-French War ends in defeat for China	1884 Actors from Peking city perform at court from this year onwards
		1890 Yü Shu-yen, Peking Opera actor, born 28 November
		1894 Mei Lan-fang, Peking Opera actor, born 22 October
	1895 Sino-Japanese War ends in China's defeat. China cedes Taiwan to Japan	1895 Chou Hsin-fang, Peking Opera actor, born in Ningpo
	1898 Hundred Days' Reform, and its suppression by Empress Dowager; Kuang-hsü placed under house-arrest	
	1900 Boxer uprising and invasion by eight foreign powers	1900 Ma Shih-tseng, Kwangtung Opera actor, born. Many theatres in Peking destroyed. Ch'un-t'ai and Ssu-hsi companies of Peking disband. Sun Chü-hsien leaves Peking
		1903 Fu-lien-ch'eng training-school for actors established
		1904 Ch'eng Yen-ch'iu, Peking Opera actor, born 4 January

229

Reign-title or Period	Political Events in China	Events in the Chinese Theatre
Kuang-hsü 1875–1908 (continued)	1905 Official examination system abolished	1905 Yüeh-lai teahouse, first urban theatre in Szechwan, built in Chengtu
	1906 Constitutional government announced	
		1907 Spring Society founded in Shanghai. Beginnings of spoken play in China
	1908 Empress Dowager and Kuang-hsü die	
Hsüan-t'ung 1909–11		1910 Ts'ao Yü, playwright, born
	1911 Wuchang taken by revolutionaries. Ch'ing dynasty overthrown	1911 Actors assist in the taking of Kiangnan Arsenal in Shanghai for revolutionaries on 3 November
Republic of China 1912–49	1912 Sun Yat-sen becomes President of China on 1 January in Nanking	1912 San-ch'ing company of Chengtu founded in Yüeh-lai teahouse.
	1913 Yüan Shih-k'ai formally inaugurated as President	1913 T'an Hsin-p'ei and Mei Lan-fang visit Shanghai
		1914 First Stage (*Ti-i wu-t'ai*), the first Western-style theatre, built in Peking
	1916 Yüan Shih-k'ai proclaims himself emperor but dies soon afterwards.	1916 Shaohing Opera first performed in Shanghai
		1917 T'an Hsin-p'ei dies in Peking 10 May

230

Reign-title or Period	Political Events in China	Events in the Chinese Theatre
Republic of China 1912–49 (continued)	1919 May Fourth Movement against betrayal of Chinese interests at Versailles Conference. New Culture Movement greatly assisted in consequence	1919 Chang Chien builds modern theatre at Nantung. Mei Lan-fang and Yü Shu-yen visit Hankow. Mei Lan-fang visits Japan
	1921 Chinese Communist Party founded in July	1921 Ch'en Ta-pei begins movement for amateur performance of spoken plays in Peking
	1923 Peking–Hankow Railway strike	1923 Beginnings of performance of Shaohing Opera by all-female companies
	1924 Sun Yat-sen holds National Congress of Kuomintang in Canton	1924 Mei Lan-fang visits Japan. Men and women allowed to sit together in Peking theatres
	1925 Sun Yat-sen dies 12 March. May 30 incident, in which twelve Chinese students are killed by police under British command	1925 Chang Chien's theatre in Nantung closes down
	1926–28 Chiang Kai-shek seizes power through Northern Expedition. Ruthless killing of Communists and leftists	
	1928 Mao Tse-tung and Chu Teh establish guerrilla base in Kiangsi. Civil War between Communists and Kuomintang in central and southern China	1928 South China Society founded to promote spoken plays

Reign-title or Period	Political Events in China	Events in the Chinese Theatre
Republic of China 1912–49 (continued)		1930 Mei Lan-fang visits United States. Training-school for actresses established in Wuhan. South China Society suppressed
	1931 Japanese occupy Manchuria, encroach on other areas of China in succeeding years	1931 Great *t'ang-hui* held by Tu Yüeh-sheng in Shanghai 9–11 June. Sun Chü-hsien dies in Tientsin 29 July. Ma Shih-tseng visits United States. K'ang Chih-lin dies
	1934–35 Communists undertake Long March that ends in northern Shensi	
		1935 Mei Lan-fang visits Europe. Liang Yu-nung, *Shao-chü* actor, dies
	1936 Chiang Kai-shek forced to agree to co-operate with Communists in resisting Japan after being captured in Sian	
	1937–45 War of Resistance against Japan	
		1938 Yang Hsiao-lou dies 14 February
		1942 Mao Tse-tung's 'Talks at the Yenan Forum on Literature and Art' in May
		1943 Yü Shu-yen dies 19 May

Reign-title or Period	Political Events in China	Events in the Chinese Theatre
	1946–49 War of Liberation results in Communist victory	
People's Republic of China 1949–	1949 Peking liberated in January. People's Republic of China proclaimed by Mao Tse-tung on 1 October in Peking	1949 Experimental Academy of the Drama founded in Peking in August. Bureau of Drama Reform set up within the Ministry of Culture in October
	1950 United Kingdom recognizes People's Republic of China in January. Marriage Law proclaimed on 1 May. China enters Korean war in October	1950 Ministry of Culture holds first All-China Theatre Workers' Conference in November and December
	1951 Movements against corruption begin	1951 East China Drama Research Institute set up in Shanghai in March. Conference of Theatre Work convened by Ministry of Culture in November
	1952 Land reform completed	1952 First National Festival of Classical and Folk Drama held in Peking in October and November
	1953 First Five-Year Plan begins. Korean armistice concluded in July	1953 Mei Lan-fang leads troupe to Korea
	1954 Geneva Conference on Indochina held in May; China participates	1954 High-level conference on drama held in November

233

Reign-title or Period	Political Events in China	Events in the Chinese Theatre
People's Republic of China 1949– (continued)	1955 Bandung Conference in April; China participates. Drive to collectivize land begins in October	
	1956 Hundred Flowers movement, marked by far wider freedom of criticism and expression, begins in May. Eighth Party Congress held in Peking in September	1956 Fifteen of Tientsin's drama troupes and sixty-nine of Shanghai's nationalized in January. Festival of Spoken Plays held in Peking in March and April. Mei Lan-fang visits Japan, May–July. Conference held by Ministry of Culture in June ushers in liberal phase of drama policy
	1957 Anti-rightist movement against critics of government begins in June	1957 First 'caravan' troupes tour Inner Mongolia. Liberalization of drama halted in July
	1958 Great Leap Forward begins in January. First communes formed in July	1958 Conference held in June and July introduces policy of 'walking on two legs' – i.e., emphasizing both traditional and modern drama. Death of Ch'eng Yen-ch'iu
	1959 Tibetan revolt in March. Communes liberalized in August. Defence Minister P'eng Te-huai dismissed in September	1959 Mei Lan-fang joins Communist Party in March. Festival of Drama held in Peking in September and October to celebrate tenth anniversary of founding of People's Republic
	1960 Soviet technicians withdrawn from China in August	

Reign-title or Period	Political Events in China	Events in the Chinese Theatre
People's Republic of China 1949– (continued)	1961 Great Leap Forward policy reversed. Sino-Soviet dispute worsens	1961 Mei Lan-fang dies in Peking on 8 August
	1962 Party Central Committee attacks Soviet 'modern revisionism' in September	1962 Ch'i Ju-shan dies in Taiwan
		1963–4 Debate over the drama results in almost exclusive performance of modern plays on contemporary themes
	1964 France recognizes People's Republic of China in January. Tonkin Gulf incident in August	1964 Festival of Peking Operas on Contemporary Themes held in Peking in June and July
	1965 Vietnam war escalates, and the United States bombs North Vietnam in February. Beginnings of Cultural Revolution in November	
	1966 P'eng Chen, Mayor of Peking, ousted in June. Red Guards take Cultural Revolution on to streets of Peking; sixteen points issued to guide them in the struggle	1966 Chou Hsin-fang dies. Ministry of Culture abolished; most theatres temporarily closed
	1967 Revolution in Shanghai against Party bureaucracy in January. Fall of Liu Shao-ch'i in March. Wuhan incident: mutiny by a division of the People's Liberation Army suppressed by central authorities (July)	

Reign-title or Period	Political Events in China	Events in the Chinese Theatre
People's Republic of China 1949– (continued)	1968 Red Guards stripped of vanguard role in Cultural Revolution in July. Fall of Liu Shao-ch'i formally recognized in October. Beginnings of May 7th schools for training of cadres, in the same month	
	1969 Serious clashes on Sino-Soviet border in March. Ninth Party Congress held in Peking in April; Lin Piao formally named Mao's successor in Party Constitution	1969 First revised 'model' Peking Opera, *Taking Tiger Mountain by Strategy*, adopted after the Cultural Revolution (October)
	1970 Canada establishes diplomatic relations with People's Republic of China in October	1970 Cultural Group established. Revised model Peking operas, *The Story of the Red Lantern* and *Sha-chia-pang*, adopted in May. Commentary in *People's Daily* on 15 July calls for popularization of model dramas
	1971 Movement against 'ultra-leftists'. Lin Piao dies in disfavour in September. China joins United Nations in October	
	1972 President Nixon of the United States visits China. Tanaka, Prime Minister of Japan, visits China and establishes diplomatic relations	1972 Movement to revive regional styles. Revised Peking operas *On the Docks, Ode to Dragon River* and *Raid on the White Tiger Regiment* adopted in January, March and September respectively

Reign-title or Period	Political Events in China	Events in the Chinese Theatre
People's Republic of China 1949– (continued)	1973 Paris accords on Indo-China signed in January. Tenth Party Congress held in Peking in August. Campaign to Criticize Lin Piao and Confucius begins the same month	1973 Revised Peking opera *Azalea Mountain* adopted in September
		1974 North China Theatrical Festival held in Peking in January and February. Campaign to denounce the Shansi opera *Going up Peach Peak Three Times* begins in February
	1975 Fourth National People's Congress held in January	

List of Illustrations

15 A representation of a seventeenth-century stage in Peking. From Chen Lin-jui, *The Peking Opera* (supplement to *China Reconstructs*, V, 7, July 1956), p. 17.

16 Theatrical performance given at a private house in Peking during the nineteenth century. From *Globus*, vol. 10, no. 2 (1866), p. 40.

17 A temporary stage in front of a temple during the Ming period. Etching by Josephine Huang Hung from her book *Ming Drama* (Taipei, 1966), facing p. 54.

18 A performance of *Ch'ien-chin chi* (*The Story of the Thousand Pieces of Gold*), by Shen Ts'ai. Seventeenth-century painting from Tanaka Issei, 'Development of Chinese Local Plays in the 17th and 18th Centuries', *Acta Asiatica Bulletin*, 23 (1972), p. 57.

19 A late nineteenth-century teahouse-theatre. From *Hsi-ch'ü lun-ts'ung* ('Theatre Digest'), 1 (1957), before p. 3.

20 A theatrical performance in a private mansion. An illustration to a seventeenth-century edition of the anonymous novel *Chin P'ing Mei*, written during the Ming period. From *Chung-kuo ku-tai yin-yüeh t'u-p'ien* ('Pictures of Ancient Chinese Music', Peking, 1959), plate 18.

21 A performance of a drama at a banquet during the Ming period. An illustration to the edition (first half of the seventeenth century) by Yang Ting-chien of the novel *Shui-hu chuan* (*The Water Margin*), by Lo Kuan-chung. From *Hsi-ch'ü yen-chiu* ('Drama Research'), 3 (1957), cover.

22 A scene from the Shaohing opera, *Liang Shan-po and Chu Ying-t'ai*. Ink drawing. From anon., *Folk Arts of New China* (Peking, 1954), p. 42.

23 Chou Hsin-fang. From Chou Hsin-fang, *Chou Hsin-fang wu-t'ai i-shu* ('Chou Hsin-fang's Stage Art', Peking 1961), frontispiece.

24 Ts'ao Yü. From Ts'ao Yü, trans. Wang Tso-liang and A. C. Barnes, *Thunderstorm* (Peking, 1964), frontispiece.

25 Chou Hsin-fang and Liu Pin-k'un in *Ch'ing-feng t'ing* (*The Ch'ing-feng Pavilion*). Ink sketch by Ch'eng Shih-fa, 1961. From Chou Hsin-fang, op. cit., facing p. 58.

26 The opening scene from one of Ts'ao Yü's best known plays, *Lei-yü* (*Thunderstorm*), 1933. From Ts'ao Yü opposite p. 22.

27 A scene from the Kwangtung opera *Sou-shu yüan* (*The Runaway Maid*). From Gladys Yang, trans., *The Runaway Maid* (*A Cantonese Opera*), revised by the Cantonese Opera Company of Kwangtung (Peking, 1958), opposite p. 3.

28 Hung-hsien-nü (K'uang Chien-lien), wife of the actor Ma Shih-tseng. From Hsiao-lien, *Hung-hsien-nü ti hung-se ch'ing-fu* ('The Red Lovers of Hung-hsien-nü', Hong Kong, 1969), frontispiece.

FIGURES

Index